2010

D0050108

Merry Christmas
   Dad

   Love,
      Cindy & Rod

HERO
OF THE
PACIFIC

Also by James Brady

The Hamptons Novels

HERO
OF THE
PACIFIC

THE LIFE OF MARINE LEGEND
JOHN BASILONE

James Brady

WILEY

John Wiley & Sons, Inc.

Copyright © 2010 by James Brady. All rights reserved

Published by John Wiley & Sons, Inc., Hoboken, New Jersey
Published simultaneously in Canada

Credits appear on page 243 amd constitute an extension of the copyright page.

For general information about our other products and services, please contact our Customer Care Department within the United States at (800) 762–2974, outside the United States at (317) 572–3993 or fax (317) 572–4002.

Wiley also publishes its books in a variety of electronic formats. Some content that appears in print may not be available in electronic books. For more information about Wiley products, visit our web site at www.wiley.com.

Library of Congress Cataloging-in-Publication Data:
Brady, James, date.
    Hero of the Pacific : the life of Marine legend John Basilone / James Brady.
        p.   cm.
    Includes bibliographical references and index.
    ISBN 978-0-470-37941-7 (cloth: alk. paper)
    1. Basilone, John, 1916–1945.   2. Medal of Honor—Biography.   3. United States. Marine Corps—Biography.   4. Guadalcanal, Battle of, Solomon Islands, 1942–1943. 5. Iwo Jima, Battle of, Japan, 1945.   6. World War, 1939–1945—Biography.   7. Marines—New Jersey—Biography.   8. Soldiers—New Jersey—Biography.   9. Raritan (N.J.)—Biography.   I. Title.
    VE25.B36B73 2009
    940.54′5973092—dc22
    [B]

                                                                            2009015922
Printed in the United States of America

10   9   8   7   6

To all who put themselves in harm's way, especially the men and women of the United States Marine Corps—then, now, always.

To absent friends and family, who are loved so well.

And for Sarah, Joe, Nick, and Matthew—your Pop Pop loves you so much!

Contents

Acknowledgments

The day after completing this book, Jim Brady died, suddenly and unexpectedly. Because he had not yet written the acknowledgments, we, his daughters, have done so for him.

Near the end of this book, our dad describes himself as "neither a scholar nor a historian, just another old newspaperman who once fought in a war." This is true enough, and yet the statement is not entirely genuine. Jim Brady was a man fiercely proud of his bond with the Marine Corps and of the extraordinary experiences and friendships that he amassed over those six decades. He was also unabashedly delighted at having made a success in journalism. He grew up wanting to write and was a working writer to the last. As difficult as his loss has been for those of us left behind, there is a true sense of joy in knowing that he was doing what he absolutely loved right up to the end.

While our dad did not have the opportunity to compose his own thank-you list, he left stacks of notes and references. Clearly, a great many people gave generously of their time, knowledge, and insights. Some are mentioned in the text, while others remain unsung. Among those we would especially like to recognize are Stephen S. Power of John Wiley & Sons, who first proposed the idea of doing the book; USMC historian Robert Aquilina, who provided what our dad called a "Rosetta Stone of sorts" in primary-source materials from within the Corps' History Division at Quantico; *Leatherneck* magazine's executive editor, Colonel Walt Ford, USMC (Ret.); Colonel John Keenan, USMC (Ret.), editor of the *Marine Corps Gazette*; Colonel Bill White, USMC (Ret.); Raritan's John Pacifico, for his invaluable ad hoc reporting skills; the *Newark Star-Ledger's* Vinessa Ermino and Jeanette Rundquist; Marine Lou Piantadosi; and Marine Clinton Watters, John Basilone's best man. Sincere thanks to *all* who contributed to the making of this book.

Fiona Brady and Susan Konig

Marine platoon sergeant "Manila John" Basilone of Raritan, New Jersey, proudly wears the Congressional Medal of Honor, May 21, 1943.

Prologue

Whatever the century, whatever the war, machine gunners have always been a different military breed, focused and lethal warriors armed with and operating a terrible weapon in a risky trade, very competent at killing en masse, pretty good at getting killed themselves.

F. Scott Fitzgerald, who came of age in the appalling slaughter that was then called the Great War, understood this, which may be why he made his iconic hero Jay Gatsby a machine gunner. We first learn about Gatsby's war as the mysterious but glamorous bootlegger reveals himself bit by tantalizing bit to narrator Nick Carraway while the two young men speed toward Manhattan in Gatsby's cream-colored roadster. Nick listens, fascinated, not sure just how to respond or what to believe, as Jay goes on in his strange, mannered style of speech:

> "Then came the war, old sport.
> "In the Argonne Forest I took two machine gun detachments so far forward that there was a half mile gap on either side of us where the infantry couldn't advance.

We stayed there two days and two nights, a hundred and thirty men and sixteen Lewis guns, and when the infantry came up at last they found the insignia of three German divisions among the piles of dead.

"I was promoted to be major and every Allied government gave me a decoration—even Montenegro, little Montenegro down on the Adriatic Sea."

A generation and a world war later, in the 1940s, another young roughneck of a machine gunner, not a character in a book but an actual Marine from Raritan, New Jersey, was similarly piling up the dead of famous enemy divisions before his guns. He would be awarded the most illustrious decoration for gallantry that we have—the Congressional Medal of Honor—for what he did in the historic battle for Guadalcanal, and later, posthumously, the prized and nearly as rare Navy Cross, for his actions on the first day ashore at Iwo Jima. This man was Sergeant John Basilone.

Basilone was for several years during World War II one of the most recognizable celebrities in the country, a national hero and quite a famous man—young, laughing and roistering, unmarried and, in contemporary terms, quite sexy. Yet today, except among the hard men of the Marine Corps, which so reveres tradition, and in blue-collar, Italo-American Raritan, where the people of his hometown still tend the flame, few Americans could tell you who Basilone was or what he did in our desperate war against the Japanese in the Pacific.

Basilone's feats of arms became such lore that nowhere in the world is there a Marine base that does not boast a building or a street named for him. At huge, sprawling Camp Pendleton, California, where all Marines including Basilone received their final combat training before shipping out to Asian wars from World War II to Korea, Vietnam to Afghanistan, a two-lane stretch of macadam called Basilone Road starts at the commanding general's house and meanders for thirteen miles. Intersecting with Vandegrift Boulevard (generals are awarded "boulevards";

sergeants get "roads"), crossing the Santa Margarita River, and finally exiting the base near San Onofre to merge into and lose its identity amid the humming multiple lanes of Interstate 5, Basilone's modest road disappears just as surely as the man himself has largely vanished from the American consciousness.

He appeared just as suddenly at a time when the Japanese, edging ever closer to our West Coast with each battle, had been, to be candid, beating the crap out of the United States of America in fight after fight, and we sorely needed heroes.

Nonetheless it took the Marines, understandably distracted by war, until May 1943 to award Basilone the first of his medals for what he'd done seven months earlier on Guadalcanal. And it was late June before the vaunted Marine publicity machine even bothered to put out a press release. A story ran in the *New York Times* under the headline "Slew 38 Japanese in One Battle; Jersey Marine Gets Honor Medal." It was a one-day story that without a little hype soon faded. Basilone returned to a pleasant obscurity and the routine of wartime garrison life near Melbourne, Australia, drilling the troops, going on wild liberty weekends, just another good, tough sergeant in a Corps full of them.

Then some bright boys in Washington realized there might be pure promotional gold in Basilone. There were already a couple of Medal of Honor commissioned officers from Guadalcanal, General Alexander A. Vandegrift and Colonel "Red Mike" Edson. How about an enlisted man? Preferably unmarried (women would like that), somewhat colorful, younger? Maybe they could put this Jersey kid Basilone, a nobody from nowhere, to even better purpose than he had shown he was capable of in a foxhole.

Despite desperate battles yet to come and a shooting war raging in the Pacific, orders were cut, and as his buddies gaped and a few fellow soldiers griped about favoritism, Basilone was ordered to the States as an officially anointed hero. He was to go on tour with a handful of other heroic soldiers and sailors, supported by a troupe of Hollywood stars—traveling salesmen assigned to show the flag, boost morale, and sell war bonds.

Needless to say, it wasn't his idea, nor did he want to leave his "boys." Reluctantly, and reportedly in tears, Basilone left Melbourne, sailed to the West Coast, and was swiftly flown east by military aircraft to New York City where the media were—the big radio networks, major newspapers, *Time* and *Life* and *Newsweek* and the other national magazines, as well as the smooth boys of the Madison Avenue ad agencies. And following a crash course, it would be there in Manhattan that Basilone would face the only formal press conference he had ever attended.

It was his first real exposure to the American public. Terrified, he turned to a Marine colonel for help. "Just tell them your story, Sergeant," the colonel said. Tell them how it was." Basilone began to talk about that terrible Guadalcanal night he fought through, barefoot and bare-chested, the tropical jungle rain coming down, the Japanese crying "Banzai!" and "Marines, you die!" and coming on toward his machine guns. Always coming on.

Basilone was a smash hit. In his halting but modest and untutored answers, he responded to the shouted questions of cynical reporters who had seen it all, and won them over with his sincerity. In the end he had them queuing up to shake his hand and say thanks. And so the road show began.

If the press and just plain civilians were impressed by their first glimpses of the heroic Marine, and they were, Basilone was overwhelmed by the enthusiastic "well dones" of his fellow Americans. In the next few months of 1943, he would learn just how supportive they were. General Douglas MacArthur, who had long ago been Basilone's commanding officer in Manila—where the young soldier achieved a first small fame as an undefeated Army boxer, earning the sobriquet "Manila John"—was jollied into issuing a statement calling Basilone "a one-man army," a brand of enthusiastic cheerleading the general usually reserved for his own greatness.

Dozens of press conferences, some orchestrated, others ad hoc and on the run, were laid on with their hurled questions: "Hey, John, how many Japs ya kill?" New York mayor Fiorello LaGuardia, "the Little Flower," welcomed him to city hall, asking where his father came from in Italy. The *New York Times* did an interview. Damon Runyon wrote a piece. *Life* magazine did an elaborate photo spread. John would be photographed wherever he went, often out of uniform and in cock-eyed or clowning poses to please the cameramen, and appeared on magazine covers, bare-chested and firing a heavy machine gun cradled in his arms. One of these pictures, a painting on the June 24, 1944, issue of *Collier's* (ten cents a copy), was the most lurid, in the grand tradition of the pulp magazines.

Basilone was trotted out by his military handlers (peacetime press agents and Madison Avenue ad men in wartime uniform) to one radio station interview after another. Famed, best-selling war correspondent Lowell Thomas, who spent World War I trekking Arabia with Colonel T. E. Lawrence, got into the act, talking about Basilone on the newsreels, mispronouncing his name to rhyme with "baloney." The sergeant was saluted from the White House by President Franklin D. Roosevelt in whose name the medal had been awarded.

As Basilone read, rather bashfully, a canned speech cobbled for him by the handlers, he got a standing ovation from nineteen thousand at Madison Square Garden on Eighth Avenue, where he had once hoped to box. He was headlined in newspapers large and small, often as "Manila John, the Jap Killer." Newspaper columnist Ed Sullivan, always on the lookout for a new sensation to co-opt, took him up, wrote a piece, and did a radio show, basking in the hero's reflected glory. Celebrity saloonkeeper Toots Shor, a notorious front-runner, got on board the "Basilone Express," buying the drinks and glad-handing him around, introducing the kid to the athletes and glamour girls, the wealthy debutantes and chinless wonders of Café Society, the showbiz people and literary types among his boldface regulars. The Navy Department and Marine handlers got him past the velvet ropes and maîtres d'hotel of the Stork Club, "21," and El Morocco, and under the El on Third Avenue, Johnny was welcomed by the barmen and serious drinkers of P.J. Clarke's. Everyone wanted a piece of Manila John.

To the people of Raritan, though, Basilone was already theirs and always would be. They renamed streets and the American

Legion post, and in time they would erect a magnificent bronze statue of him holding his favorite weapon, the heavy water-cooled Browning .30-caliber M1917A1 machine gun, which he had loved to the point of obsession.

The Basilone family was transported into Manhattan to be interviewed. A *Manila John Basilone at War* comic book for kids was published (not a dime in royalties was ever paid). Two members of the Basilone clan would write their own books, amateurish and fanciful, admiring but brief on fact. John's sister Phyllis Basilone Cutter did a fourteen-part serialized account in a local newspaper, the *Somerset Messenger-Gazette*, and her son, Jerry Cutter, and a hired writer named Jim Proser published a book titled *I'm Staying with My Boys*—Cutter admitted that when they got stuck, they "made things up." Best-selling author Quentin Reynolds wrote a magazine piece. An ambitious writer began hanging around the family home hoping to win the hero's cooperation if not collaboration on an "authorized" book, until Basilone himself told the pest to "scram."

The federal government set up a city-to-city "Back the Attack!" war bond–selling tour of the country, first in the East and eventually to go national, with Basilone supported by a handful of other decorated servicemen (he was clearly the star turn) and Hollywood actors volunteered for the task by their movie studios. It would be, said FDR's friend Louis B. Mayer of MGM, excellent, patriotic, and quite free publicity for Mayer's next releases. Joining the tour were Gene Hersholt, John Garfield, Keenan Wynn, Eddie Bracken, and a pride of actresses, beautiful young women including one fairly well-known performer, Virginia Grey, who promptly fell for the young Marine over drinks and cigarettes in a dark hotel bar their first night out on the road.

That plotline alone would have made a swell Hollywood romance of the period, the juvenile dream of every obscure young man who comes out of nowhere, becomes an overnight sensation of one sort or another, and encounters the beautiful princess, or in this case the movie matinee equivalent of royalty, a movie star, the beauty who falls in love with the clean-cut young war hero.

Garfield, one of the troupe, might not have been bad in the role of the fighting Marine.

Basilone was credited by the tour organizers for drawing crowds that bought millions of dollars' worth of bonds. In Newark and Jersey City, where Basilone and Grey first shared a moment, and at New Haven, where Yale undergrads turned out to hail the young man who never even went to high school, in Pittsburgh, Albany, and all over the East, they organized parades: mayors, aldermen, governors, retail merchants drumming up trade, leading citizens and schoolchildren lining up to touch or even just to see Manila John.

He shook hands at factory gates and inside armaments and munitions plants. At a gala black-tie dinner at the Waldorf sponsored by the National Association of Manufacturers, Sergeant Basilone was seated on the dais, mingling with influential and wealthy men, captains of industry and other tycoons, the onetime laundry delivery boy fired for napping on the job atop the soiled laundry bags. A movement was launched to get his face on a postage stamp (eventually issued well after his death). Raritan gave him a parade of its own with tobacco heiress Doris Duke throwing open her estate to handle the overflow crowd. Catholic mass was said by Basilone's old priest, Father Amadeo Russo. The snob membership of the Raritan Valley Country Club turned out, remembering fondly, they claimed, the teenager who'd worked out of their caddy shack, lugging their golf clubs for tips. Basilone was invited to address a Bar Association lunch. He visited elementary school classrooms, signed autographs, kissed pretty girls in the crowd, and greeted old soldiers from earlier wars dating back to the Spanish-American, who approached to pay their respects and, perhaps, to bore the Marine with hoary war stories of their own.

At the family home in Raritan where Basilone grew up with his nine siblings, with only three bedrooms and two baths, they were inundated with fan mail, thousands of cards and letters, mostly from women, including a number of mash notes, and even marriage proposals from girls who had never met the machine gunner. One young woman wrote, "I always wanted to marry a hero." Basilone's brother marveled, "Johnny, everybody in the country loves you." An unsubstantiated rumor surfaced, courtesy of ribald Marine tattle, and possible enlisted men's jealousy, that when a USO show came through the islands of the South Pacific during Manila John's campaigning days, he had "bedded one of the Andrews Sisters." No one held it against either him or Miss Andrews, if the anecdote was true, because in wartime such "showing the flag" might justifiably be considered patriotic.

Basilone got married, but not to a movie star. His wife was another young Marine, a cute sergeant named Lena Riggi whom Basilone met in a Camp Pendleton mess hall.

Then he was gone again, without a honeymoon, back to the fight, back to his boys. He had been offered, and stubbornly turned down, an officers' rank and posh duty stations, politicking instead for just the opposite: to get back to the Pacific. Finally, the Marines had relented and reluctantly cut new orders reuniting him with the Fleet Marine Force Pacific.

Then he was gone for good, the "unkillable" hero of Guadalcanal dead on Iwo Jima, torn apart that first February morning by Japanese fire in the shadow of Mount Suribachi, a hero once again. Then he was forgotten.

How this could happen goes beyond the passage of time simply blurring and obscuring his image. Within the violent priesthood of the Marine Corps, there has long been contention and controversy, and some doubt, surrounding Basilone. There are contradictory and incorrect accounts about what exactly he'd done that dreadful night in the rain on the ridgelines of Guadalcanal in October 1942, starting with the official record in the *History of U.S. Marine Corps Operations in World War II*, volume 1, *Pearl Harbor to Guadalcanal*:

> The Japanese continued to assault out of the jungle and up the slopes. A small group forced a salient in the Marine line to fall upon a mortar position, and further to the front [General] Nasu's soldiers worked close to a water-cooled machine gun and knocked out all but

two of its crew. Marines near the mortar position won back the tube from the enemy, and in the machine gun section Sergeant John Basilone took rescue matters into his own hands. For this action and later heroism in braving Japanese fire to bring up ammunition, Basilone became the first enlisted Marine in World War II to win the Medal of Honor.

In fact, the first enlisted Marine to earn the medal was another sergeant, Clyde Thomason of the 2nd Raider Battalion, killed in the small-scale (and ill-fated) raid in August on Makin Island. But the brief record above does convey some of the savagery and chaotic nature of the fighting that night along the ridgelines, with infantrymen of both sides grappling in the dark over a single mortar tube, and a lone Marine (Basilone) risking hostile fire to sprint out and fetch more ammo for the machine guns, the heavy ammo belts slung about his neck and bare shoulders glistening in the rain. So began the legend of Manila John.

And what really happened later on Iwo? Had Basilone destroyed an enemy blockhouse single-handedly with demolitions, while contemptuously brandishing a knife at the Japanese? In the end, how did he die, on the beach or attacking Motoyama Airfield #1? Was he hit by an artillery or mortar shell and killed instantly as his Navy Cross citation reads? Or did he bleed slowly to death from small-arms fire, as the Marine casualty report has it? Shot up with morphine by a corpsman, had he left messages for his brother, smoked a cigarette, and lived for hours? Was the Navy Cross he received posthumously awarded to make up for the near-unprecedented second Medal of Honor he was thought by some to be chasing?

Then there's this: so hard up were we for heroes that there were suspicions the government had turned to "manufacturing" them. How else to explain the convenience of Basilone—a Marine under orders who would do what he was told, including a war bond tour and morale-boosting visits to war plants? This has clearly happened in more recent wars. Remember feckless young private Jessica Lynch and Arizona Cardinals football star Pat Tillman? Both became the innocent tools of a military publicity apparatus that ambitiously turned an understandably terrified young woman and a tragic victim of friendly fire into heroic but essentially synthetic symbols of American courage under fire. The *New York Times* editorial page savaged the Pentagon's misinformation campaign for conjuring up "the false story that PFC Jessica Lynch had been captured in Iraq after a Rambo-like performance," when she'd actually been injured in a truck crash. And Tillman's mother, Mary, in a book about her son, wrote that "officials tried to hide details about the incident because . . . it made the Army look bad." Ergo the cover-up, trying to persuade a nation that Tillman "had been killed by the enemy in Afghanistan (in a battle that won him a questionable Silver Star) long after the military knew he had been killed accidentally by fire from American forces."

But even suggesting half a century later that Basilone's heroics might similarly have been concocted infuriates contemporary keepers of the Basilone flame. Men such as Deacon John Pacifico of St. Ann's Roman Catholic Church in Raritan seem ever vigilant and ready to stand up to defend the Basilone name and his legend. In May 2007, sixty-five years after the Marine's death, Deacon Pacifico angrily told Vicki Hyman of the state's largest newspaper, the *Newark Star-Ledger*, "That's not what the Army was like in World War II. That's not what the Marines were like."

Having been a Marine myself and still a working journalist and writer of books about Marines at war, I thought Basilone's story was worth telling, worth a search for the real Basilone. I've grown fascinated by Manila John, sometimes puzzled by him, and I'm still trying to get a grip on him—not the bronze statue but the real man, not the marketing image but the real hero—and what made him tick.

In the Corps, you meet natural-born warriors, live with them, fight in the next hole to them, men like Basilone. Sometimes you understand them, frequently you don't. Or there's nothing to understand; he's just another Marine you serve with but never really know. In ways, we're all the same, we're all different. Maybe you're a cowboy, a kid off the farm, a young tough, an inner-city smartass, or a college boy like me, a young lieutenant, as mysterious to the other fellow as he is to you. You have nothing in common, you and he, only the one thing: you're both Marines. You have that, and when you both have also fought in combat, you very much have that, too.

Fighting a war, especially alongside other soldiers, fighting together, you learn the password, you know the secret handshake of combat, of the Few, the Proud, the Marines. Which is why it was conceivable that before I finished writing this book I might eventually get to know a man I never met, who died when I was a schoolboy, get to know him almost as well as all those folks who loved him so.

His story begins on an island few people had heard of before 1942.

PART ONE

GUADALCANAL

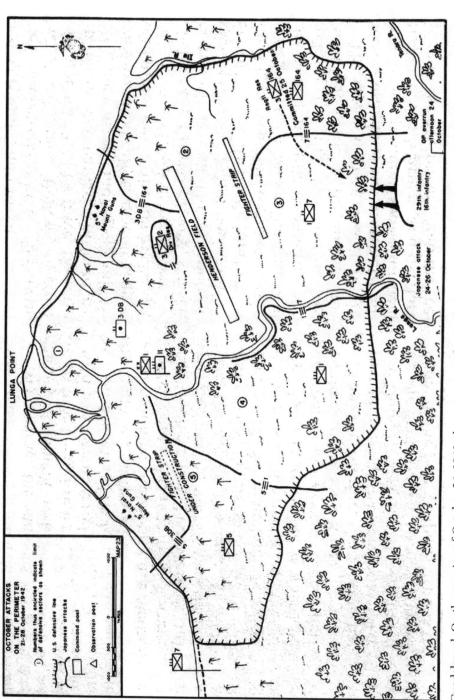

Guadalcanal. On the evening of October 24, 1942, then sergeant John Basilone made a stand on the strategically important high ground near Guadalcanal's Lunga River and south of the vital Marine-held

1

Like Johnny Basilone, the country itself back then was big and brawny, a bit wild and sure of itself, had never been defeated in war, and was accustomed to winning; still young and tough, not effete or decadent like all of those tired Europeans being bullied by dictators, caving in to and being overrun by the loathsome, menacing Adolf Hitler. Our purported allies, fellow democracies Belgium, Norway, the Netherlands, Denmark, and Greece, were already lost or in peril, and the French Army, the greatest in the world it was often boasted, had been thrashed in six weeks and Paris occupied. Britain, even with its powerful Royal Navy and gallant Royal Air Force, was isolated, under siege, its great cities ablaze, its schoolchildren evacuated, its people sheltering in the Underground.

We were different, though. This country didn't lose wars. In eight terrible years of bloody revolution the ill-trained farmers and shopkeepers and frontiersmen of colonial militias had defeated the great British Empire, with the aid of the French fleet had forced the famous Lord Cornwallis to surrender, marching out of Yorktown with his band playing "The World Turned Upside

Down." In 1812 the British were back, burning Washington, but again beaten in the end. In 1848 we rolled over the Mexicans. In the most terrible war Americans ever fought, the country defeated Robert E. Lee, who was perhaps our greatest general but did not possess quite the army of Ulysses S. Grant. Spain in 1898 was a walkover, San Juan Hill, Manila Bay, and all that. In 1917–1918 we came to the rescue of the Allies in Flanders fields and the Argonne Forest.

Yet despite our pride, despite our history and sense of destiny, for the seven months since December 1941 American Marines had done little more than die gallantly in losing causes or surrender, as they had done under fire at Wake Island, or peacefully, striking flags and stacking rifles in humiliating parade formation at the legation of Peking. Except for the air and naval battles at Midway and the Coral Sea, we had been losing and, worse, not to the powerful German army with its Luftwaffe and panzers, its economic machine, its science and technology, or to Mussolini, but to a lesser foe.

They were, to American eyes, the short, skinny warriors of a small island nation with a third of our population, a strange, derivative people known in world markets largely for manufacturing dinnerware and porcelains, knockoff gadgets, china, fine silk textiles, and cheap, colorful children's gimmickry and tin toys, a third-world country of comic-book figures stereotyped and mocked in B-movies as sinister "Oriental" villains or farcical heroes like Mr. Moto, portrayed by Mittel-European Peter Lorre as a clever little detective with outsized horn-rimmed glasses and a mouthful of false teeth, grinning and bowing and given to hissing absurd lines like, "So solly . . . yes, pliss," appealing, like the rest of our view of Japan, to our most facile racist and xenophobic chauvinisms.

What we didn't see was a people with a grand martial tradition who at the opening of the twentieth century in blizzard-swept Siberia and at sea had defeated the czarist fleet and the great peasant armies and Cossack cavalry of the vast Russian empire. And who, since 1937, had been waging another, consistently and appallingly victorious war against the corrupt but much larger

China. Instead we dismissed them as colonial snobs told us that "the Japs," or "the Nips" (lifted from their own name for their country, Nippon), as it was then permissible to call them, were cunning little fellows but not very imaginative. For instance, having years earlier purchased an old surplus Royal Navy destroyer from the British in order to learn how to build modern warships, they had then duplicated the thing precisely, right down to the dent in its bow occasioned by some forgotten collision with an inconvenient pier.

In addition, we were fighting a war like none we or the world had ever seen nor may ever see again, one we couldn't lean on our history for lessons in how to fight. Sprawled across seven thousand miles of great ocean, it featured powerful naval armadas and air forces on both sides and pitted soldiers against one another in murderous ground combat in jungles and on coral beaches, atop mountains and deep in swamps. These were some of the finest light infantry in the world, ours and theirs, Japanese regulars with their samurai traditions of courage and barbarity, their screaming banzai assaults, battling hundreds of thousands of American GIs, sailors, and airmen, and six divisions of United States Marines, who on island after deadly island were living up to their own motto of Semper Fidelis, "always faithful."

A half dozen years after that war, a young New Yorker, a Marine replacement platoon leader, a college boy turned second lieutenant, flew west out of San Francisco bound for the winter mountains of North Korea. The obsolescent Navy C-54 Skymaster carrying the replacement draft took seven days to cross the great ocean, conveniently breaking down or pausing for fuel each night, on Kwajalein, Guam, touching en route Marine holy places such as Iwo Jima of that far greater war. The young lieutenant had never seen combat, knew but secondhand about the South Pacific, beyond seeing the Rodgers and Hammerstein musical in 1949 and attending college with men who had actually fought that war. Now he would be serving alongside many of the seasoned Marines who had defeated the Japanese. For the next year the young officer would fight with the 7th Marines (Basilone's old regiment) against the Koreans and the Chinese army, and would himself come of age in combat at the other end of that greatest of oceans, the Pacific.

In the snowy wartime autumn of 1951, I was that kid lieutenant. A Marine tracking the steps of other, earlier Marines, including Manila John Basilone, but never in war or in peace getting to the obscure Pacific island where his story really begins.

Guadalcanal, whose name derives from the hometown of a long-ago Spanish adventurer, is nearly three thousand miles southwest of Hawaii and one of the larger of the Solomons. It was an appalling place to fight a war, but it was there that we would finally take the ground war to the enemy, give Japan its first land defeat in a half-century of combat against westerners and prove that, mano a mano, American troops were as good as the Japanese Imperial Army.

According to the official records of the United States Marine Corps, the *History of U.S. Marine Corps Operations in World War II*, volume 1, *Pearl Harbor to Guadalcanal*, "Not a single accurate or complete map of Guadalcanal or Tulagi [the tiny neighboring island] existed in the summer of 1942. The hydrographic charts, containing just sufficient data to prevent trading schooners from running aground, were little better."

Aerial photography might have been helpful, *Marine Ops* conceded, but there was a shortage of long-range aircraft and suitable air bases from which they could take off. A lone flight was made, "the beaches appeared suitable landing," another aerial-strip map was scraped up in Australia, and that was deemed it. Estimates of enemy strength were put at 1,850 men on Tulagi and 5,275 on Guadalcanal. "Both estimates were high," Marine historians later admitted. As for the place itself, and its stinking climate, "Rainfall is extremely heavy, and changes in season are marked only by changes in intensity of precipitation. This, together with an average temperature in the high 80s, results in an unhealthy climate. Malaria, dengue, and other fevers, as well as fungus infections, afflict the population." The well-traveled novelist Jack London was once quoted as saying, "If I were king, the worst punishment I could afflict on my enemies would be to banish them to the Solomons."

By the autumn of 1942, "banished to the Solomons" to join that "afflicted population" of those unhappy islands were nearly 20,000 Marines and a smaller number of American soldiers, fighting the equivalent number of Japanese troops. One of those Marines, Robert Leckie, gives us a more intimate and personal description of the place in his book *Challenge for the Pacific*: "Seen from the air, it was a beautiful island, about ninety miles in length and twenty-five wide at its waist, and traversed end to end by lofty mountains, some as high as eight thousand feet." In domestic terms, the place was roughly the size and shape of New York's Long Island but with mountain peaks far taller than any New England ski resort. It was when you got closer up that you recognized the differences.

Leckie quotes one of the local "coast watchers," brave men who stayed behind to report back by radio after the first Japanese landed in the midsummer of 1942, an event that caused most Europeans and Chinese to flee. The coast watcher, British district officer Martin Clemens, described the place for Leckie: "She was a poisonous morass. Crocodiles hid in her creeks or patrolled her turgid backwaters. Her jungles were alive with slithering, crawling, scuttling things; with giant lizards that barked like dogs, with huge, red furry spiders, with centipedes and leeches and scorpions, with rats and bats and fiddler crabs and one big species of land-crab which moved through the bush with all the stealth of a steamroller. Beautiful butterflies abounded on Guadalcanal, but there were also devouring myriads of sucking, biting, burrowing insects that found sustenance in human blood; armies of fiery white ants. Swarms upon swarms of filthy black flies that fed upon open cuts and made festering ulcers of them, and clouds of malaria-bearing mosquitos. When it was hot, Guadalcanal was humid; when the rains came she was sodden and chill; and all her reeking vegetation was soft and squishy to the touch."

Clemens does not mention the big sharks, cruising just offshore and feeding on the bodies, American and Japanese, of sailors, soldiers, Marines, and airmen who fell, alive or dead, into the coastal waters. With about two dozen warships and other vessels of each side going down during the five-month battle, there was plenty for the thriving sharks.

It was the coast watchers who reported that the Japanese were building an airstrip there with Korean slaves, one that would endanger both Australia and New Zealand, our allies whose own forces were largely in action against the Germans half a world away, the famed ANZAC divisions fighting Rommel in North Africa. So they needed our help here on their own doorstep. The Japanese had northern Australia in their path, especially if enemy airpower and the Imperial Navy controlled the shipping routes and opened the way for their infantry.

The U.S. Navy had against all odds defeated the Japanese fleet at Midway, and now it was the turn of American Marines to do the job on land—*if* they were up to the challenge. On August 7 the 1st Marine Division landed by surprise and unopposed. Within a day it encountered and skirmished with Japanese infantry, igniting a terrible battle that would rage for the next five months on land, in the air, and on the surrounding sea.

2

Neither Lieutenant Colonel Lewis B. "Chesty" Puller nor Sergeant Basilone of his 1st Battalion of the 7th Marines had been on Guadalcanal when the 1st Marine Division invaded the island and began their grueling campaign. Fearful that the Japanese were still on the move elsewhere, perhaps against Fiji or the Samoan islands, elements of the 7th Marine Regiment, including Puller's battalion, were dispatched in late summer to defend Samoa against possible invasion. That was where Basilone and his mates groused about having missed the fun, if that's what it was, during those early weeks on the 'Canal.

Samoa wasn't bad duty, though entirely antithetic to the Marine culture of attack. The Marines in Samoa weren't anywhere near the enemy, nor were they about to launch a first offensive against the Japanese; their mission was strictly defensive. And why not? The Japanese were pitching a shutout in the western Pacific, taking one island, one battle after another, and why would they stop short now? No one in Washington or the Pacific knew just where the enemy would strike next. Samoa was certainly a potential target. So the Marines detached to defend it against a proximate invasion dug in and set up their gun emplacements, not only artillery and mortars but those heavy machine guns of Basilone's platoon. When and if the Japanese arrived at Western Samoa, the Marines would be ready to defend the islands, to hold the islands. They'd stacked arms and surrendered at Peking, gallantly lost Wake, burned their colors and asked for terms in the Philippines; they weren't going to lose Samoa without a fight.

Guadalcanal wasn't yet on anyone's charts. No intelligence had come in about the Solomon Islands. And the Japanese had not made up their own minds. They might not yet have recognized the strategic value of the 'Canal for an airstrip. In May when the Marine defense forces landed at Apia, Samoa, there were intelligent men both Japanese and American studying the situation, assessing the region, marshaling their forces, moving prudently closer to each other, but neither side knew precisely what was going to come next.

The Japanese moved first, landing on Bougainville, in the northern Solomons, and then on May 4 taking undefended and minuscule Tulagi, twenty miles across the water from Guadalcanal. In June, they finally made their decision: they would build that famous airstrip in the jungle.

Samoa knew nothing of this. Meanwhile, the Marine defense detachment's job had its fringe benefits. Samoa was "cake . . . a piece of cake," as Marines of the time put it. Basilone, having seen duty in tropical outposts as a younger man while in the Army, would have a basis for comparison. According to his sister Phyllis's serialized newspaper account, Basilone remarked, "Compared to Tent City [in North Carolina], our five month stay in these beautiful islands was a luxury. Not that we didn't continue our training. We got it every day, only now it was real jungle warfare, camouflage, the works." After all, "the Japs were coming, the Japs were coming." Weren't they?

Well, yes, or they had been. Those had been the Japanese plans. But when American naval and air forces defeated the enemy at Midway, June 4–7, Imperial General Headquarters in Tokyo scrapped plans to invade Midway, Fiji, New Caledonia, *and* Samoa. Meanwhile, on Samoa, which was now *not* being invaded, Basilone remarked, "There were some good times. The native women were eager to help the Americans and for months I don't think a single Marine had to do his laundry. Fresh eggs and butter were plentiful and for once the griping subsided.

"By this time I had been promoted to sergeant and my boys were the best damn machine gun outfit in the Division. All sorts of scuttlebutt was drifting into the boondocks and the men were getting restless. We all had thought we would see action first. One morning about the middle of August 1942 word trickled back that our buddies from Quantico and Tent City had already locked grips with the legendary and superhuman Japs."

That last we can take as Basilone sarcasm, but the fact was that a week earlier, on August 7, elements of two Marine infantry regiments, the 1st and 5th Marines, and the 11th Marine artillery regiment, the 1st Marine Raider Battalion, and the Parachute Battalion had landed on the islands of Guadalcanal, Tulagi, and nearby Gavutu. While at Samoa and other backwaters and aboard transport ships, Basilone's own 7th Marine Regiment was scattered over miles of the Pacific and had not yet been committed to battle. Needless to say, the 7th Marines were not happy. When Basilone complained to a Captain Rodgers about his men's impatience, he was told, "For the next few days we are going to run the men ragged. I know they'll bitch and gripe but I still want to hear them gripe *after* their first action."

The captain was true to his word. Said Basilone, "The next few days were hell. All day long we practiced storming caves, then were routed out in the middle of the night to repel imaginary Japs behind our lines. While the men complained bitterly, this practice paid off handsomely in the months to come. Instead of the confusion our buddies ran into, we profited by their misfortunes. I have no doubt many lives were saved with the series of codes and signals we adopted. We became so proficient that not a man of our outfit was shot at by one of his buddies as had been the case during the initial landings on the 'Canal."

August wore on, yet for Manila John and his mates this was not yet even the overture to battle. Guadalcanal was still about twelve-hundred miles away to the west, three or four days by ship, and even there the war had scarcely begun, while on Samoa most of these young Marines were combat innocents. That included Sergeant Basilone, the crack machine gunner Manila John, the salty veteran of three years in the prewar American Army and a few skirmishes with bad men in the backcountry of the Philippines.

We tend to think today of the 1st Marine Division by its nick-name, "the Old Breed," salty, battle-tested vets, hard men who broke the Japanese in the Pacific, and later fought desperate battles in North Korea against Chinese regulars at the Chosin Reservoir. They would fight still later in Vietnam, and more recently in the Middle East. But in 1942 they were only kids, young Marines largely untried. In point of fact, the division had only been created in February 1941, eighteen months before it hit the beaches of Guadalcanal, with few of its 20,000 members blooded in actual combat, just some older officers and senior NCOs who had fought in France in 1918, and a few regulars who had chased bandits and fought rebels in Haiti or Nicaragua during the so-called Banana Wars of the later twenties and early thirties. Basilone himself must have been painfully aware of how little fighting had actually gone on outside the boxing ring during his U.S. Army tour in the 1930s in Manila.

Everything changed for John and his machine gunners on September 18, when, some five weeks late, the 7th Marine Regiment, plus some smaller units, went ashore on Guadalcanal to be greeted with the usual catcalls and derision from men who'd been there and fighting since early August. The 7th had been the first regiment of the division to go overseas but ironically the last to go into combat. Their arrival brought the Marine count on the island up to authorized strength, and the division's commander, General Alexander A. Vandegrift, wasted no time throwing these fresh troops into action. Historian Henry I. Shaw Jr. tells us in his monograph *First Offensive* "Vandegrift now had enough men ashore on Guadalcanal, 19,200, to expand his defensive scheme. He decided to seize a forward position along the east bank of the Matanikau River, in effect strongly out-posting his west flank defenses against the probability of strong enemy attacks from the area where most Japanese troops were landing, First, however, he was going to test the Japanese reaction with a strong probing force. He chose Puller's fresh 1st Battalion, 7th Marines, to move inland along the slopes of Mount Austen and patrol north towards the coast and the Japanese-held area."

But what was all this about Vandegrift's being on the defensive? Hadn't he and his division landed against light or no opposition? How were the Japanese now holding much of the coastline of Guadalcanal? What had happened since August 7 when the invading Marines seemed to have gained the initiative?

Shaw, who wrote about those early days and weeks on the 'Canal, explains the situation. "On board the transports approaching the Solomons, the Marines were looking for a tough fight." Estimates of Japanese strength ranged from 3,100 to just over 8,400. In actual count, there were only a total of 3,457, and of those 2,500 were mostly Korean laborers, not actual fighting men. Said Shaw, "The first landing craft carrying assault troops of the 5th Marines touched down at 0909 [9:09 a.m.] on Red Beach. To the men's surprise (and relief), no Japanese appeared to resist the landing. . . . The Japanese troops . . . had fled to the west, spooked by a week's B-17 bombardment, the pre-assault naval gunfire, and the sight of the ships offshore [those twenty-three transports and their escort vessels]." The U.S. assault troops were reported to have moved "off the beach and into the surrounding jungle, waded the steep-banked Ilu River, and headed for the enemy airfield." That airfield was the point of the entire operation, and on their very first day ashore the U.S. troops were nearly there.

But the Japanese enemy was nothing if not resilient. Heavy combat raged on the small nearby island of Tulagi where the enemy consisted of the Japanese equivalent of Marines, what they called "special naval landing force sailors," and those babies weren't running from anyone. On Tulagi that first day the Raider Battalion suffered ninety-nine casualties; a rifle battalion had fifty-six. When night fell on Gavutu, the enemy stayed in caves as the first wave of parachute Marines came ashore, and brisk fighting ensued as they emerged, with the Marines having to fall back for a time. On August 8, the airfield was taken, but more Japanese forces were on their way, by air and naval surface ships. On the several small islands near Guadalcanal in one day the Americans had suffered 144 dead and 194 wounded. On the second day Japanese airplanes sank the destroyer *Jarvis*, and in dogfights over the two days twenty-one Marine Wildcats were lost. Guadalcanal was not going to be a walkover. But there was worse to come, and swiftly.

On the night of the eighth an enemy cruiser-destroyer force off Savo Island proved themselves our superior at night fighting, sinking with no loss to themselves four Allied heavy cruisers, three American and one Australian, and knocking off the bow of a fifth heavy cruiser. About 1,300 U.S. and Aussie sailors died that night, with another 700 badly wounded or severely burned. These losses were such a shock that a panicky Admiral Jack Fletcher asked for and got permission to withdraw his carrier force. The supply and other amphibious support vessels were also pulled from the area, in effect leaving the Marines ashore on their own and without the heavy artillery that had been due to be landed, to follow the assault waves and reinforce the lighter field artillery already ashore. As for ammo and rations, the 1st Marine Division had only a four-day supply of ammunition for all weapons and, even counting captured Japanese food, only seventeen days' worth of chow.

All this as still half-filled supply ships steamed away from the beaches, fleeing the island and the enemy at flank speed. Their departure was so hasty that several small Marine units that should have been landed were still on board and didn't rejoin the division until October 29. Worse still, on August 12 a sizable Japanese force of reinforcements for Guadalcanal was massing at the huge Japanese base of Truk, only a thousand miles away in the Carolines. On Guadalcanal through August and into September there was heavy fighting, continued combat and recon patrolling, strongpoints and beachheads that changed hands several times over, nightly bombing, naval shelling by ships of both sides, and mounting Marine casualties, as well as the first cases of malaria. No wonder Vandegrift had gone over to the defensive before the 7th Marines, and Sergeant Basilone, even got to the 'Canal and the war.

On that first battalion-sized "probing" by Puller and his men on the 'Canal, what would be for many their first firefight, Marine historian Shaw gives us the details: "Puller's battalion ran into Japanese troops bivouacked on the slopes of [Mount] Austen on the 24th [of September] and in a sharp firefight had seven men killed and 25 wounded. Vandegrift sent the 2nd Battalion, 5th Marines, forward to reinforce Puller and help provide the men needed to carry the casualties out of the jungle. Now reinforced, Puller continued his advance, moving down the east bank of the Matanikau. He reached the coast on the 26th as planned, where he drew intense fire from enemy positions on the ridges west of the river. An attempt by the 2nd Battalion, 5th Marines, to cross was beaten back."

Heavy machine guns are defensive weapons that don't usually play much of a role in a probing patrol like this one in rough enemy country, but if this was Basilone's first serious combat, it wasn't dull. What had begun as a "probe" was becoming something else. The 1st Raider Battalion was now involved, and so was Colonel Red Mike Edson, the former Raider who now commanded the 5th Marine Regiment. Vandegrift on the twenty-seventh ordered Edson to take charge of the expanded force that included Puller's fresh but inexperienced battalion. When faulty intelligence caused Red Mike to believe that one of his battalions was advancing when in actuality it had been stopped by Japanese who crossed the river by night, he ordered Puller to take his men by small boats around the enemy flank to land and move inland.

It was a clever tactical idea, but too complicated, and the relatively green 1st Battalion soon found itself cut off on the beach and, covered by gunfire from a convenient American destroyer, was forced to evacuate by sea (Puller himself having gone out in a small boat to the destroyer *Ballard* to make the arrangements and signal back to his men on the beach) and find its way back to the perimeter. The fighting was confused and uncoordinated, and along with the newly arrived 7th Marines (Basilone and his comrades), both the Raiders and the 5th Marines also were forced to pull back from the Matanikau. It was typical of combat at that stage on Guadalcanal that the three-day battle didn't even rate a name. But all the to-ing and fro-ing gained no ground and cost sixty Marine dead and a hundred wounded. The newly arrived Marines were learning, and it was a painful schooling.

Welcome to the war, Manila John.

3

In September 1942, a month after the fight began, Manila John and the 7th Marines finally left Samoa, sailing in convoy to join up with the other two Marine regiments fighting on Guadalcanal. For Basilone's arrival at the war we have to turn from the historian Henry Shaw to Basilone's sister Phyllis Basilone Cutter's serialized newspaper account, written well after the fact and by a civilian who didn't seem to understand the difference between the 7th Marine Regiment, which was John's outfit, and the 7th Marine Division, which never existed, then or now. Such criticism may seem trivial and somewhat hard on a family member, but since numerous articles, one monograph, and a hardcover book have been published that are to an extent reliant on Phyllis's recollections, an analysis of her work is justified. Here then, caveats established, is how she describes, supposedly in her brother's words, the time just before he reached the island: "The Japs were putting reinforcements in nightly and now the talk was maybe our boys would be driven off the island and into the sea. We could not understand where our Navy was. Why couldn't they have stopped the Jap transports? We didn't know our Navy had taken quite a beating, even though they won the sea battle, the losses were costly and the Japs were still pouring in." If John here is referring to the battle of Savo Island, our Navy didn't win the sea battle; it had been massacred, losing four heavy cruisers.

"Suddenly on Friday morning September 18, 1942, the loud-speakers blared," Basilone recalled on the transport, "'All Marines go to your debarkation stations!' We climbed the narrow ladders to positions on the deck above the cargo nets draped over the side and heard the squeaking of the davits as they were swung out and landing craft lowered. The whole length of the ship was swarming with Marines scrambling down the nets into the boats. One by one the boats scooted off to the rendez-vous areas where they awaited, circling. Breaking out of the tight circles, wave after wave sped for the beach.

"Our landing was unopposed and we poured in."

Marine Ops reports simply, "The reinforced 7th Marines unloaded its 4,262 men," as three other transports, also peacefully, delivered aviation fuel, ammo, engineering equipment, and the like along the same tranquil stretch of coastline.

Phyllis's account of her brother's landing makes it sound dramatic, while the official account dismisses it as a mere "unloading." Her newspaper series, with Basilone now ashore on the embattled island, then wanders into pulp magazine fiction, and it seems reasonable to suggest that some of the Basilone lore about his combat experiences from this point on derives from his sister's fanciful journalism and not necessarily from the facts. If there are Marines and others who question any of Basilone's feats of arms, they should consider that the man himself wasn't making these absurd claims; it was his loving sister many years later who conjured up the theatricals.

A week would pass before the 1st Battalion, 7th Marines, was sent into concerted action (on September 24), in the so-called probe by Chesty Puller, as recounted by Shaw. With so many men involved and in rough country, there surely must have been a few earlier skirmishes and spontaneous firefights and shelling. But

Phyllis has young Johnny Basilone, new to battle, starting to take over the war. Still quoting her brother: "This was the morning of the 24th [a week or so after their landing] and after about five hours of the toughest trail-breaking imaginable, we halted for a breather. Our advance scouts sent word back that a heavy patrol of Japs was on the trail ahead. We had not expected to encounter the enemy this side of the Matanikau River."

Here is where the writing really takes glorious flight: "Captain Rodgers [the company commander, it appears] felt we could try to entrap this patrol by encircling them with a ring of machine gun fire. At the same time being fully aware of the enemy's reputation for trickery, he decided he would call on the 2nd Marines for help. Calling me to his side, the Captain said, 'Sergeant, take three machine gun crews up to try and clean up that nest of Japs.'"

This entire passage is ridiculous. Marine company commanders issue their orders through their lieutenants, not their machine-gun sergeants, unless in extreme circumstances. Why would a Marine officer send out three heavily burdened machine-gun crews in thick jungle country to encircle or ambush anybody, especially a number of enemy troops described as "a heavy patrol"? They would send lighter-burdened, faster-moving riflemen, possibly a four-man fire team or squad, depending on the situation. Once the riflemen located the enemy, the machine guns could be brought up or sited on high ground to support an assault on the enemy with overhead fire. To use heavily laden machine-gun crews as scouts far out ahead of the swifter riflemen goes against reason.

And no Marine captain would confide to a sergeant that he was about to go outside the chain of command and his own battalion commander to ask yet another regiment, the 2nd Marines, to back him up—especially not with a battalion commander as fearsome as the terrible-tempered Puller.

The rest of Phyllis's account has Basilone wiping out enemy soldiers right and left. He had been a week on the island, and already "all the newness was worn off by now. We were dirty, tired and mean." The generally sensible Bruce W. Doorly, in his monograph about Basilone, the privately published *Raritan's Hero*, seems to have bought into the Phyllis Cutter version in his own variation on the incident:

"A U.S. patrol had spotted a small group of Japanese on a scouting mission. John was told to bring three machine gun crews and wipe out the enemy, hopefully leaving no survivors that would bring information back to enemy headquarters. Guadalcanal was jungle with low visibility. John and his group snaked their way quietly [dragging those heavy guns?] toward the location where the U.S. patrol had seen the Japanese. Luckily the Marines spotted them undetected. Basilone led the group, moving in closest to observe that the Japanese had stopped to eat, obviously unaware of his presence. Moving back toward his men, John instructed them to set up in a half-circle around the unsuspecting enemy. He cleared his forehead, wiped his eyes. Then started firing his machine gun. The rest of his group also opened fire. John observed the Japanese reacting as they were shot. He later said, 'They seemed to be dancing up and down. I forgot to realize the impact of heavy bullets was jerking them into all sorts of crazy contortions.'"

The new-to-combat Marines had been warned about treachery and enemy tricks, playing dead, for one. "John decided to take no chances. He walked around, finishing off the enemy, making sure they were dead by firing a short burst from his machine gun. One of John's men, Bob Powell, said, 'Jesus, Sarge, what the hell are you doing? Why waste ammo on dead ones?' Just as Bob finished his words, a supposedly dead Japanese soldier jumped up with his gun in hand. Another of John's men quickly shot him down."

Wrote Doorly, "On the way back to camp two of his men got sick. This was everyone's first taste of war. They were very fortunate . . . they suffered no casualties."

While Doorly's version of that first real firefight is more controlled than that of sister Phyllis, there appears to be a need here among Basilone chroniclers, fans if you will, to make him even from the very start somewhat larger than life, bigger, braver, deadlier. But neither account of a first Guadalcanal firefight by Basilone rings true.

Manila John needed none of this tarting up. He was an authentic hero, the real goods. He was a warrior who fought with an extraordinary courage and resolve, with strength and an instinctive canniness far beyond what might be expected of a man of his background and age (he was twenty-five at Guadalcanal), killing a lot of seasoned enemy troops, and he would be rewarded by a nation with medals and gratitude. But people apparently felt they had to create a Basilone of their own, to concoct and exaggerate, regardless of the hard reality, however difficult it was to ascertain entirely who John really was. And phony yarns gained currency, when really there was no need, only this compulsion to inflate and imagine. It may be that units of Puller's battalion, possibly including John and some of his gunners under Captain Rodgers, did actually stumble across some Japanese carelessly eating lunch without any perimeter security and wiped them out with machine-gun fire, but it borders on the fantastic to accept that the action came about when a machine-gun unit was sent on a combat patrol unaccompanied by riflemen, or that one of Puller's captains would breach the chain of command, asking support from another regiment. And in a machine-gun platoon, their sergeant doesn't have "his" machine gun. He directs the fire of others. But here Basilone does most of the firing himself. In that far-fetched "first fight," if it ever happened, the legend of Manila John began to emerge.

He and his gunners were certainly part of that very real and quite bloody "probe" by Puller's battalion in which the Marines took 160 casualties. But with versions of the incident surfacing here and there that have the Japanese caught at lunch, you have to consider the possibility that Basilone had gotten through at least one efficient if rather one-sided firefight *before* Puller's battalion completed its somewhat screwed-up first probe.

Battle, especially for green troops, is always confused, chaotic, frightening, and few men remember its details in precisely the same way. Quite possibly not even Manila John, still new to combat, could tell you precisely what happened in his first firefight and when. The problem is simply that the vision of Basilone wielding a fifty-pound heavy machine gun delivering the coup de grâce to wounded enemy soldiers, firing bursts into their prone bodies, is patently absurd. No Marine with any combat experience will fail to recognize gaps in the narrative. And there is no mention of the incident in Shaw or *Marine Ops*.

There would be more heavy fighting for the lately arrived Marines on October 9 when they crossed the Matanikau River and attacked north. In a three-day fight Puller's battalion (with Basilone) and other units were credited with killing or wounding 799 members of the Japanese 4th Infantry. General Alexander Vandegrift knew the Japanese were building up for a major offensive—reinforcements were being landed on the 'Canal almost every night under cover of darkness—yet another attempt to retake Henderson Field, as the Marines had named their captured Japanese airfield (to honor Marine pilot Captain Lofton R. Henderson, killed flying against the Japanese fleet at Midway).

As has long been Marine infantry philosophy, Vandegrift intended to use constant aggressive combat patrols, raids, and probes in force to upset Japanese plans, unbalance the enemy, render it more difficult for them to build up and attack in great force. Of Basilone's regiment, the official USMC operations history notes, "In the short time that men of the 7th Marines had been ashore on the island, they had earned a right to identification as veteran troops. So with a complete combat-wise Marine Division of three infantry regiments, the 1st, 5th, and 7th by now on hand, plus an artillery regiment, the 11th—and Army reinforcements on the way [their good 164th Infantry commanded by Colonel Robert Hall was already on the island and being gradually fed into the line]—Vandegrift and his staff made plans to meet the strong Japanese attack that was bearing down on them." It would likely be a defensive battle with General Vandegrift and his officers relying on heavy machine guns, such as those of Basilone's platoon.

Thus was the situation in mid-October, the awful terrain and even the weather, with two powerful forces roughly in balance and about to clash, as summed up in the *History of U.S. Marine Corps Operations in World War II*, volume 1. The Japanese moved toward Henderson Field along the jungle track named, rather grandly, the "Maruyama Trail," for their apparently vain new general, scratched out of the inhospitable bush by Japanese engineers. At the terminal of the trail Japanese troops would assemble for their assault on what would come to be known as Bloody (or Edson's) Ridge, where Puller's battalion and other Marine units would make their stand. From *Marine Ops* here is the situation from the enemy's point of view: "Heavy rain fell almost every day. The van of the single-file advance often had completed its day's march and bivouacked for the night before the rear elements were able to move. Troops weakened on their half-ration of rice. Heavy artillery pieces [vital to the siege tactics lying ahead] had to be abandoned along the route, and mortars also became too burdensome to manage. Frequently unsure of their exact location in the jungle, the Japanese by 19 October still had not crossed the upper Lunga, and Maruyama [their new commander] postponed his assault until the 22nd. Meanwhile, General Sumiyoshi's fifteen 'Pistol Petes' [Japanese aircraft] pounded the Lunga perimeter, air attacks continued, and Imperial warships steamed brazenly into Sealark Channel almost every night to shell the airfield, beaches, and Marine positions."

Now, from our side's vantage point, according to *Marine Ops*: "The tempo of action was obviously building up for the counteroffensive, and Marines and soldiers worked constantly to improve their field fortifications and keep up an aggressive patrol schedule. Patrols did not go far enough afield however to discover Maruyama's wide-swinging enveloping force, and recons to the east found no indications of a Japanese build-up on that flank. Thus General Vandegrift and his staff were aware only of Sumiyoshi's threat along the coast from the west. There the first probe came on 20 October."

It was in the Bloody Ridge area on the Lunga River line that the Japanese began testing the Marine lines and outposts, searching for soft spots and lack of security, with infantry patrols and a few tanks. An early probe on the west bank of the Matanikau turned back when one tank was hit by 37mm fire from the 3rd Battalion, 1st Marines. For weeks General Hyakutake had tried but failed to take Henderson Field and so end the thing, and now a new general, Maseo Maruyama, who had flown in to command the 17th Japanese Army, was determined that this offensive would be successful. He was confident he would retake the airfield and swing the battle for Guadalcanal his way. He commanded a famous Japanese outfit, the crack Sendai Division freshly arrived from the big enemy base of Rabaul, to spearhead the effort, and at noon on October 24 he issued a battle order that contained an ominous, if somewhat grandiose, sentence: "In accordance with plans of my own, I intend to exterminate the enemy around the airfield in one blow."

One of the units waiting for him, and for that menacing "one blow," was Chesty Puller's 1st Battalion of the 7th Marines.

4

On the twenty-third, the Japanese attack on the Matanikau River had been beaten back, the attackers cut to pieces. Ironically, 1st Marine Division commanding officer Alexander Vandegrift wasn't even on Guadalcanal during the crucial fighting of October 23–25. Instead, he was in Noumea for a meeting with Admiral "Bull" Halsey. In his stead, Major General Roy Geiger, though an aviator, but being senior man on board, was left in command. And Geiger knew that despite the enemy's appalling losses of the twenty-third, they would be coming back, however many times it took. That was how the Japanese operated and one reason they were so formidable. Everyone knew the little airfield was at stake, the battle was now in the balance and could swing either way— and with it might go the entire Guadalcanal campaign.

At sea the heavyweights were also squaring up. Admiral William "Bull" Halsey, having succeeded a dilatory commander (Robert Ghormley), was now running the overall Guadalcanal campaign, land and sea, and senior Marine officers who knew his hard-charging reputation were delighted. With Halsey on the case, the Navy and Washington itself would be paying attention to a distant front too often on short rations and a slim budget. Halsey and his fleet were now at sea following the parley at Noumea, steaming toward the Solomons with two carriers, two battleships, nine cruisers, and twenty-four destroyers. Arrayed against them, Admiral Isoroku Yamamoto, Japan's top naval commander, had sailed with four carriers, five battleships, fourteen cruisers, and forty-four destroyers. Aircraft from both sides were up. Clearly some sort of major clash of arms was coming, on the island and in the air and sea above and around it.

Chesty Puller's 1st Battalion of the 7th Marines had a mile and a half of ridgeline front to defend. Such a long front held by a single Marine rifle battalion, a thousand men or so, was painfully stretched, with little depth. Out in front of the main line of resistance, the MLR, Chesty had a few outposts, and he was nervous about those. The 2nd Battalion of the regiment (my own outfit eight years later in North Korea), commanded on the 'Canal by Colonel Herman Hanneken, had been pulled out of the line guarding Henderson Field on the south and sent toward the Matanikau, which was why Puller was spread so thin. Hanneken, a former enlisted Marine, soft-spoken but dangerous, an officer who would himself pull a weapon (Mitchell Paige in his book reports that Hanneken once shot a sniper out of a tree with a single shot from a handgun), had previously fought side by side with Puller, the two men so very different in style and temperament but both of them fighters.

Robert Leckie in his *Challenge for the Pacific*, describes Puller's demeanor before the battle as he worked to get everyone in the battalion except the mortarmen up into the thin green line of his lightly held front: "In the morning and afternoon [of October 24] Puller roved his lines, chomping on his cold stump of pipe, removing it to bellow orders ('We don't need no communications system,' his men boasted, 'we got Chesty!'), or speaking through teeth clamped firmly around the stem. Puller's manner was urgent because a young Marine who had fallen behind a patrol that morning had seen Japanese officers studying his position through field glasses. Puller urged his men to dig deeper, but when he came to one position he pulled his pipe from his mouth, pointed at the hole with it, and grunted: 'Son, if you dig that hole any deeper, Ah'll have to charge you with desertion.'" The Marine grinned, and Puller strode on, pleased to see that Manila John Basilone had fortified his "pair of machine guns almost in the exact center of the line."

This is an interesting moment. Leckie, who fought on Guadalcanal and later wrote about it, may have recorded the first interaction of Puller, the legendary battalion commander, with Basilone, the machine-gun sergeant. Marine battalion commanders usually know, or know of, most of their men at least by sight, but such precise recognition by a colonel of a single sergeant on the eve of battle is hardly typical. Given that machine guns play such a crucial role in a battalion's tactics on defense, however, Puller would understandably take more than a casual interest in Basilone and the placement of his weapons. In any event, that is what Leckie reports happened early in the day of what would be, for Manila John, the climactic moment of his young life, and for the colonel, one of the epic combat commands of the war so far. And for anyone who questions just how professional a Marine Basilone had been, that perfect positioning of his guns is telling.

In the Marine Corps a battalion commander holding a defensive line is personally responsible for the location of all of his machine guns. No platoon commander or even company commander has that responsibility, and certainly no sergeant. But here we have the veteran Puller with all his combat savvy, his Navy Crosses, his experience in the "Banana Wars," approving Basilone's placement of his machine guns at precisely the right spot. Where did Manila John pick up that much tactical know-how? Maybe the son of a peaceful Italian tailor in Raritan was just an instinctive warrior. Back home, at Gaburo's Laundry or the country club's caddy shack, who would have thought?

Unknown to the Americans, Japanese general Maruyama had issued orders for the attacking assault troops to jump off against the Marine line of resistance that afternoon at five p.m. Leckie continues reporting on Puller's behavior as the fight neared: "Colonel

Puller returned to his 'command post'—not much of a place but simply a field telephone hardly ten yards behind his line—to repeat his request for permission to withdraw his outpost platoon. He was convinced the enemy was coming, and he feared that the forty men on outpost would be needlessly sacrificed. But his argument— couched in ungentle roars—was unavailing. The men stayed outside the line. "Finally, Puller had all of the field phones opened so that every company and platoon could hear every message. And then the rain came down."

To those of us who open umbrellas when the first drop falls, the sheer weight, volume, and shattering noise of a tropical rain squall is likely beyond our experience. The rain blurred vision and intensified the jungle gloom. Under its battering, men blinked and ducked, squinting as daylight turned to premature dusk, the ground beneath their feet becoming slippery and then viscous slime, and soon sucking, clotting mud. The rain fell that afternoon not only on the Marines but on the Japanese preparing their offensive. And the newly arrived General Maruyama had no conception of what the downpour might do to confuse and disconcert a large body of troops traveling by foot through hard country on their approach march to battle in dense jungle conditions and fading light.

Five o'clock came and went without the scheduled and anticipated attack. It's possible to imagine the thoughts of rain-soaked Marines as they waited for their rendezvous with the enemy and with their own fate. The 7th Marines knew the quality of the Japanese troops they were fighting, and were by now reasonably confident of their own abilities and resources; John Basilone's tactical placement of his guns was evidence of how Puller's battalion had matured to veteran status.

Combat soldiers can rarely agree on just what happened and when in a firefight. And consequently there exist different versions of just what Basilone and his machine gunners did and how they performed in the crucial battle about to commence.

5

Can a single night define a man's entire life? There are a half dozen accounts of just what John Basilone did that Saturday night on Guadalcanal on October 24, 1942, some conflicting, others confused and contradictory. Let's assess them all and pass our own judgments. But take in and remember what his battalion commander, Lieutenant Colonel Lewis B. "Chesty" Puller, believed he saw and to which he later attested in his recommendation for a medal. You may even choose to argue with Chesty, although few Marines would.

Here is the situation. Late in the afternoon the 1st Battalion, 7th Marines, learned they were not only facing General Tadashi Sumiyoshi's command but another, and unexpected, flanking move by Maseo Maruyama, when an enemy officer was spotted on high ground south of the airport studying Bloody Ridge with field glasses, and then a scout-sniper report came in from that same quarter of "many rice fires" two miles south of Puller's extended line. *Marine Ops* acknowledges that at this moment, with the fight not yet begun, the Marines seemed to hold a significant advantage in heavy weapons. As noted, the Japanese had left behind, strewn along the difficult Maruyama Trail, all of their heavy artillery and had even discarded most of their mortars. While the entrenched Marines were supported by all of their own mortars and heavier guns, there was some early hope of moonlight to aid the gunners in zeroing in on enemy targets. But though the rains slackened briefly toward seven p.m. (according to Robert Leckie), heavy rains came again and full darkness settled in on the front. Yet it was then that Maruyama ordered his left-flank regiment, the 29th Infantry, forward toward the main line of resistance.

Leckie reports that Sergeant Ralph Briggs Jr. called in from the outpost and reached Puller. Speaking softly, Briggs said, "Colonel, there's about three thousand Japs between you and me."

"Are you sure?"

"Positive. They've been all around us, singing and smoking cigarettes, heading your way."

"All right, Briggs, but make damned sure. Take your men to the left—understand me? Go down and pass through the lines near the sea. I'll call 'em to let you in. Don't fail, and don't go in any other direction. I'll hold my fire as long as I can."

"Yes, sir," Briggs said, and hung up. Crawling on their bellies to the left, he and most of his forty-six outpost men got out. The Japanese caught and killed four of them. This was about nine-thirty p.m. Soon the enemy had reached the tactical barbed wire in front of the 1st Battalion and began to cut lanes through it.

Toward eleven o'clock, still in heavy rain, the main body of the Japanese force attacked Puller's line amid the usual screaming of "Blood for the Emperor!" and "Marines, you die!"

The Marines responded with, "To hell with your goddamned emperor!" and, hilariously, "Blood for Franklin and Eleanor!"

Writing years later in New Jersey, Bruce Doorly provides us a first mention of Basilone that crucial night about ten o'clock: "The field phone rang. Having waited for days, they thought it must be just another outpost getting lonely. However, when John answered the phone he heard trouble. It was one of his men from a post closer to the front line. He screamed, 'Sarge, the Japs are coming.' In the background John could hear the sound of explosions and gun fire. 'Thousands of them, my God! They just keep coming, Sarge, they just keep coming.' The phone went dead."

This reputed exchange doesn't entirely make sense. Basilone headed a two-machine-gun section of perhaps six or eight men total. Why would he have an outpost of his own reporting to him? Wouldn't an outpost Marine with the enemy that close have whispered and not screamed?

Doorly then writes, "John Basilone took control. He turned to his men and said, 'All right, you guys, don't forget your orders. The Japs are not going to get through to the field. I'm telling you that goes, no matter what!'"

Doorly cites battle descriptions by Basilone that "were often very descriptive and at times comical." Doorly pictures the first assault wave this way: "They could soon hear the Japanese cutting the barbed wire. Unfortunately, they could not see the Japanese in the dark as they had hoped. Their first line of defense, the barbed wire, was already falling. Basilone set the strategy for his unit. He told his men to let the enemy get within fifty yards and then, 'let them have it!' They fired at the first group of attacking Japanese, successfully wiping them out." He quotes Basilone as saying, "The noise was terrific and I could see the Japs jumping as they were smacked by our bullets. Screaming, yelling, and dying all at the same time. Still they came, only to fall back, twisting and falling in all sorts of motions, as we dispatched them to their honorable ancestors."

That first enemy charge was only the beginning of the overall attack. The enemy charged again. The dead began to pile up. "One thing you've got to give the Japanese, they were not afraid to die, and believe me, they did," Basilone is quoted as saying. Grenades flew into the Marine lines and "one Japanese soldier got to within five feet of Basilone—here Basilone used his pistol, killing the attacker."

Leckie picks up Basilone's fight:

"Now the attack was veering toward dead center. The Japanese hordes were rushing at Manila John Basilone's machine guns. They came tumbling down an incline and Basilone's gunners raked

them at full-trigger. They were pouring out five hundred rounds a minute. The gun barrels were red and sizzling inside their water jackets—and the precious cooling water was evaporating swiftly. 'Piss in 'em. Piss in 'em!' Basilone yelled and some of the men got up to refill the jackets with a different liquid.

"The guns stuttered on, tumbling the onrushing Japanese down the incline, piling them up so high that by the time the first enemy flood had begun to ebb and flow back into the jungle, they had blocked Basilone's field of fire. In the lull Manila John ordered his men out to push the bodies away and clear the fire lanes. Then he ducked out of the pit to run for more ammunition. He ran barefoot, the mud squishing between his toes. He ran into Puller's CP and ran back again, burdened with spare barrels and half a dozen 14-pound belts slung over his shoulders."

By now, the enemy was drifting west, overrunning the guns to Basilone's right. "They stabbed two Marines to death and wounded three others. They tried to swing the big Brownings on the Americans but they only jammed them. They left the [gun] pit and drove further to the rear. Basilone returned to his pit just as a runner dashed up gasping. 'They've got the guys on the right.' Basilone raced to his right. He ran past a barefoot private named Evans and called 'Chicken' for his tender eighteen years. 'C'mon you yellow bastards!' Chicken screamed, firing and bolting his rifle, firing and reloading. Basilone ran on to the empty pit, jumped in, found the guns jammed and sprinted back to his own pit. Seizing a mounted machine gun, Basilone spread-eagled it across his back, shouted at half of his men to follow him—and was gone."

It must be noted here that a "mounted machine gun," the gun and tripod mount, exclusive of ammo, weighs 49.75 pounds—the gun 31 pounds, the tripod, pintle, traversing, and elevating mechanisms the rest—not including the 14-pound belts of ammo, and Manila John was running around in the rain and mud lugging this thing on his bare back. As Basilone and his squad ran they blundered into a half dozen Japanese and killed them all. Then, at the pit, Basilone dropped one gun and lay flat on his back trying to unjam the other guns and get them working again. It isn't clear here (via Leckie) just how many machine guns he had by now, two or three.

By one-thirty in the morning Basilone had the guns fixed. And by now the Sendai Division was attacking once more. Puller phoned the artilleryman Colonel Pedro del Valle for support and was told the big guns were running short of ammo and when what they had was fired there would be no more shells for tomorrow. Puller informed the artilleryman coldly, an infantryman chiding a gunner, "If they get through here tonight, there won't be a tomorrow." And when a Captain Regan Fuller told Puller he was running out of small-arms ammo, Puller responded, "You've got bayonets, haven't you?" "Sure, yes, sir." "All right then, hang on."

The fight went on all night despite the staggering loss of life, especially on the attackers. Bit by bit American Army soldiers were fed into the cauldron as reinforcements for the Marines, firing the new eight-shot semiautomatic Garand rifles the Marines had not yet been issued (they were still armed with the five-cartridge-clip, bolt-action World War I '03 Springfield). There was a wonderful exchange between Puller and his Army counterpart Colonel Robert Hall, who arrived at Puller's post, guided through the darkness by a Navy chaplain named Father Keough who was ministering to his Marines. Puller thanked the cleric for his assistance and then turned to Colonel Hall. Leckie gives us this dialogue: "Colonel, I'm glad to see you. I don't know who's senior to who right now, and I don't give a damn. I'll be in command until daylight, at least, because I know what's going on here and you don't."

Said the sensible Hall, "That's fine with me."

6

Fresh troops were arriving, but the deadly night was decidedly not yet finished, and Manila John Basilone was still fighting. Using the heavy machine gun cradled in his arms, apparently still attached to the tripod, he killed several infiltrating Japanese, the hot barrel burning him as he did so. At another point some enemy infantry were wriggling toward him on their bellies through the long grass. To get lower and in a more effective firing position, Basilone took the big heavy off its tripod and steadied it in his arms, his own belly flat to the ground, and from that prone position fired bursts as low as he could to chop down the Japanese snaking toward him. As he later remarked, he had "mowed down the crawlers." At the same time the professional machine gunner who knew the gun better than most, in the dark, in the rain, and in combat, continued coolly to instruct his men on using the other guns, finding a jammed gun and reminding them, almost pedantically, "the head spacing is out of line." This is pretty cool stuff under fire, as the Japanese mounted yet another charge, shouting their banzais as they came. One Marine, perhaps not yet a true believer, asked Basilone as the long, exhausting night wore on, increasingly lethal, "Sarge, how long can we keep this up?"

According to Bruce Doorly, Basilone himself was wondering the same thing. And ironically, considering the downpours, they were short of drinking water, some canteens holed by shrapnel, with Marines running dry.

"The attacks kept coming, even in the heavy rain. John told two of his uninjured soldiers, Powell and Evans, to keep the heavy machine guns loaded. He would roll to one machine gun and fire until it was empty, then roll over to the other one that had been loaded while he was firing the first one. When that one was empty he went back to the first one which had now been reloaded. The tactic was used against the remaining Japanese attacks. Just when the Marines could not keep up the pace any longer, the Japanese would retreat to regroup. The enemy would then predictably charge again, in groups of 15 or 20, Basilone letting them get close and then mowing them down. As they were hit, screams filled the night.

"Another Japanese soldier managed to sneak up to their position and jumped right at them with a knife. Again, John got him with his pistol [it must have been a .45, the standard-issue sidearm for a machine-gun sergeant]. The pistol would see more action through the night, as it was the best weapon for those who crept in close by crawling. Some grenades exploded close to John and his fellow Marines, but none hit them. It was a long night and some of the early kills started to decompose. It brought on a nasty stench."

This sounds to me like rather rapid decomposition, but it was, after all, the tropics and these were the dead.

"Later in the night, Basilone saw an incredible sight. The Japanese had taken their dead and piled them up high in front of them to form a wall to protect the living Japanese soldiers who set up their machine guns behind the pile of their dead comrades. To counter the new enemy 'wall,' John decided to move his position to get a better angle. Later, in a break in the fighting, John sent one of his men to push over the wall of dead bodies."

It's worth noting that Bob Leckie has the Japanese bodies piling like a wall in the course of action, while Doorly has them being piled up deliberately. According to Robert V. Aquilina, head of the Marine Corps History Division reference branch at Quantico, and Colonel Walt Ford of *Leatherneck* magazine, there is ample historical precedent, going back to antiquity, for the former, and the piles would have included dying as well as dead enemy soldiers. As for the latter, yes, it could well have happened, but Colonel Ford suggests that it's "more the sort of detail that somebody only knows from having been there." Such variations are illustrative of the challange inherent in accurately reporting accounts of battle—the so-called "fog of war."

By three a.m. the Marines were once more running short of ammo. And the Japanese kept coming. Here is what Basilone's nephew Jerry Cutter and writer Jim Proser have to say about what Basilone did that night, the genuine heroism he displayed, the losses of men close to him that he suffered. While much of their book is inaccurate and somewhat misleading, it does convey something of the chaos and has its moments: "Evans fed the ammo and tried to keep mud off the belts. He also kept an eye on the rear of our position where we turned our .45s on the Japs coming up behind us. A hail of TNT and grenades fell all around us and our ears rang from the explosions so we couldn't hear ourselves yelling from inches away. The concussion was like getting socked in the head by a heavyweight and made it hard to keep your vision clear."

Basilone knew about being "socked," having boxed, often against harder-hitting men. Proser wrote, quoting Basilone, "We were seeing double, and things were moving around. So that we couldn't draw a clear bead on a target. The dead piled up in front of us obscuring the firing lanes. Both guns jammed. I tore mine open and cleared the receiver of mud. Powell did the same. In the process, Evans yelled just in time and we shot two more Japs coming at us from behind. Garland was frantically trying to clean the mud off the belts but it was tough work. We were getting low again on ammo and were out of water completely. The water jackets were smoking again which meant they were low or out of water too. If we didn't get water for the guns the barrels would burn out and never last the night. I got mine firing again but I was hitting only corpses piled high in front of us and others hanging on the wire further back."

"Hanging on the wire." The lethal phrase may sound innocent, meaningless, but men "hanging on the wire" are usually dead attackers, shot to pieces by the machine guns of the defense. The war doesn't matter—the trenches of Flanders in the Great War, so many other infantry battles in World War II. Maybe Grant's and Lee's men had to clear the dead as well. The first dead men I ever saw in combat, five or six North Koreans, were "hanging on the wire" of snow-covered Hill 749 in November 1951. Basilone's and Powell's and Evans's and Garland's dead happened to be Japanese of the Sendai Division. And when there are too many of them obscuring your aim, it is the gunners who have just killed them who are forced to do the undertaking as well, the tidying up of corpses. Listen to what are said to be Basilone's words:

"I ordered Garland to go down and clear the firing lanes. He looked at me and I looked back at him. It could easily be a suicide mission. The latest assault backed off. I didn't have to tell Garland twice. He was up and out of the hole. Evans and I covered him in bursts of fire that kept the field clear on either side of him. He slid down the hill on his butt and pushed the piles of bodies over with his feet, keeping his head below the pile. That did the trick. He slid over to another pile and did the same maneuver. We had a clear field of fire again. He slithered back up the hill while we sent streams of bullets a few inches over his head. For the life of me I didn't know why we hadn't been cross-haired by artillery and concentrated mortar fire by now, but I guess that's where luck comes into it."

Obviously John wasn't aware of all those heavier weapons discarded by the enemy struggling through the jungle along the Maruyama Trail and unable to keep moving under the load. If that was luck, it was what infantrymen pray for, who know the damage good artillery and big mortars can do to men in trenches or foxholes open to the sky and vulnerable to the vertical fall of high-trajectory weapons.

"Garland got back in the hole. I was out of ammo. The boys all needed water as well as the guns. Powell was back on duty sighting down the ridge [with machine guns the most effective killing fire is not straight ahead but across the front, *along* the ridgeline, hitting the enfiladed attackers on their flanks]. The latest wave had retreated. I had to make another run for ammo, and this time for water, too. Down the ridge, there was movement. The Japs had almost the same idea I did. They crept up to the piles of their dead comrades and pulled them on top of each other like sandbags. They had a machine gun up behind the human barricade.

"'Move out,' I ordered. We scraped our weapons out of the mud and hopped out to the left to get an angle on the new advance position of the enemy. Within a few minutes, they had our hole cross-haired and landed mortars on the bulls-eye, but we weren't there anymore [so the Japanese had gotten a few mortars up the Maruyama Trail after all]. We concentrated fire on the new position and wiped out the gunners. There was no fire coming from Bullard's hole over to the left, and I led what was left of my squad over there. When we got there, all my boys were dead. We pulled Bullard and the rest out and took up firing positions in the new hole. The field phone was still open to the CP and I called in our situation—no water, no ammo, the position to our right flank was now out of the fight. We were all that remained of C Company." This surely is an exaggeration, as along the length of an extended company front of perhaps eight hundred yards, no one machine gunner would know his entire company was gone. And according to post-battle casualty reports, the assertion that C Company had been wiped out is false.

"I told Powell, 'If I ain't back in ten minutes, put an ad in the paper for me.' I left the three in the new hole and took off again toward the rear.

"Sniper and mortar fire was constant now and half the time I couldn't tell if the shadows across my path were enemy or not [*what* shadows at night in heavy rain?]. I just kept running. A grenade or mortar knocked me to the ground but didn't knock any more holes in me that I could tell. I was bleeding from several places but none seemed too serious. I got up again and kept moving."

Again there are contradictions here. As for his being hit several times and "bleeding from several places," other accounts marvel that Basilone came out of the fight surprisingly unscathed. Bruce Doorly writes that when Basilone and his remaining men left the field next day to rest, Basilone "realized he had not eaten for 72 hours" and at Henderson Field wolfed down what they had, crackers and jam, and ate them "like it was Thanksgiving dinner." There is no mention of seeking out a corpsman and having his "wounds" treated. The records show no Purple Heart being awarded Basilone. Mitch Paige, in contrast, was awarded both decorations in the continuing fight the next night.

Basilone's account, via Cutter and Proser, goes on: "At the ammo depot I pried open ammo boxes and draped six of the fourteen pound ammo belts [about eighty pounds!] over my shoulders. I picked up another of the boxes and started moving out. Then I remembered the water. I was a fully loaded mule and couldn't do much better than a fast walk with all the weight hanging on me. I passed the CP and called in for water. Someone came out and draped a few canteens on belts around my neck."

This is confusing. Puller's CP was previously described as being nothing more than a field phone on the reverse slope of the ridgeline. What was the "out" someone came out of? There were no structures or caves on the ridge that we know of.

Basilone does describe overhearing "Chesty . . . giving hell to someone over the phone." This sounds about right. The Cutter and Proser book continues in Manila John's voice: "I was back onto the trail in the darkness with my heavy coat of bullets banging against my knees, my hands full with the ammo box. I shuffled along as fast as I could. If I ran into Tojo in the dark, I'd have to drop the ammo box to reach my .45 on my hip. I ran behind the ridge crest but that didn't stop sniper fire from whining past my head. They were behind our lines and by the amount of fire, there must have been quite a few of them. I thought, if they can't hit a slow-moving target like me, that must mean my number isn't up, at least not tonight. I soon couldn't think about anything but about somehow making it a few more feet. The whole trip was about six hundred yards and I didn't stop once for a breather. Every thought and scrap of strength I had, was focused on just making a few more feet down the trail. I slipped under the weight several times, covering the belts with mud.

"I made it to the hole and made the call sign, 'Yankee Clipper,' as I came up from the rear so they wouldn't shoot me thinking I was a Jap infiltrator. I dropped what I had, 1500 rounds, and jumped in behind it. Powell was out of ammo on his gun. He grabbed a belt and I took over his trigger just in time. The next wave was on its way up the ridge. With Garland and Evans covering our flanks with their rifles, Powell and I leap-frogged from one gun to the other. The water wasn't nearly enough to fill the water jacket of even one of the guns, so I had to fire one of the guns while the other one cooled, and while Powell cleaned the next ammo belt and reloaded. We were able to keep a fairly constant rate of fire doing this and also make the Japs shift their targeting from our right gun to our left. It was hours after the first attack and they were still coming, wave after wave screaming 'Banzai!' and 'Marine, you die!' and we kept killing them. Evans and Garland threw grenades down the hill until they were barely able to lift their arms [it is unlikely there would have been that many grenades in a single machine-gun position]. The boys drank all the water in the canteens and when they could, pissed into the water jackets. Another wave of men ran up the ridge, broke and died in front of us. Some had gotten through. We could hear the firing to our rear. I wasn't sure our guns would hold up under another attack."

As the night fight continued, Basilone is said to have made yet another run to the rear, a water run, this time to A Company on C Company's flank. "Who the fuck are you?" someone demanded when he called out the password. Typical Marine response. But when Basilone returned to his own position and the guns, "Garland was dead. He was a big boy, a quiet type and brave."

Page 212 of Cutter and Proser's account reports Garland's death as a fact, but Doorly's book lists Garland, with "Powell, Evans and La Pointe," as having been ordered by Basilone the morning after the fight to return to Henderson Field while he remained behind "at his post in order to help the new men," who must have been replacements, during the less severe fighting and mopping up that continued on October 25.

At my request Bob Aquilina at Quantico looked up Garland's "death." He found seven or eight Marines named Garland who died during various Pacific campaigns, but none on Guadalcanal in October 1942. The "death" of Garland remains an enigma.

Young Marine officers and NCOs are taught, "Don't over-identify with your men. Know their military strengths and weaknesses, but not which guy has a kid, or an old gray-haired mother at home. When you send a man out on the point, the riskiest position, you send the best point man, the sharpest-eyed, canniest scout you have. Otherwise, you weren't going to lose just him to enemy action, but maybe your own life."

There was also the inarguable truth that every death of one of your men, a "Garland," tears a piece out of your own psychological hide, diminishes you as surely as one of John Donne's clods: "If a clod be washed away by the sea, Europe is the less." Clearly, as his NCO, Basilone would mourn Marine Garland, his man, his machine gunner. You hear it in his words: "a big boy, a quiet type and brave." We recall his assessment of the man, and the professional: "That night, when I told him to go down the hill, he hesitated just long enough to read my face. He looked to me just long enough to know I wasn't kidding, then off he went." But had Garland really died that night? It remains one of the narrative's puzzles.

Now, unexpectedly, on the twenty-fifth fighting erupted again with new massed Japanese assaults. This time it wasn't Puller's and Basilone's turn but the 2nd Battalion of the same regiment, the 7th Marines, commanded by Lieutenant Colonel Herman Henry Hanneken, that found itself grappling with the attacking Japanese infantry in lethal close combat, and it would be

Mitchell Paige, another, and quite different, machine-gun sergeant whom Basilone actually knew, who would be at the heart of
the most horrific fighting and would himself be nominated for a
Congressional Medal of Honor. More on that later.

About four on Sunday morning, the twenty-fifth, the Japanese
punched another hole in the Marine lines between Basilone's C
Company and A Company, but that was the end to his hard fighting for the moment. Proser describes his getting the crackers and
the jam, and quotes Basilone as saying of himself and his handful of hungry but surviving men, "We were all wounded." I find
no independent proof of this. Customarily, unless a wounded man
is treated by a medic (a Navy corpsman) who notes the fact, no
Purple Heart is awarded. Myriad cuts, burns (Basilone's scorched
arms, for example), and scratches are often ignored, overlooked
by the Marine himself. Despite his words about being "wounded,"
the records indicate he earned only the one Purple Heart for
wounds, for those suffered at his death on Iwo Jima on February
19, 1945, some three years later. Nor does his citation for the
Medal of Honor mention his being wounded on the 'Canal, which
such carefully vetted citations customarily do.

Marine Ops doesn't break out daily USMC casualties for each
night of the three-day battle of Bloody Ridge but says "sources"
put the entire three-day cost to the 7th Marine Regiment at 182
dead. Basilone's reference to C Company's having been wiped out
and his handful of men the only ones left is clearly an exaggeration.
And his service record book notes that Basilone "joined Company
D, 1st Battalion, 7th Marines May 29, 1941," while Puller's
own written citation for the Medal of Honor calls Basilone a
member not of C Company but of D Company. It seems to me
axiomatic that Puller would know one of his rifle companies from
another. And surely Basilone would have no such doubts about his
own outfit. Blame confusion in battle, but family and other remi-
niscences are replete with such perplexing errors of fact.

As for the Japanese, their losses at Basilone's machine-gun
position are put at thirty-eight dead by PFC Nash W. Phillips of
Fayetteville, North Carolina, who was in Basilone's company on

the 'Canal. Total enemy losses on October 23–26 are recorded as 3,500 dead, including one general, Yumio Nasu, and his two regimental commanders. Puller's citation for Basilone's medal (countersigned by Chester Nimitz himself) refers to a thousand dead Japanese buried or left unburied in front of 1st Battalion's position.

7

Basilone's own terrible night was succeeded only hours later by the equally desperate nightlong fight by the 2nd Battalion in which Mitchell Paige distinguished himself and would be written up for a Congressional Medal by his own commanding officer, Colonel Herman Hanneken. In a 1975 book by then Colonel Paige titled *A Marine Named Mitch*, he recalled a temporary lull in the aftermath of the October fighting, including his own, on the Guadalcanal ridgelines: "The next day Chesty Puller came up to see me. He sat down next to me after we shook hands and he told me about the big attack they had down at the airport on the night of the 24th [Paige's own battle was fought late on the twenty-fifth]. He also told me he had just seen Colonel Hanneken at the Division Command Post before he came to visit with me. He told me that he read a report that Colonel Hanneken was preparing, recommending me for a medal. 'Chesty' went on to tell me that that [sic] his sergeant was also a machine gunner and that our actions were similar. I said, 'wonderful, is this sergeant someone I may know?' 'I don't know,' he said, 'but his name is Basilone.'

"I said, 'Johnny Basilone?' And he said, 'Yes.' I had made platoon sergeant just before we left the States and I told Chesty that I had recently seen Johnny when we were moving positions and I had asked him when he expected to be made platoon sergeant, and he said soon he hoped. I told Chesty that I hoped this would help Johnny get promoted to platoon sergeant. I had met Johnny originally back in New River, North Carolina, just after he joined the 1th Battalion, 7th Marines. He told me he was better known as 'Manila John,' and then I said, 'you must have been in the Philippines,' and we had a lot to talk about as I told him I had been stationed in Cavite [the big U.S. naval base on Manila Bay] for some time. Johnny had been in the Army and was stationed in Manila, thus the name 'Manila John.' We had a friendly greeting when I would call him 'Doggie Manila John,' and he would jokingly call me 'Cavite Mitch.'"

There are suggestions that in the months between the time both sergeants were "written up" for decorations and the day months later when they actually received their awards (the Medal of Honor) in Australia, someone up the line of command in Washington decided these two enlisted men had legitimate "hero" potential. After all, two Medals of Honor for Guadalcanal heroics had already been awarded to senior officers, and wasn't it time for enlisted men to be recognized for what the Marines had accomplished in handing the Japanese their first defeat since ground fighting began?

John Basilone's sister Phyllis takes up the story in her brother's voice, recounting his telling of what happened on Guadalcanal and how Chesty Puller had recognized not only Paige's but also Basilone's own pivotal role:

"As dawn came, the last frenzied attack, preceded by their now familiar cries, 'Marines you die, Banzai, Marines you die!' By now we were all light-headed as we sent back our songs of death . . . towards the end I had to stand up with my 'chopper' [the heavy Browning] cradled in my arms to fire out over the rising pile of dead. The attack was growing weaker and weaker and suddenly the last desperate charge petered out at the wire. I rested my head on the ledge of the emplacement, weary, tired and grateful the Lord had seen fit to spare me. Then I heard my name being called. Looking up I saw Lieutenant Colonel Puller, my commanding officer, standing with his arm outstretched. He shook hands with me and said, 'I heard you came back for ammunition. Good work.'"

There was considerable hard fighting left on Guadalcanal for Manila John's outfit, but on the following night, a Sunday, the brunt of it would fall not on Puller but to the east, where Colonel Hanneken and his 2nd Battalion, 7th Marines, fought off another all-night assault by the Japanese, and where Paige, though wounded, held his position as tenaciously as Basilone had.

Basilone has his own, surprisingly modest, count of casualties on the night fight for which he will ever be remembered and on which he won the famous Medal of Honor. Compared to the earlier inflated estimate that C Company (of perhaps two hundred men) was "wiped out," the Jerry Cutter and Jim Proser book once again contradicts itself. Here is their quote from Basilone: "In the whole 1/7 [1st Battalion, 7th Marines] we lost 19 boys that night. Another 30 were wounded and 12 were missing." Then John says, "Twelve of my boys were dragged out of the mud that day, some of them in pieces. They were just about everybody I knew on the island." Does this account, supposedly in his words, really make any sense? Nineteen Marines in the entire battalion dead and twelve of them were Basilone's "boys," his machine gunners? Out of the other eight hundred or thousand men in Puller's 1st Battalion, there were only seven Marines killed who didn't work with or for John Basilone? Despite the bloody setback those two nights, the Japanese had not quit.

In postwar depositions in 1946, Japanese senior officers cavalierly swapped insults and blamed one another for the loss of Guadalcanal, for failures in strategy and tactics during the period of October 23–26, but no one, especially not the Americans, suggested the enemy couldn't fight. October phased into November, when there was more bloody combat with both Puller's 1st Battalion (Basilone included) and Hanneken's 2nd (with Mitch

Paige) again engaged in heavy fighting. At sea, the two fleets fought, usually out of sight of the other, trading heavy losses to air attacks. In one battle, seventy-four American planes and more than a hundred Japanese aircraft were lost, warships went down, and the coastal sharks feasted. On land, the fighting ebbed and flowed, men continued to die, and Henderson Field was bombed and shelled and threatened again on the ground, but it never fell.

Tokyo must at last have been having second thoughts about whether this one relatively insignificant island was worth the loss of so many ships, planes, and irreplaceable pilots, to say nothing of thousands of veteran infantry. Gradually as November ran its course, the Japanese brass stopped sending in reinforcements, no longer dispatched their capital ships in harm's way, and in the end began to evacuate. The battle became one of hot pursuit, as the Americans, Marines and soldiers, chased and attempted to trap the remaining enemy infantry. Every Japanese soldier who died on the 'Canal would be one man they wouldn't have to fight on some other hostile shore. There were fewer pitched battles, fewer banzais screamed.

The American Army was in growing numbers taking over the Marine positions, and on December 7, the first anniversary of Pearl Harbor, elements of the 1st Marine Division began leaving the island. The last Japanese to quit Guadalcanal, harried and pursued by American GIs, were evacuated on the night of February 7–8, 1943. No one knows how many died, but sources say more than 14,000, with another 9,000 missing and presumed dead. And these were only the ground forces. Japanese naval and aviation casualties are not included.

The official history of *Marine Ops* compiled the following casualty figures for the 1st Marine Division from the landing on August 7 to early December: 605 officers and men killed in action, 45 died of wounds, 31 MIA and presumed dead, 1,278 wounded in action. Another 8,580 "fell prey to malaria and other tropical diseases." As is often the case in war, illness took more lives than combat.

Speaking of which, as early as October General Alexander Vandegrift at the Noumea conference was already lobbying to get the 1st Marine Division "to a healthier climate" as soon as possible. The Japanese offensive of October 23 and the following days rendered consideration of that a purely academic exercise; the Marines couldn't be spared. But now that the Army had arrived and the Japanese were trying to leave, where the division would go next had become a concern. Phyllis Basilone gives us some insight into her brother's state of mind toward the end there on the 'Canal. Basilone, for all his heroics, was now having nightmares.

During the firefight on the long night of October 24, a lone Japanese soldier somehow broke through their position. Someone shouted, "Look out, Sarge," and Basilone saw the man disemboweled by a Marine's machete and Basilone and his gun were splattered with the man's red blood "and blue guts." Despite all he'd seen and experienced already, this particular incident seemed to have shaken Basilone. According to his sister, he threw up and was trembling uncontrollably. The machete killing was but a single event during a night of such horrors. But this one shocking moment among so many had its impact, coming back to haunt his dreams. The previously imperturbable sergeant was shaken, having trouble sleeping, and haunted by wild dreams of combat, drenched with night sweats and shivering. Was this malaria or what they call battle fatigue? Phyllis tells us that Basilone himself wondered.

The scuttlebutt was that the division was headed for Australia, which, with its "people like us," the girls, the cold beer, and especially the temperate climate, sounded to the Marines like Eden, and especially to Manila John with his tour in the Philippines and memorable R&R in neighboring New Zealand, where the young Americans fell in love with the people and the land. As Basilone waited to ship out, away from the 'Canal and its horrors, he sounded pensive, waxing philosophic, which would be something new for him, a facet of his makeup not previously remarked on at Raritan, the Philippines, or in his Marine experience. Combat can do that.

Listen to Basilone in his sister's account as the troopship carried him and his unit out of the war zone and toward what they expected to be a period of rest, refitting, and getting well: "Looking about me during the long voyage to Australia was heart-rending. Where only a few short months ago they were only boys in their teens, now they appeared old, far beyond their years. Their sunken eyes reflected the pain and misery they had been subjected to. I was no different. My family on seeing me at this moment wouldn't even recognize me. The only thing that kept us from just collapsing on the deck and going into a shell was the gratifying thought we had met the feared enemy, defeated him on his own ground, and poured the flower of his troops back into the earth and sea."

This sounds a bit poetic for Basilone, but his sister goes on with his description: "After a long trip during which we soaked up the sunshine and fresh sea air, with nary a Jap sub to bother us, we dropped anchor off Brisbane, Australia, the city we had been told would be our rest camp." Located on the northeast coast of the continent, it was hundreds of miles closer to the tropics than the other big Aussie cities of Sydney, Canberra, and Melbourne, with their more moderate climate in the country's south. It was hardly the cooler, healthier "temperate" rest camp area Vandegrift had requested.

Some rest. Some camp.

8

Down Under, the Marines might have expected to go "Waltzing Matilda," but Australia turned out to be a shock to men you'd think were beyond shock.

"None of us realized the weakened condition we were in, and that the camp set up outside Brisbane was only temporary," Basilone is reported to have said. Instead of a rollicking good liberty or a more extended leave, the Marines were marched to a hastily thrown-up military tent city. "We soon learned we were supposed to set up permanent defense positions along the Australian coast." Where they would presumably confront a Japanese invasion, if and when. And this would be along the hot, fevered, mosquito-blown northern Australian coast, only a hundred miles from New Guinea where the enemy was already established. In the inverted world of the Southern Hemisphere, the south was cool, dry, and moderate, while the north was hot and pestilential like the 'Canal. On top of that, Australia both needed the Americans and resented them.

Here is John's account of that first, disillusioning view the Marines would have of their new home, as recorded by Phyllis Cutter: "Coming all that distance cramped in transports, we could hardly believe our eyes when we finally marched and were carried into our rest camp. If we bitched about 'tent city' we were sorry. This was even worse. Guadalcanal was paradise compared to this swamp [surely this is typical Gyrene hyperbole!]. Goony birds and mosquitoes made sleep impossible. Our breaking point was not far off. General Vandegrift was furious and after having southern Australia scouted for a more suitable location, he proposed the Division be moved to Melbourne where the climate was cooler and free of the giant mosquitoes. Having decided on the new location, Vandegrift found that the Army could not spare any ships for transporting the men."

Marines are celebrated for the profane eloquence of their wrath, and Vandegrift was a celebrated Marine. These were *his* men who for months had been abiding in hell and, despite everything, had met and defeated the Japanese and captured one of their islands after nearly a year of seeing the Japanese invade and occupy our islands. And now this worn-down, fevered corps of heroes had been billeted in a swamp and barred from more salutary precincts by a lack of Army shipping! The situation did nothing to endear the U.S. Army to the Gyrenes or to their general officer commanding. Alexander Vandegrift's righteous rage swiftly reached the United States Navy, and more to the point, it got to Bull Halsey, a man who appreciated a good exchange of oaths, who on the spot issued orders to send Navy transports to Brisbane to pick up the 1st Marine Division and deliver it to Melbourne. When the Marines out there in the swamp heard the news, they cheered Halsey's name.

Said Basilone, "Our first sight of Melbourne as we docked in the harbor brought tears to our eyes, it seemed so much like home. That is, the home we knew, the Golden Gate in Frisco, the Statue of Liberty in New York Harbor, Chicago on the Great Lakes, St. Louis and the mighty Mississippi. We disembarked and with the Division band in the foreground, we paraded through Melbourne to the cheers of thousands of friendly people. During our march through the city our eyes drank in the sights. We had forgotten what a simple thing like a wide city street looked like."

To men who for months had been slogging through swamps and along narrow jungle trails, such things were startling in their commonplace loveliness, as were the lighted streetlamps of a city not blacked out by night, to say nothing of the dry barracks and clean bunks following the morass of "tent city" Brisbane.

And the girls, the girls! Basilone marveled at them as well. "They weren't jealous like girls back home, they'd simply ask each other if they'd had a nice time. It was a little confusing, don't get me wrong, they were nice girls and wonderful company even if your ego was dropped a bit."

"We had by now gotten over the first flush of liberty," Basilone is quoted as saying, which sounds rather tame considering that, even today when Marines are asked how a liberty weekend had gone, the cheerfully vulgar but standard response might be, "I got screwed, blew-ed, and tattooed." Basilone added that he and his buddies now, for the first time, "began to look around and enjoy the people. They were without question the most honest and sincere people we had ever met. They threw open their homes to us and most of the men took advantage of their generous hospitality. Some of the boys fell in love, some lived with families, especially the boys from the Midwest, who really had a ball. They did all the farm chores and, while exhausted, they enjoyed it."

One local favorite to which the Marines never got accustomed was mutton for breakfast, or pretty much at any meal and anytime. But as Basilone noted, despite mutton, "We were slowly but surely getting back our strength and, with it, our desire to live." Part of that desire, naturally, was sex.

"There were never enough girls to go around and it was a rat race to get a date and hold it. I did pretty well." At this somewhat modest boast from the newly arrived but hardly bashful Marine sergeant, it might be well to go to Basilone's nephew Jerry Cutter on the subject. Cutter quotes Basilone about those early days at Melbourne: "Strangers were buying us drinks, taxicabs gave us free fares and women came out of their houses to meet us. Now the women, what can I say about the women? To begin with they weren't shy. They stood up square to a man and told him straight out what they liked, didn't like, and how they expected things to go. And things certainly did go. One of the things going around camp after that [first] night was, 'what they say about Atabrine [that it rendered a man impotent] ain't true.' One thing I learned about nearly dying is that it gave me a hell of an appetite—for everything. The last time I had anything close to this much sex, I was nineteen years old and paying for it. I ate, drank, and screwed like a wild pig, and didn't feel bad for one second about any of it."

The good times wouldn't roll forever. They lasted, in Basilone's words, "until the Ninth Australian Division returned home from the Middle East. They were a wonderful bunch but you couldn't blame them for flaring up. Here we were solidly entrenched in their homeland, had the market on their women, the corner on money and we spent it, how we spent it, as if there was no end to our supply." After all, for those months on the 'Canal, there was nothing to buy, nowhere to spend a man's pay. "As a result, fights flared up all over town. Many a pub was wrecked in short, furious fist fights. The Aussies were hard fighters, and once we understood their methods, we more than held our own. They were clean fighters in the sense they did not use anything but their fists but they would not fight alone."

Apparently if you duked it out with one Australian, you had to fight every Aussie in the room. "The whole situation was well on its way towards getting entirely out of hand. We got so we wouldn't travel alone. While this cut down on the number of fights, there were still plenty of bad ones. Finally the whole mess was laid before [Marine] General Rupertus. The general, in an effort to ease the situation, decided that the 1st Marine Division would host the Aussies with the biggest party they had ever seen. The only precaution Rupertus took was the directive be issued that the beer was to be served in paper cups. He even had the courage and conviction to order that the MPs not attend. This party, more in the nature of a peace conference, was a huge success. At least ten thousand men attended, half of them Australian. For the occasion, the Melbourne cricket grounds were turned over to both armies. We got to know the Aussies better and believe it or not the fights in the pubs stopped. Shortly after the 'peace conference,' the Aussie Ninth was pulled out and sent to New Guinea [where the enemy held perhaps half the vast island, the second largest in the world]. With all the fuss and fights, we were sorry to see them go. Our money was getting low and the Aussies were always good for a beer or two."

Bruce Doorly in his monograph, *Raritan's Hero*, recalls one of those earlier evenings, before the pacifying beer bust at the cricket grounds: "One night John got into a situation over a girl in a bar, with an Australian soldier, John tried to back off but the other guy would not. Using his boxing experience, John hit him with a straight left causing the Australian to fall to the floor. He got back up and came at John again, this time with two of his friends. Basilone's buddies joined in and a small riot erupted. Military police got the riot under control relatively quickly."

Considering Basilone's boxing prowess (nineteen wins in nineteen fights at Manila for his Army unit before the war), his fearlessness, his appetite for women and their obvious interest in him, and his adventures in the Marines and civilian life, you wonder at how few brawls there were. The man was a fighter, in every sense, but not your usual barroom brawler, bellicose or easily riled. There was an admirable prudence, the realization that his fists could be considered lethal weapons, and he disciplined himself in their use, which probably made him even more effective and dangerous when he did occasionally lash out.

Wartime Australia, menaced by the Japanese, was hardly a normal situation for a young soldier from any country. There were rational and understandable reasons for a love-hate relationship. The Yanks were here and their own boys weren't. As the Brits put it when Americans flooded into the United Kingdom by the hundreds of thousands in the buildup to D-Day, "The trouble with the Yanks is, they're overpaid, oversexed, and over here." The British understood we were there to help them beat the Germans. That still didn't make the reality entirely palatable. The Australian situation was analogous. Tens of thousands of young Australians, including their best troops, weren't here facing the Japanese, protecting their own country, their wives, the kids, and their homes. But the Yanks *were* here, and that wasn't quite the same thing.

"The bloody Japs aren't a hundred miles away across the Torres Strait, their planes are bombing Darwin [on the northern coast], and our lads are half a world away fighting the bloody Eyeties [Mussolini's Italians]." There was considerable truth to all of this. It was late 1942, early 1943, and the Americans had landed and fought their way through the Vichy French at Oran and Casablanca and near Algiers to open a second front against the Germans and their increasingly insignificant Italian partners. The Aussies (and New Zealanders) were also in North Africa with the British Eighth Army, and soon to be joining up with the new Allied invaders to the west. But in the meanwhile, the Brits and their empire were fighting full-time against Rommel and his Afrika Korps. So until their own 9th Division sailed home for a break, the only sizable forces back home Down Under would be the "bloody Yanks."

And waiting for them the glories and creature comforts of Melbourne, with its lonely, lusty, and compliant women, to welcome the nearly 20,000 men of the recently landed 1st Marine Division, malaria-ridden, exhausted, wasted, haunted, but randy, womanless, and by now battle-hardened. These Yanks, at least, had proved themselves able to "kill Japs." A mixed blessing indeed!

There is no indication that Manila John understood such dynamics or cared. All he knew was that he and his machine gunners were out of hell and, like Sydney Carton, in "a far, far better" place, a civilized country much like their own, where, drained and tired and haunted as they were, they could expect to recover and live once more as men and not animals of the field. But just how thin, in wartime with its stresses and losses, might be this veneer of civilization, even in a country as lovely as Melbourne and its agricultural environs? These were a grand people and this Australia a gorgeous place; there was beer to be drunk, liberty to be enjoyed, girls to be loved, money to be spent. Cutter reports further on "Uncle John" Basilone's revels amid the hospitable people of Melbourne: "They'd find a bald-headed Marine dead drunk, planted face-first in their petunias, and they'd bring him into their home, clean him up, and introduce him to their daughter."

Basilone had singular memories of his own. "I woke up one morning in my bunk and had no idea how I got there. I didn't remember the trip back or how I got my arm all bloodied. Somebody had wrapped it in white gauze so I figured I must have been in the sick bay at some point. All I knew was that my head hurt like hell. My mouth felt like mice had made a nest in it, and my arm hurt as bad as my head. I got myself cleaned up and had to shave with my left arm because my right was so sore. I still couldn't remember how I had banged it up. At chow Powell looked up at me over his coffee and smiled like the cat that just shit in the corner. 'Death Before Dishonor, sarge,' he said.

"'What the hell was that?' I was thinking but didn't say anything.

"'Let's take a look at it,' he said.

"'At what?' I said. I still wasn't too fast on my feet before coffee. Then it all started to come back to me. The drinking contest on Flinders Street, the cab ride and the little shop by the docks with drawings of dragons in the window. Powell nodded at my arm. Then I saw the rest; the tray of black inks, the needles, and the bald top of a man's head bent over my arm as pain shot through me. Powell was kissing a very heavy, brown-skinned girl and watching us. I peeled back the bandage on my arm, and saw the scabbed-over letters in blue ink, 'Death Before Dishonor' and some other design that was covered in dried blood. I liked it.

"'Death Before Dishonor,' I repeated to Powell. 'Who paid for it?' I asked because I didn't remember that part.

"'Beats me, but somebody did,' he said. It was done now and I was pleased with it."

Not every night was tattooed, drunken, or lecherous. The local girls also loved the new American dance, the "jitterbug," and were mad to learn more about it and work on their technique. There were families that took in some of the boys for domestic, warm, family-style meals and small, relatively sober parties. Men fell in love and got married, some were "adopted" by families and helped out the households with a little cash, and they learned to drink tea, sitting around the kitchen table as they'd done at home. They taught the Aussies our songs and learned theirs. To this day Marines who served Down Under can recite the lyrics of all four stanzas of "Waltzing Matilda" and do a pretty good job on its close harmony. American farmboys vanished for days at a time and then wandered back to the base explaining they'd been helping a local farmer get the crops in. Basilone fell for the younger children of one family and found himself playing on the floor with a little girl who reminded him of a niece in the Reisterstown, Maryland, home of his sister Phyllis Cutter and her husband, Bill.

The Marines who came to Australia, as well as others who went to New Zealand in those days, were there for rest and relaxation and recuperation, to cure the malaria and purge the intestinal worms. To come back from the dead. So that soon they would be sufficiently fit to fight the Japanese all over again on some other lousy island. Or maybe right here up north in the swamps and on the beaches of the northern coast with its malaria and crocodiles. Military bases thrive on rumor, on scuttlebutt; gossip was the circulating blood of every-day garrison life, and here at Melbourne the talk was of when they might be leaving, where they would be going next, about the order of battle and terms of engagement the next time out.

And now, in the spring of 1943 (which was autumn Down Under), other rumors began to circulate through the 1st Marine Division, not about the future but about its so recent past, some of it about Manila John Basilone and his exploits last October on Guadalcanal. There had already been some talk, earlier rumors, the morning after the fight on Bloody Ridge, especially about how Chesty Puller himself had gone out of his way to recognize Manila John and give him a "well done" for having gone back for ammo under fire at the worst of the enemy attack. Basilone heard the talk, of course, but refused to put much stock in it. After all, as he said, "There were thousands of boys fighting and dying. Why should I be singled out?"

Then in May 1943 the scuttlebutt ramped up.

9

Perhaps the best account of the time and the place comes not from Basilone family accounts or from neighbors and boyhood chums at Raritan, and certainly not from the taciturn John himself, but from another Marine who was there, the "other" Marine machine-gun sergeant from Guadalcanal, Mitchell Paige.

In January 1943, Paige, a more buttoned-up NCO than the casual, carousing Basilone, had been commissioned a second lieutenant in the United States Marine Corps, his date of rank backdated to October 1942, which meant a nice packet of back pay. Basilone, only slightly junior as sergeant to Paige, was not offered a commission. Later, he would be given several such opportunities, but not in early 1943. Not that he wanted or had politicked for an officer's gold bars. Manila John was happy being a sergeant. Paige, in his own postwar book, writes about that May in Melbourne where some quite extraordinary things had begun to happen. Fortunately for us, if Basilone wrote very little, Paige took notes or had an exceptional memory.

"One day we received word that a very distinguished person would be visiting our camp at Mount Martha. We were all busy with our machine guns when we saw the inspecting party coming through our area. We were instructed to continue our work. This was a great departure from the standard practice of a troop formation and formal inspection for a visiting dignitary. But Eleanor Roosevelt, the President's wife, only wanted to see the camp and see the troops in training. She stopped by our platoon and shook hands with us. I never dreamed that again one day I would shake hands with the First Lady in the White House in Washington.

"[Another] day the entire camp went on parade. There were to be presentations and awards. A group of us were assembled along the parade ground waiting for instructions when Colonel 'Chesty' Puller came smartly over to us as we all came to attention and rendered a snappy salute. Chesty grabbed me by the arm and said, 'Sergeant Paige, you're senior here, oh, yes, now you're a looie,' as he twisted his jowls to one side and with a warm smile said, 'You'll always be a sergeant to me. You know the backbone of the Corps is the non-commissioned officer.' Then he said, 'Sergeant Basilone, you will march next to Paige,' and then he lined up the rest of our group. The band struck up a march number and Chesty marched us front and center as my spine tingled with pride, being with such men. Chesty halted us directly in front of the Division commander, General Vandegrift. My citation was read and then in the name of the Congress and of the President of the United States, General Vandegrift placed the Congressional Medal of Honor around my neck. After which, I stepped over next to Colonel Merrill 'Red Mike' Edson and I continued to stand at attention as Johnny Basilone's citation was read and he, too, received the Congressional Medal of Honor from General Vandegrift. The 1st Marine Division Band and all the troops then passed in review as General Vandegrift, Colonel Edson, myself and Johnny Basilone received the honors—all four of us with the Congressional Medal of Honor and all for Guadalcanal."

Here, from the official records, is how Basilone's citation read:

For extraordinary heroism and conspicuous gallantry in action against enemy Japanese forces, above and beyond the call of duty, while serving with the First Battalion, Seventh Marines, First Marine Division, in the Lunga Area, Guadalcanal, Solomon Islands, on October 24 and 25, 1942. While the enemy was hammering at the Marines' defensive positions, Sergeant Basilone, in charge of two sections of heavy machine guns, fought valiantly to check the savage and determined assault. In a fierce frontal attack with the Japanese blasting his guns with grenades and mortar fire, one of Sergeant Basilone's sections, with its gun crews, was put out of action, leaving only two men able to carry on. Moving an extra gun into position, he placed it in action, then, under continual fire, repaired another and personally manned it, gallantly holding his line until replacements arrived. A little later, with ammunition critically low and the supply lines cut off, Sergeant Basilone, at great risk of his life and in the face of continued enemy attack, battled his way through hostile lines with urgently needed shells for his gunners, thereby contributing in a large measure to the virtual annihilation of a Japanese regiment. His great personal valor and courageous initiative were in keeping with the highest traditions of the United States Naval Service.

The citation was signed by Franklin D. Roosevelt.

Chesty Puller, that legendary Marine, would eventually, in the time of Korea, win his fifth Navy Cross, but he never possessed what Paige and John Basilone now had, the Medal of Honor.

That night, tired of being gawked at in the barracks, Basilone and his closest buddies visited their old haunts on Flinders Street and, in Basilone's words, "got shit-faced" as he clowned about, wearing his cap sideways and mugging. Newly minted second lieutenant Paige, now an officer and gentleman, presumably celebrated in more decorous fashion.

Paige continued, "A couple of days later Johnny came to see me and said, 'Listen, we've got a ticket home right away.' That afternoon a jeep pulled up to our battalion headquarters and I was summoned to Colonel Amor LeRoy Sims' office to see General Vandegrift and Colonel Edson. The general told me that Basilone was going home and that we had another campaign coming up. For several days following my visit with General Vandegrift, Colonel Edson and Colonel Sims, reporters and war correspondents continued writing stories about me. I was advised my picture was going to appear on the cover of LIFE magazine [then a very big deal, *Life* being that era's print version of network television, with one of the largest circulations in the business] while holding a machine gun in my arms with a belt of ammunition over my shoulders, as had been told them by Captain Ditta and others whom they had questioned about our action on Guadalcanal. . . . For some reason, my picture never appeared."

A note of possible jealousy here? There would be many such photos and a sculpture of John Basilone in a similar pose, machine gun cradled in his arms, the ammo belt slung across his shoulders. Paige continued, "I always felt hesitant about talking with them [the journalists], as I wasn't interested in publicity, and medals had never really entered my mind." Within days Puller would be awarded a third Navy Cross and another lieutenant colonel named Conoley was also given the cross. At the ceremony, Paige stood with Conoley and Basilone with Puller. In this section of Paige's book, he goes into no additional detail on why Basilone may have been selected to go home and why it was assumed Paige himself would stay in the Pacific for that "next campaign." All Paige would add about his friend Johnny was a gracious little passage of *l'envoi*: "Manila John went home to sell war bonds and two years later he had volunteered to go back overseas. Johnny joined the 5th Marine Division which went to Iwo Jima. A few minutes after they hit the beach in the opening assault, on February 19, 1945, Johnny and four of his men were caught by Japanese mortar fire and were killed. My good friend, Manila John Basilone, was awarded the Navy Cross posthumously for that action."

Almost three weeks went by at Melbourne before, on June 12, Basilone bothered to write home about the famous medal, and he did so briefly and simply: "I am very happy, for the other day I received the Congressional Medal of Honor, the highest decoration you can receive in the armed forces. Tell Pop his son is still tough. Tell Don [John's kid brother] thanks for the prayer they say in school [for soldiers overseas]."

For all the talk about "a ticket home," the famous medal around his neck, and the brief flurry of publicity, as May became June and then July, Basilone was still in Australia, routinely drilling his machine gunners, marching in step, and dutifully saluting officers, including brand-new shavetails, young second lieutenants who'd never heard a shot fired in anger. They, too, were saluted and were to be obeyed. The more sensible young officers knew how absurd the situation was and restrained themselves, playing it cool and trying to learn from these salty and combat-hardened enlisted Marines and NCOs, not throwing their rank around with guys like Basilone. Basilone's new and raw young machine gunners were impressed by their betters, the veterans of the 'Canal, and were eager to listen and to learn—which was what Sergeant Basilone wanted, young men to be taught the hard, deadly lessons of combat.

Manila John had announced prematurely to Paige in May that they had that "ticket home." But in July he was still there, training troops, making formation every morning, doing whatever it was he did each night as the weeks passed. And the Pacific war went on. For a time it wasn't really a Marines war at all. The only substantial fighting by late May was in far-off Attu in the Aleutians where the Japanese had dug in and the American Army, the GIs as they were now widely called in the headlines, were taking significant losses trying to dig them out. The Aleutians were cold and windswept, isolated and only thinly populated, really not very strategically important. But they were part of territorial Alaska and therefore American ground. And that was sufficient emotional and political reason to take them back, regardless of the cost. Fighting continued in the Solomons, though not on the 'Canal, and it was mostly a naval fight and an aviator's war. Henderson Field remained vital, and the once tiny, beleaguered, potholed little airstrip was now capable of launching a hundred American warplanes at a time to harass and sink Japanese shipping, to shoot down Zeroes, to take the bombing war to other of the Solomons still in Japanese hands. Henderson Field had indeed been worth fighting for.

On May 30, Attu fell. The ghastly count read 600 Americans dead, 1,200 wounded. True to their tradition, only 28 Japanese troops, all of them wounded, survived, with 2,350 dead, many of those suicides. Across the world the Russians were chewing up the Germans in fierce spring fighting, Tunisia still held out against the Allies, while plans firmed up for the invasion of Sicily, Patton and Monty and all that. In the Atlantic we were now sinking German U-boats in almost equal numbers to Allied losses in the convoys.

Closer to Australia and New Zealand where the Marines like Basilone trained, played, and waited, the island-hopping resumed with GIs and Aussies fighting in increasing numbers on New Guinea, and the 4th Marine Raider Battalion prepared to land on New Georgia, the first real confrontation of U.S. Marines and Japanese infantry since Guadalcanal was finally "secured," Marine terminology for "job well done." As was said in wise-guy USMC lingo, "There's no cure like see-cure!"

Basilone, in the Jerry Cutter and Jim Proser account, takes up the story: "We were back on maneuvers, gearing up for some scheme they were cooking up with Mac's [Douglas MacArthur's] 6th Army stationed up in Brisbane, probably the same swamp we left behind [an ironic note of delight to the Gyrenes, surely]. The wheels were turning again, slowly. Each day new equipment arrived and more shaved-head 'boots' a few weeks out of Basic filled out our ranks. It was a good mix in a way because we could fill in the new boots on the real world of jungle warfare, not what they heard in scuttlebutt. I wished somebody like us had been there on the 'Canal to take us aside and tell us the real dope. I could tell we were going to keep a few of these kids from getting killed because they listened to every word and we never had to tell them something twice."

Reading such sensible, and even rather noble, stuff from Manila John, you have to wonder as he drilled these kids on his beloved heavy Brownings, stripping and reassembling them in the dark, had he earned a few bob competing with them, as he had done during his Army days, stateside as a Marine, or on Samoa?

There is another reference to home: "George [another of John's brothers] had joined the Marines. He was headed to the Pacific, too, so maybe we'd meet up somewhere. Everyone was doing fine and they were praying for me every day. The whole town was. That was supposed to make me feel better because a lot of angels were watching over me. If that was true, I'd have a few things I had to answer for when I got to heaven. *If* I got there."

There is a new, uncertain tone here, pensive, less impulsive. He was getting older, maybe growing up. In May, when he was awarded the medal, he'd declared, almost in glee, that the famed medal meant a "ticket home." That moment was now forgotten, the jubilation vanished. He was reconciled to the idea of going back into combat, taking on another campaign, landing on another hostile beach. That was what Marines did. And Basilone was certainly a Marine before he was ever a Medal of Honor laureate. Paige would be going back to war, Puller would be going, Bob Powell and the rest of them, and this "mix" of youngsters fresh out of boot camp and old stagers from the 'Canal would be going to the war. And why wouldn't Manila John be with them?

The warrior in Basilone seemed at peace with the notion of another fight. He was not at all restive or apprehensive.

Suddenly in Melbourne, there arrived new orders. Manila John was being pulled out of his battalion, was leaving the division and shipping out for the States, where an entire country at war was about to meet and embrace him. Many there were as yet unaware of just who the guy was, where he came from, and what he had done in his short and eventful life beyond killing people and winning medals.

If you really want to know about Johnny Basilone, though, you start with a small town in New Jersey.

PART TWO

HOMETOWN

Basilone in his service uniform.

10

John Basilone's family boasted no martial tradition, and John was a fairly unruly kid, not overly given to discipline, so he had no reason to believe, not then, that he just might have been born to soldier.

In fact, his boyhood was unremarkable small-town stuff. According to Bruce Doorly: "Basilone's mother Dora Bengivenga grew up in Raritan, born in 1889 to parents Carlo and Catrina, who had recently emigrated to America from Naples, Italy. Carlo was a mill worker. In 1901 Dora's parents purchased a house in Raritan at 113 First Avenue for $500. This would later be where John Basilone grew up. The house was built in 1858 and in 1901 was a single family home, but later additions would [make] it a two-family house. John's father, Salvatore Basilone, had come to America from just outside Naples in 1903 when he was 19. He went to work in Raritan and made friends among the other Italian Americans."

There were church parties and neighborhood gatherings, and it was at one of these that Salvatore met Dora. They dated for three years, saved some money, got married, and moved in with Dora's parents on First Avenue. Salvatore worked as a tailor's assistant, and their first five children were born in the family home. Looking for more work than Raritan offered, they moved north to Buffalo, New York, where young John, sixth of the Basilone children, was born not in a proper hospital but at home, very much in the family tradition, on November 4, 1916. But the Buffalo interlude was brief. Whether it was the long winters or a slump in the tailoring trade, the family returned to Raritan in 1918. By now Salvatore had a tailor shop of his own, and they were living in one-half of the two-family house. There was one bedroom downstairs for the parents, and two more upstairs, one for the girls, the other for the boys. There were usually several kids to a bed and the house had a single bathroom. The Basilones certainly weren't living grandly.

Growing up, John enjoyed the usual scrapes, black eyes, tossing rotten tomatoes, swimming "bare-ass" in the Raritan River, silent movies, later talkies, mostly westerns and serials, in a local movie theater kids called the "Madhouse" for its boisterous matinees punctuated by loud boos, hisses, cheers, and thrown popcorn. Half a dozen sources recall one Basilone caper that was hardly ordinary. At age seven and eager for adventure, he climbed a pasture fence and was promptly chased and knocked over by a bull. No damage was done to either boy or bull.

Doorly reports that St. Bernard's parochial school yearbook described John as "the most talkative boy in the class" and that "conduct was always his lowest mark." His sister Phyllis admitted the boy had difficulty in grammar school, couldn't seem to "buckle down" to his studies. When he graduated, at age fifteen (most graduated at thirteen or fourteen), Basilone opted to drop out, not to go on to high school. He confessed, apparently to his adviser, Father Amadeo Russo, that he might be a "misfit," that school just wasn't for him. John's father objected strongly to the idea of working at the local country club, but the boy assured him he could make a little money caddying at the club, shrewdly pointing out he'd be outdoors getting exercise and plenty of fresh air. At the Raritan Valley Country Club, according to the Cutter and Proser book, it was while caddying for a Japanese foursome that young John had one of his early "premonitions," of a war one day when the United States would have to fight the Japanese. No one else in Raritan can recall Basilone's ever having spoken of such a premonition. "He wasn't that sort of fellow," one said. On rainy days or when caddying was slow, John and the other boys played cards. John turned out to be a natural at it, becoming a lifetime gambler, canny and adept, winning more than his share of the usually small stakes.

When the golf season ended, John got a "real" job, working as a helper on a truck for Gaburo's Laundry at the corner of Farrand Avenue in Raritan, delivering clean clothes, a job he actually held on to for a year before being canned for sleeping on the job. According to Doorly, future Raritan mayor Steve Del Rocco, who knew Basilone, called him "a happy go lucky . . . [who] enjoyed everything he did."

But John was restless. And with his lack of education and difficulty with books, in a down economy, at some point he must have concluded that going into the Army (a private received twenty-one dollars a month; a uniform; a pair of stout, hard-soled shoes; and three squares a day) might be a way of escaping depressed and jobless Raritan. Not yet eighteen, he needed parental approval, and that took considerable convincing. According to sister Phyllis, their father, Salvatore, "tried to reason with him. 'Johnny, you're crazy. You're only a kid. There's no war, why do you want to join the Army?'" Raritan was a small town, and John's mother was reluctant to see her boy leave home and go out into a very large and unknown world. He argued, though without any evidence, "I'll find my career in the Army."

Wrote Phyllis, "He explained to papa that with the Depression all about us, it was almost impossible to get a job. Army life might be just what he was looking for, he said. Then again, when his enlistment ran out, conditions might be better." On that point, Salvatore, an employed tailor but very well aware of the lousy job market, who'd been pressuring John to start a career in something, *anything*, reluctantly had to agree with his son. Doorly writes that the senior Basilones may have concluded the military could be "a good match" for a strong, active, out-of-doors kid like their son.

We know to the day the date on which John would later join the
Marine Corps, but there is a debate on when, even in what year,
he earlier joined the prewar U.S. Army in the mid-1930s. Doorly
believes John joined up in June 1934. Cutter tells me that by his
reckoning, John enlisted "about three months before he turned
eighteen [on November 4], which would have been August of '34.
I know his parents had to sign on." His Marine Corps records insist
he had joined the Army early in 1936. His 1935 Army service in
the Philippines, thoroughly documented, indicates the Marine data
is incorrect. But the military records that might solve this small
and perhaps unimportant question were destroyed by fire in 1973
at the Military Personnel Records Center in St. Louis, Missouri,
where the archives were held. According to Marine historian Bob
Aquilina, Marine and U.S. Navy records went untouched in the fire
but Army records of the time were burned.

There may have been additional arguments within the family
about John's enlistment, some fits and starts along the way, since
with the requisite records missing, some contradictory evidence
suggests that John didn't actually enlist until he was nineteen.
The Marine Corps, which apparently keeps files on just about
everything, even the other military services, reports on John's
military service record that he joined the Army on February 5,
1936, and served on active duty with consistently excellent fitness
reports until being discharged back into civilian life and the U.S.
Army Reserve on September 8, 1939. Since there is reasonable
proof that as a young soldier still on his first enlistment John
arrived in the Philippines in March 1935 to start a two-year overseas tour of duty, we can conclude that, at least this once, the
Marine Corps got it wrong.

All we get is a fanciful line or two supposedly from "Johnny"
to Phyllis Basilone as he left home for the Army. She describes
his getting on the train at Raritan for Newark and then traveling
under the Hudson River into Manhattan, no date given. "Well, Sis,
I'm on my way. I wonder if this is what I really want; everybody's
advice is still ringing in my ears." After all, the boy may not yet
have turned eighteen.

11

When the Raritan Valley local pulled into its last stop one January morning in 2008, the three local men were waiting for me out in the cold in a red Lincoln truck because the station's waiting room was locked. We'd arranged for me to meet with some people in New Jersey who could tell me about John Basilone, his home and family, his roots. The men were John Pacifico, a Roman Catholic deacon for twenty-five years at St. Ann's Church on Anderson Street; Herb Patullo, who was driving the truck and who owns a historic piece of high ground in the nearby Watchung Mountains on which Washington and the Continental Army once encamped in a blocking position to mask Philadelphia from the British; and Peter Vitelli, a large, talkative man who used to be in sales and marketing in Manhattan and recalls that at age six at St. Joseph's parochial school in Raritan, he once shook Basilone's hand when the nuns trooped the returning hero around to the classrooms to greet the children in 1943.

Pacifico, Vitelli, and Patullo, are members of the Basilone Parade Committee, three of those who tend to Basilone's memory and reputation and still stage the march in his honor every September, commemorating the day he returned on leave from the Pacific wearing the Congressional Medal of Honor. Raritan erupted (no other word will do) in a spontaneous welcome as he took a jubilant stroll through the town, the kid who once delivered their laundry, carried their golf bags, and had now become an American folk hero.

The men saw to it that I got a place in the truck, and it turned out they knew me from the page I wrote every Sunday for *Parade* magazine, a sort of accreditation as a professional that gave them a small assurance that I wasn't just another nosy parker but a reporter who *might* be trusted. I was hoping there would be a station coffee shop where I might get a wake-up cup of coffee, but no such luck. These men were focused, however, and they knew precisely why I was there, and so we drove on.

Our first stop was the Raritan Public Library, a small, trim white-framed building where on the second floor up the carpeted wooden staircase is the Basilone Room. It is nothing fancy, just a place where they collect and keep memorabilia about him. On a table were three white leather-covered photo albums filled with mostly black-and-white photographs: Basilone, in uniform and out, at various stages of youth (after all, he was still in his twenties when he died), pictures of his family, of friends, of the more or less famous movie stars who traveled the war bond sales route with him. I recognized John Garfield, who would play a Marine in a wartime picture, Eddie Bracken, Louise Allbritton. Vitelli leaned over my shoulder to identify people. He pointed out Virginia Grey. She was the woman who had caught Basilone's eye, and he hers. There were casual shots set in a soda shop. Basilone, they said, was known to be "the biggest ice-cream soda drinker" in town, while his schoolboy hobby was "chewing gum," and his ambition was "to be an opera singer"—if not a heavyweight boxing champ appearing in Madison Square Garden like his hero, a huge, strong, but awkward Italian fighter named Primo Carnera. There were pictures of Basilone in uniform, sometimes squared away and crisply tailored, or more casual on liberty with his "piss-cutter" overseas cap jauntily cocked or turned sideways. Beneath the uniform, there were two tattoos: "Death Before Dishonor" and a heart pierced by a sword.

We then took off in Patullo's red truck for a tour of the place where Manila John Basilone grew up, crossing the John Basilone Veterans Memorial Bridge over the Raritan River. "That's the Doris Duke estate over there," someone said, indicating a smooth, grassy, handsomely treed lawn that seemed to go on and on without ever a house in view. The place was so large you could hide a mansion on it. It had been a relatively warm and damp winter, and for January, everything was very green.

"He was actually born in Buffalo," someone said, "November 4 in 1916." Halfway through World War I, I calculated hastily to orient the time frame we were discussing, "and at twenty-eight he was dead." My guides showed off buildings where Basilone family or friends had at one time lived, other places of significance to Basilone, anxious to be helpful and at the same time to provide me a positive slant on their town. But not phonying it up. They took turns at talking or sometimes all spoke at once. I scribbled notes.

"New York City police commissioner Ray Kelly (also a Marine, of the Vietnam era) was here for the Basilone Parade one September, and he called Raritan 'a Norman Rockwell sort of town.' It's really a blue-collar town. Back then most people worked at Johns Manville. Or the Raritan Woolen Mills. Raritan started out Dutch, then it was Irish, and at the turn of the century the Italians and Slovaks came in. The Irish controlled all the justice system. Oh, sure, there was bias (established Irish versus the arriviste Italians), a couple of incidents.

"There's the statue, at Somerset Street and the Olde York Road, the stagecoach road between New York and Philly."

We pulled over and got out of the truck to look at the town's big monument, the outsized statue of John Basilone, a few yards from the Raritan River. "How tall was he?" I asked one of the men. "Five eight, five nine." Someone else said, "Maybe five ten."

Proud of their hometown boy, I think they kind of wanted him to be taller. The statue itself was big and bronze, maybe seven or eight feet high, a muscular young man, bare-chested as he had been in that fight on the Lunga River on Guadalcanal. His arms cradled a heavy machine gun, the weapon he loved, his weapon for killing.

He fought that night barefoot in the mud for better traction, but the sculptor had added what looked to me like modern Army combat boots. The replicated Medal of Honor on the statue was also, alas, a mistake, the Army version of the award, not the slightly different Navy version, as is appropriate for a Marine. Patullo pointed out for my tutelage the minor design distinctions in the two versions of the medal. That's how sensitive these men are about "their guy" John.

Next, we swung by Bridgewater-Raritan High and parked at John Basilone Memorial Field. We went into the athletic building and were greeted by a huge mural, maybe ten feet wide and about eight high, of Gunnery Sergeant Basilone. Out the other side of the building we walked onto the athletic field made of artificial turf, and the impressively modern composition running track surrounding it. Some boys in the infield played touch football while other kids, boys and girls both, in running shorts or sweats, sprinted or jogged laps. On the exterior walls of the athletic building looking out at the field were replicas of the two citations, the one for the Medal of Honor, the other for the Navy Cross Basilone was awarded posthumously on Iwo Jima.

We stood there reading the citations. Once again, talking up Raritan as a fine place, someone said, "Out of six thousand people in Raritan, nine hundred or a thousand went into the service during the war." They meant World War II, it was clear, not Iraq.

It was obvious that Raritan remembers almost everything about its hero. "He went to St. Bernard's grammar school. It burned down years ago. St. Ann's was his parish. Father Russo was his priest. Amadeo Russo." I noticed no one bothered to use Basilone's name with me anymore. They realized by now I know who "he" was. As in, "He never went to high school."

After grammar school Basilone caddied at the Raritan Valley Country Club. "Could I see that?" I asked. "Will they let us in?" The answer was, "Sure."

"Raritan Valley C.C. was very elitist then," I was informed, once again with a possessive local pride about *their* country club. "And the only way kids could make a living was to caddy. It was the Depression." I was interested in knowing more about the caddying, about Basilone's own golf. "John was good, but his brother Carlo was better." I'd also read that the young Basilone had premonitions, that he foresaw things, including his own death in war. And that when he was caddying for a foursome of Japanese businessmen in the 1930s, he had one of his premonitions. Because the men were taking snapshots, Basilone sensed there was going to be a war one of these days and America would have to fight Japan. "Ever hear any of that stuff?" I asked. No one I spoke to in Raritan was buying it.

Nor did they see anything sinister about the golfers. "Johnson and Johnson [of nearby New Brunswick] was just getting started off the ground and they built here. That's why there were Japanese here then. They were okay." Vitelli interrupted. "Tony Farese was the pro back then so he might know about premonitions, but he died recently at ninety-five. There was also a story Basilone once caddied for David Niven when he played Raritan. Niven told that to Pete, the bartender at P.J. Clarke's, and Pete told it to me. Niven was supposed to have said it might have happened, but he couldn't swear to it. Raritan was a very social club. A lot of people played here."

The Basilone house at 605 First Avenue (Basilone's Marine service records insist 113 First Avenue) in Raritan is now a small office building housing a fire alarm company, All-Out Fire Protection. What kind of house was it then? I asked. "Just a normal up-and-down house." How did they fit ten kids in there? My guides shrugged. It was Depression time, people made out somehow. We looked over the house and drove past sister Mary's home and where brother Alphonse used to live over there on the right, on to Gaburo's Laundry, the outfit that canned young Basilone from a delivery job for crapping out on the job, literally napping atop some piled-up laundry bags. Our next stop was at Basilone Place, a short residential street with small, neat houses on each side and carefully tended lawns, all of them very green in winter. This was where Joe Pinto still lived, and we were going to see Joe.

My guides had phoned ahead and Mr. Pinto came to the door and welcomed us. He is a slender, very small man bent nearly double at the waist, and very old. In the old days, I was told, he owned the Raritan Liquor Store.

We all took chairs and Mr. Pinto began to talk. "I grew up with him, more or less," he said of Basilone. "I'm ninety-nine years old now, and there couldn't have been a better guy. When he came home from Guadalcanal there was a parade here. He wore his uniform and he went all around town, and I was one of the guys he hung out with, his father and Chief Rossi of the police, Rocky Calabrese whose family had the department store." I asked what Basilone drank. "Beer, soda, not so much wine, but he'd drink anything. We went up to Villa Firenze one night, a regular night, John and me and two girls, and I was driving a car I'd just bought [probably used, since wartime Detroit wasn't making any new automobiles] and we had a flat up front. No jack, no lights, and two in the morning after a night of drinking. We're standing around there, lighting matches so he could see, and John's pumping the front tire with a hand pump, and we got going again. He was a regular guy, he'd do anything. A happy-go-lucky guy, about twenty-six years old.

"He left to go back [to the war] and got married out in California. He never brought his wife back."

What was it like when you heard he was dead? I asked the old gentleman.

"It was as if everyone in town went to hell. Everyone knew him, from his time as a laundry deliveryman," he said. "I had a business, ran a liquor store, came up here in thirty-six. So I knew him, a happy guy, always razzing with the kids." When I asked, Joe said, "No, he didn't find the laundry job demeaning." I asked other questions, about John's boxing, reports that Madison Square Garden wanted him, that a promoter wanted him to go pro, did he and Pinto ever box? I asked again about his supposed premonitions. For a man his age, Pinto was very crisp in his responses.

"I never sparred with him, and don't think he ever gave a thought to turning pro. As for premonitions, no, I never heard any of that. And he was not a guy to brag about the past, what he did [in the Pacific]. A handsome guy, but he didn't have much time for girls [others disagree bluntly on that point], and not a fancy dresser. I think he had one suit, and his father was a tailor, a man who would fix anything, no charge. His mom was a good looker and very nice. A nice, close family. I don't think you will ever find another man like John. A good guy, and anyone saying 'not' ought to be shot. John was the kind of guy some people can hate because he was so right. They had a funeral mass right here for him at St. Ann's."

On that exit line, we shoved off to meet the man who buried John Basilone, Raritan undertaker Anthony Bongiovi, ninety-six years old, whose home is attached to the funeral parlor and who received us in his blue wool bathrobe while reclining on a settee in the living room. He began by apologizing. "I've got this breathing thing." He paused to take a breath. Then he went on with a long rambling story, not about Basilone but another wartime casualty, an Air Corps officer killed in a plane crash and how his mother was hysterical and demanded the mortician open the sealed coffin. "The mother is screaming, 'I want to see my son, I want to see him!' In those days they held a wake at home, in the living room. So I didn't want to see that with the Basilones. But I get a call from the Basilone family and I know [Mrs. Basilone's] not going to be able to see her son." It was three and a half years after his death before he was disinterred from an Iwo grave and sent home. So obviously there was nothing left that a mother should be shown.

"I go to see the family at their home and I say, 'What the hell!' This is a local guy and the only one ever receiving a Medal of Honor, so I said, why not bury him right here at Raritan? At the house I calmed Mrs. Basilone. I said we could have John right here at home on the first floor [for a viewing of the casket]. I knew it would be a lot of work for me but what the hell. So I had the body shipped from Dover, Delaware."

This is confusing. The evidence indicates the body was sent directly from Delaware to Arlington, Virginia, site of the big national cemetery, with the government and the undertaker making the arrangements, the idea of burying John in Raritan having been scrapped. Bongiovi went on, at least in part clarifying the situation. "The funeral mass was said at St. Ann's in Raritan with the burial to follow at Arlington."

The old man paused again to catch his breath. This was clearly tiring him, but he wanted to keep going. He was very clear about the last part of his story.

"I had my own limo and the chief of police drove another car and the family rode with me and some others drove behind. I had it timed out so that in three hours [Bruce Doorly says it was four hours] we would meet at Arlington. I had never met John Basilone but it had to be right. We got to the cemetery and expected to see a firing squad and a casket with the flag on it, but when we arrived we got the Marine Corps band and a firing squad and a lot of generals, who they were I don't know, and I said to myself, 'What is this?' I introduced the family to the higher-ups and we had the funeral. And that's why, ever since, we celebrate this young guy's death."

We thanked Bongiovi for his time and help and said our good-byes, his daughter graciously apologizing for not having her dad all dolled up for us. There were cars and limos pulling up outside his funeral home now for another wake as we left the old undertaker and went out into the midafternoon sun. The following month I got a phone call from Raritan that Mr. Bongiovi himself, the undertaker who buried John Basilone, had died on February 1 at nearby Somerset Medical Center.

Before I left Raritan on the late afternoon train into Manhattan, I also learned about Basilone's "double-dating with a buddy named Augie Sena at Chichi's pizzeria in nearby Bound Brook before he left for the Army," and about "a red-haired girl named Josephine Cianciella, a local babe who went out with John in the late thirties, after he got out of the Army. He was dating Josephine and then he left to go back to the war. Her father was the local druggist."

But when we phoned, Augie Sena wasn't available, nor were several other promising sources, so I provided Pacifico a list of questions for the deacon to ask if he could nail any of the sources down and convince them to sit still for a tape-recorded grilling.

12

As good as his word, later that month John Pacifico sent from Raritan an audiotape of three interviews he'd conducted.

First was ninety-four-year-old Augie Sena, who said he'd lived all his life in Raritan. As to when he and Basilone met, he said, "In the late thirties at the Raritan Valley Country Club, we both caddied there together. I didn't know him that good. We lived on different streets. He was very friendly, made friends with a lot of people." About sports, Sena said, "I knew him as a football player out there. No, I never knew him as a fighter." Nor did he remember any premonitions about the Japanese golfers. "We caddied for the Japs because they played a lot of golf there. I think [he went into the Army] for the excitement. He wanted to travel. But [contradicting Joe Pinto] he had a lot of girls. He was a good-looking fella. So he had a lot of girls as far as I know."

Sena remembered Basilone when he came back from Guadalcanal with his medal. "I knew him back then, knew him pretty good. He used to deliver my laundry. A lot of times we used to meet at the Checker Diner around the circle in Somerville and we used to talk a lot. They had a big parade for him and then after that we were having coffee one day together and he was telling me he was going back [to the Pacific war] and I told him he was foolish. He would sever a lot of bonds like that. He told me he had to go back, wanted to go back. I don't think he changed much from when he went in and when he came back [from the war]. He liked to go back to the Army [Augie meant the Marines], he told me. He had an easy go and was selling bonds and he didn't have to go back, and I asked him why he wants to go back. He said he had to go back. That's what he told me."

Pacifico asked Sena whether he and Basilone discussed combat. "No, we never talked about that." Was it patriotism that had John out selling war bonds with movie stars? "No, he didn't think it was patriotic. He'd rather go back and fight. He'd rather go back with his buddies, he said. That's what he told me. He was anxious to go back, he told me. I told him he was foolish but that's what he said, that he wanted to go back. He really wanted to go." Augie kept stressing that. And when the brass said okay? "He really wanted to go back. It was the last time we had coffee and he was telling me he was leaving the next day, and that was the last time I seen him and I never seen him no more after that."

And when Sena learned his friend and neighbor had been killed? "I think Steven Del Rocco told me. He told me John Basilone got killed on Guadalcanal [actually Iwo Jima]. I'm pretty sure Steve told me on Anderson Street." And his memories of Manila John? "That he was a good person, that's all. He fought for the country. He had to go back. He died for his country. He was a good man, that's all I could tell you."

Former mayor Steve Del Rocco is eighty-nine years old and a lifelong Raritan inhabitant. He recalls, "I grew up with John and the whole family and got to know John pretty well on the golf course at Raritan Valley C.C. where he excelled in golf and he was a very good golfer. He was a very ambitious kid. [The family certainly didn't think so, and his father was forever asking John what he was going to do with his life.] He was always looking to do something, like he had ants in his pants and he couldn't stand still. Always looking to do something. Times were tough then. It was during the Depression, the biggest depression of our lifetime. The sport that I know he was the best in was golf. One of the best golfers in town. Every Monday was caddies' day and John would always be there, playing golf. He was a real good golfer. He played for a little bit of money and the more he played for, the better he was. Other sports, I'm not familiar with."

Did Del Rocco believe Basilone went into the Army because there were no jobs, or for excitement and travel? "I think he went in because [he] wanted to do something and there was nothing [here] to do. It was a depressing time those years in the thirties and I think it was a great challenge for him to go into the Army." And after that tour in the Army? "We knew him. He used to hang around what they called the joint down Ellison Street, and that's the last time I saw John [before the war]. We were playing cards there that night and he was leaving the next day to join the Marines, and that's the last time I saw him. He looked like he was anxious to get in the Marines, he thought it was something a little tougher, or something better. He would like it better than the Army, and I'm sure that he found it a better place to go. That is, for him. What motivated him, you know, he worked in the laundry, and I remember he got the job there and he stayed around for a while, and he got a little tired of the job and I think that's why he left."

And after Guadalcanal and the medal? Was he still one of the boys or distant? Scarred by the war or something like that? "Well, he wasn't scarred by the war. The only thing I can say about that is that I knew he missed it. He wanted to go back to it. He wasn't very happy selling war bonds. That wasn't his forte. He couldn't wait to get out of here and go back into the Marines. He never talked about combat. We never, one of us, brought it up. I think that was what drove him back to the Marines that he didn't want to sell war bonds. He just didn't want to do it. He wasn't up to it. He'd much rather be with the boys he left behind. Very anxious to get back, to get back in the worst way. He had a chance to spend the rest of his life as a Marine without going back to battle, but he chose to go back to battle to be with his friends, and that's something you got to admire."

And when the future mayor learned his local pal was dead? "I got a telephone call from I forget who it was who called me and told me about it and I didn't know anything about it until this phone call, and of course the next day it was all over the papers. That's when I knew for sure. There's not much I can say except to say his love for his country, to go back when he didn't have to go back. He could have stayed here and laid around and lived a good life, but he chose to go back and sacrificed his life for his country."

Del Rocco was one of the pallbearers, "the last pallbearer still alive. The big regret," he said, "that John's mother passed away before his body came back to Raritan or was taken to Arlington. [Not so; Dora Basilone attended her son's funeral at Arlington.] But when anybody was killed or died in the service, ten thousand dollars was given out to the family, and at that time John was married to a Marine girl from California and when she got the check for ten thousand dollars she turned it over to the Basilone family in respect of John Basilone. "She returned ten thousand dollars to the family."

Lena Riggi's niece later confirmed that story to me that her aunt, John's widow, gave the ten thousand dollars to the family. That didn't mean there wasn't some family hostility toward the widow, for whatever reason. Later I would get some insight into that.

Pacifico also got another neighbor on tape. Joe Sian is also eighty-nine and a lifelong friend of the Basilone family but one with a special perspective: "During the war when he got killed at Iwo Jima, I was there at the time [aboard a Navy warship providing naval gunfire support to the Marines ashore]. Yes, I heard it the same day because I was in the radio gang and when it came over our speaker I knew about it. It was the same that day as every day with that invasion. You were there two days of bombarding, day and night. And then we went back to the Philippines."

How did Sian feel about the news, knowing Basilone as he did? "I knew about him because when he came to Raritan [in 1943 after Guadalcanal] I was at the parade and all that stuff when they had the big time at Duke's Park. Everybody was buying bonds. My father bought bonds. Then we all went to [Doris] Duke's and had a big ceremony. I only met him once, when we were kids. I saw him in town. I was no friend of his. I just knew of him."

Pacifico pressed Sian, but he didn't know much. "Because, like I said, he's on the other end of town so we were not friends."

And about Basilone's selling war bonds? "Well, he didn't care too much for that. He didn't care for the big shots because he was going to Orlando's bar a lot with Gaburo. Al Gaburo was with him at that time, from when he was delivering laundry for Gaburo's Laundry. He was pretty cocky later, let's put it that way. I used to see him around town, not that I was friends with him."

Did he talk then about combat, or about going back? "Combat, no, and yes, he really wanted to go back." And at Iwo, did Sian ever land or remain aboard ship? Stayed on board. "Bombarded for two days and two nights. I knew he wanted to go back because he was going around this bar a lot and that's when he used to talk about it a lot. I didn't know he was on the island when we were bombarding and we found out he got killed when we got it on the radio."

Pacifico continued asking about Joe's relationships with the Basilones after the war. "Well, Dolores was a good friend of mine. She lived with me for a few months. She was the second youngest of the family. She went someplace. She had to take Donald with her. Donald's the youngest and he's still alive in Florida, and Dolores died. She died four and a half years ago. And that's about it."

There's an authentic small-town American feel to much of this, my own interviews and what's on the Pacifico tape, really less a profile of the most celebrated man in town than a last-century portrait of a provincial town and its people, a modest place only an hour from Times Square. In Raritan, if you lived at the other end of town, or on a different street, you weren't friends. You met people at bars. You worked local jobs, attended Catholic schools. You didn't belong to the country club but probably caddied there. In Basilone's town almost everyone seemed to have an Italian surname, they prayed at the same churches, drank at the same bars, had the same favorite Italian restaurants, dated some of the same Italian girls, fell for a guy's sister, worked at some of the same jobs. And most of the boys joined up during the various wars. They all knew who John Basilone was and remembered him. But how many really knew the man, the machine gunner who in passing through a damp tropical hell killed so many enemy soldiers and became famous?

The other thing about these Raritan interviews was the insistence over and over that Basilone hated the war bond tour, and wanted sincerely to return to the Pacific, to the fighting, to his Marine buddies. Everyone noted it.

Over the past year or two I searched for Basilone, for which of several overlapping or contradictory versions of the man and his war might be the real one, the true John Basilone. I visited Marine bases where he is anything but forgotten, the local libraries, museums, the archives of New Jersey's largest daily newspaper— the *Star-Ledger* in Newark—and other newspapers, local and large. I interviewed friends, his fellow Marines, the citizenry of Raritan, his old neighbors, schoolmates, drinking buddies, the mayor, and then in a phone call, the one surviving of ten Basilone children, seventy-eight-year old Donald in Florida.

"So you're the youngest of the Basilones," I said as we began, and Donald responded, somewhat amused by the irony, "The youngest and the only."

As noted, I'd gotten to see even the old undertaker, Anthony G. Bongiovi Sr., who buried John at Arlington. And, yes, Jon Bon Jovi was of the same family, albeit with a different spelling, but according to my Raritan guides, definitely a cousin. There had been something of a family falling-out early in Jon's career, a disagreement over his dropping a family marketing and commercial connection as his reputation grew. A neighbor in Raritan congratulated me for having been just about the last reporter to see the undertaker, to ask about Basilone and do an interview. And now I was going to have somehow to arrange an interview with Donald Basilone in Florida, the kid brother, the only Basilone left.

That subsequent, gracious, rather sad phone call reminded me not to dawdle. The people I had still to talk with or to visit (mostly Marines) weren't getting any younger (nor was I myself, to be candid). And gradually, as I went, a picture was emerging of small-town 1930s America where their hero came of age.

13

John Basilone, for all his restlessness, turned out to be a dream recruit. He was strong, tireless, not homesick, and for once, eager to learn. Once the drill instructor realized the young boot wasn't just brown-nosing, he took note of and encouraged the lad. Basilone's first outfit was Company D of the 16th Infantry stationed not on some hostile frontier or distant military post, but perched right out there in the middle of New York harbor, on Governor's Island at Fort Jay. According to retired Marine Colonel John Keenan, editor of the *Marine Corps Gazette*, in the United States Army between the world wars, and specifically in the thirties, there was little or no formalized recruit depot or boot camp such as in the Marines. Recruits were usually assigned to an existing regiment of the regular Army, there to be trained and then incorporated into the ranks of the regiment, depending on its needs and the new soldier's aptitude and skills, if any. This, on Governor's Island, was to be whatever recruit training he would receive.

Jim Proser quotes Basilone as delighted with Governor's Island, comparing the place to a country club, noting that it even had a small golf layout where he might hit a few balls. I'm not sure anyone ever filled him in on the island's history, purchased hundreds of years earlier from the Indians for two ax heads and a few iron nails, and then doubled in size to 172 acres by landfill from the excavation of tunnels for the city's brand-new subway system. In World War I a small airfield was built and pilots trained there to fly military aircraft. At some point German sailors were interned here.

But it was also on Governor's Island that, for a variety of reasons, Basilone fell in love with his weapon of choice, the water-cooled .30-caliber heavy machine gun. For the usual enlisted grunt, the gun is far too heavy to be at all lovable or to become a man's personal weapon as it would become Basilone's. The Jerry Cutter and Jim Proser book takes up Basilone's affection for the weapon, purportedly quoting him: "All through the summer [of 1934] I worked on my two specialties, machine gunning and poker. I also had a very active hobby across the harbor in Manhattan when we had passes [recruits aren't usually issued many passes] off the base. This involved young ladies who seemed to be attracted to men in uniform. All in all, the Army was shaping up to the kind of life that was tailor-made for me.

"Even my specialty, machine gunner, suited me down to the ground. When I imagined myself in some future battle, even though I had no idea what a real battle was like, I only knew what I'd seen in the movies. I knew I wanted to be behind a machine gun. Outside of a tank, I figured that was the most powerful weapon on a battlefield, and I was damned if I was getting into a tank if I could help it. I couldn't stand even being in a room all that much. I wouldn't last ten minutes inside a tank."

Was there a suggestion of claustrophobia? "The first time we rolled our 1917A Browning water-cooled .30 calibers out of the old fort's magazine on their caissons, they looked to me like something I could handle. They were human-sized. They weren't complicated. We rolled them out to the gunnery ranges and spent the next six weeks of our boot camp learning the weapon."

No one else refers to Fort Jay as a boot camp. But Cutter and Proser press on, describing John's passion for the weapon: "You could see the rest of the boys getting excited as the sarge went through the ins and outs of the machine. He seemed to go on forever—by the book. The 1917A, its military purpose, capabilities, operating procedure, safety procedure, parts, and assembly—it went on all day. By the afternoon we were ready to get our hands on one and try it out. Sarge went on, the strategy of infantry assault, interlocking fields of fire, trajectory, care and maintenance. Just before chow, we set them up on the range and squeezed off our first rounds."

In 1951 in North Korea with Dog Company, 2nd Battalion, 7th Marines, commanded by Captain John Chafee (the future senator), I was briefly in charge of a Marine machine-gun platoon, and this account of a first day's training with the heavy guns sounds like nonsense. This is not to blame Basilone but the family amateurs who wrote about him. For a young soldier, after less than a full day's training in a weapon as complex and deadly as the machine gun, actually to be firing live rounds without even the usual dry runs and "snapping in" without live ammo doesn't ring true. Or is this simply my being a Marine and overcritical of Army procedure? To be sure, I checked with one of my own former machine gunners, Charles Curley, at his home in Olean, New York. After I read him the passage, he went into detail on the education of a machine gunner. "Oh my God, lieutenant. In my case we were trained at Camp Pendleton on the gun, and then before I ever fired a live round, I had to work my way up, from ammo carrier to assistant gunner to gunner. It was never accomplished in just one day. You had to drill on the gun, take the gun apart, reassemble it, name all its parts, even tell them how many air holes cooled the jacket of the air-cooled gun. You learned all that, then you lugged the ammo, before you ever fired a round of live ammo." Maybe during the ensuing six weeks of machine-gun drill, Basilone actually fired the damned thing, but it surely wasn't that first afternoon.

Basilone, in the Cutter and Proser book, goes on: "For me, it was a God-given moment [those first rounds squeezed off]. It was pure thunder in my hand. The most awesome personal weapon ever built. With correct technique, the gun could fire almost continuously for days before the barrel had to be replaced. It could fire in all weather, in all directions and accurate at 150 yards [This is also silly. The gun's sights are graduated to 2,400 yards and the effective maximum range almost half that and not the meager 150 yards impressionable recruit Basilone supposedly believed.] I was safe and nobody else was. I was like the God who throws thunderbolts." The mock literary allusion doesn't really fit the Basilone we know.

His enthusiasm wasn't feigned, however. This wasn't just a kid's normal excitement over a new and elaborate toy. Basilone truly loved the machine gun. The passion began right there on Governor's Island and would continue through his army years, the first overseas tour at Manila, his Marine Corps hitch, on the 'Canal, and he would still be lugging a Browning machine gun, fiddling with its head space, fretting over its care and feeding, using it to kill people, up until Iwo Jima, on the last day of his young life.

But long before then, there was that other youthful enthusiasm which also sounds genuine; there were the girls. Just a pleasant ferry ride away, the city of New York, with its millions of women, its Third and Sixth Avenue bars under the elevated trains, the Greenwich Village joints, the German beer cellars, the brauhauses of Yorkville on the Upper East Side. So passed a pleasant season, machine-gun drill, poker, ferry rides, and Manhattan honeys.

And sometime early in the new year of 1935 the young soldier was, for the first time, about to travel at government expense, to begin seeing something of the great world beyond Raritan and neighboring New York City. Basilone was being transferred, first sent to the West Coast, and then overseas, to the distant shores of the faraway Philippines. Had a restless small-town kid really found a home in the Army?

14

John Basilone had been a soldier long enough by now to have put aside any youthful illusions. You think it was easy earning that twenty-one dollars a month in the Depression-era Army? The corporals and sergeants chivvied and hassled you from reveille to Taps, the officers lorded it over you, and if you cursed back, hit out, or even gave anyone ranked higher than you a sour look, the MPs beat the shit out of you and you went to the stockade where they beat up on you some more. But what were the options? Where were you going to go? There was no money and little hope or opportunity beyond the CCC (Civilian Conservation Corps) or the Army, only the unemployment lines, the soup kitchens, and the hobo jungles with the rest of the tramps, where the strong screwed boys and weaker men, because there were no women, and thugs would beat a man to death for a pint of rye whiskey or his mulligan stew. As hard as the soldier's life was in the thirties, were you really going to give it up for that and go out on the tramp?

Phyllis Basilone Cutter's story details her kid brother's travels as he departed the garrison at Fort Jay for California and then across the Pacific to Asia. She makes it sound a pleasant idyll.

"The group of us were herded into buses for the quick trip to the Pennsylvania Station in New York. Arriving at this tremendous station our sergeant for the trip counted noses as we filed out of the buses and stood at attention on the walk. To the curious onlookers we must have presented quite a sight as we marched through the station, down the steps to the lower level where our train lay waiting. I was anxious for a window seat as I had never traveled much before and did not want to miss the view. Approaching the vestibule of the Pullman car, I broke ahead and ran for a window seat which I fortunately got. In a few minutes we heard the conductor's 'all aboard,' the peep-peep of the signal, and we were on our way. I got into my seat, hunched back and munched on my goodies, and we were on our way.

"Reaching Chicago, we passed over a maze of tracks and had a tiresome three-hour layover waiting for the West Coast Limited. Finally we were made a part of this super train and heading westward. Looking back, the huge buildings and skyscrapers of Chicago faded in the distance as our train picked up speed. The trip was uneventful. As I watched the countryside speeding by, milepost after milepost, I was amazed and felt small indeed as the vast panorama spread itself before my eyes. I had never been on such a long trip. I soaked up the ever-changing landscape like a dry sponge, for which, during the dark and anxious days still to come, I thanked God because it gave me strength when I needed it most. Just to feel that I was a tiny part of a vast country that we all more or less take for granted, until we sense the danger of losing it, was the spark that kept us going in the face of odds that seemed insurmountable. So you see, folks, we young-uns do think seriously on occasion."

There is much in this passage that's both phony and yet quite sweet, natural, and rather innocent. Maybe it was just a protective big sister's efforts years after the fact to shape the narrative in ways to make her kid brother sound better. The phony part isn't simply that self-consciously corny "young-uns" line, but the reference to those "insurmountable odds." In 1935 as John set off for the coast on his first serious travels, there was no war going on; that was still six years ahead. Such passages, written long after Basilone's much later voyage to a real war in which he would fight heroically and be killed, suggest that his sister was imagining what a boy on his way to war might have felt, translating his wartime emotions to a much earlier, long but essentially uneventful peacetime train ride across a tranquil nation. But some of the passage does ring true: a young man's excitement at embarking on a long trip and seeing the big country for the first time, hustling to find a window seat, munching his goodies—chocolate bars and peanut brittle—gawking at the landscape speeding past, marveling at a first glimpse of Chicago. He was, after all, still a boy, but if it was all a long way from Raritan, Johnny Basilone was to travel farther, and further, much, much further.

The Jerry Cutter and Jim Proser parallel account of that same train ride is juicier, somehow more credible, even when contradictory. In their book, Basilone leaves for California from Grand Central Station instead of Penn Station. Here's their account leading up to and of his trip west following a couple of days leave in Raritan:

"In July there was a machine gun competition on the base. My unit, D Company, walked away with the pennant. I was in a company of 58 winners. I could easier spend a year with these guys than a weekend at home. They were my family now. This was my home and the army was my life. I was a soldier.

"We shipped out to San Diego on the Super Chief out of Grand Central Station. You might have thought of it as the Wild West by what went on in the saloons in the station. The closer it got to 'all aboard' the wilder things got. Fellas who never smoked or drank in their life were doing two at a time. That went for women, too. I'm not proud of the way we acted but I won't pretend we were choirboys either. We were warriors and likely off to war [once again, a war that wouldn't begin for them until 1941]. Orders were for the Philippines. Soon enough, the MPs cleaned the places out and got us on the train. They were some of the roughest sons of bitches I ever met, those MPs. If you didn't hear them the first time they said something you might never hear anything again. They used those white batons the way Ted Williams used a ball bat. [Williams was at this time, in 1935, still an unknown schoolboy, not the major league star who hit .400, so the reference simply doesn't work.] Five or six boys got dumped into the train bleeding or doubled over with the wind knocked out of them. I hadn't really seen that kind of rough stuff before. In camp nobody was ever gotten beaten like that, that bad. In a way, after all the ceremonies, and speeches after basic training, this was the real graduation. We were trained for violence and here it was. Every one of us who could still walk wanted to jump off that train and smash those MPs in the face. That's who we were now. We were violent men. We were a hunting pack and our blood had been spilled. We were ready for our first kill."

What first kill? No one was fighting; there was no war.

"A long train with soldiers holding full pay envelopes was like a dream come true. The first crap game started before we cleared Grand Central. I was in no hurry because the money wasn't leaving this train for the next four days. I wanted to see the country since I'd never been outside New York and New Jersey.

"We slept in our seats and washed over a basin the size of a soup bowl with one foot wedged against the bathroom door so we wouldn't get knocked around by the swaying of the train. By the second day we were starting to smell like goats. Civilians who got on the train didn't stay around us long. We were irritated as hell from not getting any decent sleep and arguments were breaking out every hour or so. If it weren't for gambling, I'm sure we would have been at each other more than we were. The fact we still had three days to go didn't help. We had our choice of three kinds of sandwiches, ham, cheese, or ham and cheese. Pretty soon we weren't a crack fighting force, we were a gang of squabbling chiselers and malcontents. The Army made sure we were going to get to California alive, but they weren't worried about morale. The unfunny joke going around was they were going to put down straw for us and give us hay instead of sandwiches at the next stop. I lost interest in the passing scenery. It all looked the same. I just wanted to get off that train and away from my brothers-at-arms. After the third day of sleeping sitting up and eating stale sandwiches, we were all miserable. Liquor bottles, puke, and cigarette butts covered the floor in some cars. The porters wouldn't come near us anymore, and neither would any civilians. We were stuck with each other in our filth and stench. We sat shoulder-to-shoulder unshaven and hung over. All we thought about was getting off that train. Fights broke out and almost nobody tried to stop them."

Then, suddenly and miraculously, everything changed. They were in California, and after getting off this cross-country train, they traveled south along the coast. As Basilone is supposed to have said in his nephew's postmortem account, "The Pacific Ocean slid into view and I'd never seen anything quite as beautiful before."

The Pacific. Where John Basilone would come of age, where he would fight the Japanese in two pivotal battles, where he would become a living American legend, a famous man, where he would return a second time to the battle, where he would die and be buried. Did any of this occur to the restless kid from Raritan, still a teenager and an untried soldier, or did he marvel only at the great ocean's splendor?

Phyllis's account resumes. "The arrival at San Diego, California was quiet. After a few days of getting settled and outfitted, we started our basic training."

Can this possibly be correct? Basilone had already been in the Army for months, probably since the previous summer, had served with an established outfit at Fort Jay, Company D of the 16th Infantry. Whatever training they did at San Diego soon came to a close, and one night (the date is elusive) at eight p.m., machine gunner John Basilone and his outfit were mustered and marched aboard the USS *Republic*, a military transport that would take them to the Philippines. The Jersey boy had crossed the country by train and now would be leaving it entirely by ship to continue his Army career on the other side of the Pacific, 8,000 miles away. A band played, the transport slipped its lines, and the lights of San Diego slowly fell off and faded astern. Stifled by the close quarters below, Basilone slept that first night on deck, at a vacant spot near the stern.

"Making myself as comfortable as was possible, I stretched out. Looking up I could see the sky with its thousands of stars blinking, so close you felt you could reach up and touch them. Well, I thought, this is better. Outside of one rainy night, that was my bedroom the remainder of the trip." He was eighteen years old, a child of the Great Depression, on the first leg of a long voyage en route to an eventual glory.

15

The Philippines had become an American territory following the Spanish-American War with a promise eventually to be granted independence. But in the mid-1930s with an elected president of their own, they were still very much subject to Washington's wish and whim, so much so that a retired American general, Douglas MacArthur, now cruelly considered a back number, commanded their armed forces, such as they were—a handful of what were romantically called "Filipino Scouts" and some 16,000 U.S. Army regulars and naval personnel—a "corporal's guard" to a man of General MacArthur's towering and magisterial self-opinion. His actual title was Military Adviser to the Commonwealth Government and his rank that of a lieutenant general in the Philippine army. For MacArthur, this was something of a professional and career comedown, since he had fought famously in World War I, and in the last hours of that war to end all wars had been promoted to flag officer rank as a brigadier general by his commanding officer, General of the Armies "Black Jack" Pershing. (It was said MacArthur had desperately twisted arms for that eleventh-hour promotion, on the grounds that once the fighting ended, so too would all promotions to general officer in the shrunken peacetime Army sure to come.)

MacArthur had later in the uneasy peace between the world wars been promoted our own Army's commander as Army chief of staff, in which role and on the president's orders he had brutally smashed the so-called Bonus Army of aggrieved war veterans camped out in the parks and streets of the national capital. Now, himself abruptly among the unemployed, the man on horseback had been stunningly dismounted.

But for MacArthur, Manila was hardly an unpleasant exile. There were powerful family ties to the islands. His own father, Arthur MacArthur, had commanded in the Philippines, and the son had lived there when he was a little boy. Now another Arthur MacArthur was growing up there with *his* parents, Jean MacArthur and "the General," as Mrs. MacArthur habitually called him, in vice regal comfort in postcolonial Manila. There was always with MacArthur, even in economically straightened times and on a more modest scale, plenty of "pomp"; it was the "circumstance" that was missing in the Philippines.

Now in March 1935, John Basilone of Raritan who had the circumstance but hardly the pomp, was about to join the MacArthurs. Not, of course, as anything approaching a social equal, but more the equivalent of a young caddy carrying for wealthy and select country club members.

Aboard the USS *Republic*, Basilone sailed into Manila Harbor past landmarks that would within a few years be sandblasted into the American consciousness, the fortified island of Corregidor, the Bataan Peninsula, the big naval base at Cavite, delivering the young soldier to his duty station for the next two years, as a machine gunner under one of the most celebrated of all American warriors, Douglas ("Gawd Almighty Himself") MacArthur. But here also young John would flirt for the first time with the idea of marriage, to a local girl named Lolita, and he would make something of a reputation as a fighter, not in war but in another arena, as a jock on the boxing team of a peacetime Army garrison.

Eight thousand miles from San Diego, and in a time of strained military peacetime budgets, the replacement draft that included Basilone was short of just about everything: proper uniforms, decent rations, and, for some reason, soap. (Since there was no rationing, the shortage of soap must have been the result of a logistics foul-up or an incompetent supply officer, or a supply sergeant down the line who was on the chisel and selling soap to the locals for cash.) The undersupplied troops were armed not with the old bolt-action 1903 Springfield rifles of World War I (Sergeant York, and all that) but the even older Boer War Enfield.

Out of sheer hunger, soldiers fleshed out mess hall chow with Filipino fare, goat meat becoming a staple. Some of the troops were adopted by local Philippine families or got part-time jobs in Filipino shops and businesses, or moved in with native girls. Others started up local, off-base businesses of one sort or another, of which Jerry Cutter and Jim Proser quote Basilone as saying, "For the first year or two I didn't go in for that. I was still U.S. Army and kept my nose clean as far as all that." Some troops took up wearing Philippine civilian clothes, a few deserted entirely, or cracked, "went Asiatic." Not Basilone, though he complained that only the constant card games got him through the boredom of that first year in country.

There were bandits up in the hills and a few rebels of one persuasion or another, and you might think that MacArthur would have had his troops constantly out in the field, aggressively patrolling, in order to train and season his men and eliminate boredom, if not the bandits. No such luck. Perhaps budgetary constraints limited such exercises and prohibited the general from issuing orders that would have benefited both his men and his entire command. These were hard times, and this was an Army on the cheap. They counted cartridges, so that firing-range practice, something you'd think to be essential, was curtailed. Or maybe MacArthur was simply getting older, saw little future in his career, and, inertia being what it was, just didn't bother ordering units into the field.

Basilone recalled that from time to time shots were fired at the Army encampments from beyond the perimeter security. There might then be a halfhearted attempt to track down and capture the "guerrillas," but the Americans never caught anyone in the rough terrain of the countryside. And there might have been the odd firefight, though how did you chase bandits through the bush lugging a Browning water-cooled heavy machine gun, basically a defensive weapon, and with its tripod, water jacket, elevating and aiming devices, and the pintle on which everything turned, weighing when loaded nearly a hundred pounds? The answer was, you didn't, so it is highly unlikely the young machine gunner ever fired a shot in anger in the Philippine years.

For the bored, card-playing, womanizing, and randy young Basilone, there were, however, the attractive charms of the petite, dark-haired, dark-eyed local women, who he thought resembled some of the handsome Italian-American girls he'd known at home in Raritan. There were plenty of compliant "amateurs," and there were the favorite girls at the local bordellos. According to a few dubious, entirely unproven allegations, Basilone actually became a junior partner in running one of these establishments of easy virtue. I found no credible evidence of that, but almost surely he patronized the brothels. The whorehouse "management" rumors may have derived from the small "nightclub" he and his girl, Lolita, set up inside her uncle's bicycle shop, which sounds colorful and fun but reasonably innocent.

All of MacArthur's troops looked forward to their R&R stints every six months in New Zealand, with its temperate climate, pretty girls, local beers, and "people a lot like us." Some of the farmboys and ranchers among the enlisted men spent their R&R, and voluntarily so, living with families and working without pay and happily on farms and cattle stations (ranches). The Yanks found New Zealanders wonderful, but really they would have welcomed almost anything to get them out of the Philippines for a time. Some of Basilone's fellow soldiers, their enlistments up, instead of going home to the States returned to New Zealand to marry local girls.

Beyond his acknowledged skill as a machine gunner, there was at first little to distinguish Basilone's first overseas tour of duty, apart from his card-playing expertise and a penchant for going barefoot in monsoon season. Army-issue wool socks, when wet, itched, and men developed fungus and jungle rot. Cotton socks sent from home rotted quickly. Basilone had a simple cure—go without—and was regularly chewed out about it. But his feet toughened up, he developed surer footing, and he didn't itch anymore. Going barefoot was just about all that set him apart from his mates—or it was until he began to box.

In the jock-happy prewar regular Army, service athletes, especially competent boxers, might do pretty well for themselves. MacArthur, who served once as superintendent of the Military Academy at West Point, understood the constructive role military athletics could play in a bored peacetime Army and encouraged the athletic culture. James Jones wonderfully (and tragically) portrayed the scene in prewar Hawaii in *From Here to Eternity* with fighter and trumpeter Robert E. Lee Prewitt as his hero. Young Basilone's experience was more rewarding. He began boxing, horsing around at first in ad hoc fights. "A lot of steam had been building up in my head."

Part of that "steam" was a professional and rather patriotic frustration. The soldiers had been told that if the Japanese (the closest, perhaps the *only* potential enemy) ever attacked, the plan was for American regulars of MacArthur's little Army to retreat to Corregidor and fight it out from there. As Jerry Cutter reported the situation from Basilone's point of view, "I didn't like sitting around waiting for an attack just so we could run for it. And I didn't like that we were stuck on this island [Luzon] and we weren't even important enough to get soap. Sparring let me blow off steam and kept me sharp. Being a fighter got you privileges sometimes like an inside bunk and credit at card games—which I didn't usually need." Based on his success in those pickup bouts, he volunteered for the unit's organized boxing squad, and as a muscular young athlete in good shape, he began fighting in service bouts as a 160-pound middleweight. He was now nineteen, and thanks to being physically more mature, a year older, and with regular workouts, conditioning, and better chow, had soon grown into and was fighting as a light heavyweight (175 pounds). He soon caught on to the racket. "Once I started winning I started getting steaks and pork chops stolen from the Officers' Club. My fellow soldiers began to see me as a money-making enterprise."

Soldiers, and especially other gunners and his buddies, not only backed him with cash in side bets but volunteered as sparring partners, medics as cut men, others as corner men, trainers, managers, and cheering squads. Gambling picked up and money changed hands. Basilone was becoming a popular local character on whom a man might make a buck.

There were organized bouts twice a month, and Basilone won them. Never lazy, he trained hard, running up hills or in the soft, yielding sand of the shoreline of Manila Bay. Parallels to the much later and fictional Rocky Balboa are irresistible. For all Basilone's casual, card-playing ways, there is an impressive discipline about the slimly educated youngster, the newly minted soldier. One weekend when a fellow soldier named Smits was arrested for being intoxicated, Basilone and some buddies conjured up a scheme to break him out of the drunk tank of a Filipino police station by ramming a stolen truck into the prison wall early on a Sunday morning, the clever reasoning being that the cops, being Roman Catholics, would be at their devotions and attending mass. Whether the Sunday-morning ploy was Basilone's or a group decision, they got Smits out and weren't caught themselves. The plan worked.

Following two knockouts in Basilone's first three winning formal bouts, the brass began coming by to see him fight, even MacArthur on one occasion stopping by to wish him luck. He eventually ran his record to eighteen wins, no losses. According to Cutter and Proser, the adulation went slightly to Basilone's head, and he started thinking of his undefeated record and himself as a sort of "mascot" for the general, someone to whom MacArthur, with his ego, could justifiably point in an otherwise unimpressive little command. Reputedly, word of Basilone's ability trickled back to the States, and offers to turn professional came in from New York fight managers and promoters, though no one I spoke with in Raritan could provide any names or details about what probably was just wishful thinking. But a fighting nickname, "Manila John," seems to have stuck. And MacArthur was pleased as the kid's perfect ring record improved, with a big possible fight against a Navy boxer coming up.

It was always an occasion, the whores and the saloons especially rejoicing, when the fleet sailed into Manila, and with Army and Navy rivalry heightening, officers trading boasts and placing bets, they staged Basilone's last Army bout, matching him as a soldier against a formidable American Navy tar, "Sailor Burt," a tough machinist's mate, "a fucking Dane . . . a shoveler of shit," as the troops rudely put it. Manila John's buddies placed their own bets, warning him he'd "better win" or they'd be broke till next payday. He tried, prudently, to warn them off. Sailor Burt was tough and Manila John could guarantee nothing. But the soldiers didn't listen.

The day of the big fight arrived, and with it a lunch that wasn't the usual dreary mess hall chow for the gladiator, but a steak, French fries, sliced Bermuda onion, topped off by apple pie, and steaming black coffee. With a cheering, foot-stamping audience of sailors and soldiers, including the brass from both services, Basilone and Burt went at it, trading knockdowns, both men nearly out. In the end it was a twelve-rounder and yet another knockout, as "Manila John" won again, running his record to 19–0. His commanding officer was jubilant, and even the disappointed admiral came back to the lockers to congratulate the foe, the Army boy who knocked out Sailor Burt.

With his Army hitch nearing its end, the young man was torn. He hated the boredom, the weather, not enough to eat even of the usual lousy food, the malaria, the bugs, the chiggers, the snakes, but most of all those "standing orders to retreat" in case of war, the prospect of a fallback to Corregidor if and when the Japanese came ashore. And John *knew* they were coming. He liked the discipline and much of the structure and purpose he found in the Army but hated some of it. He's quoted on how enlisted men were handled: "They trained us to be fighters and treated us like convicts."

John thought he might be in love with Lolita, even considered staying in the islands with her and starting a real business outside the bike shop cum nightclub. But in the end when his sergeant asked if Basilone planned to re-up for another tour, he said no. Twenty-one years old, he headed home to Raritan, as adrift as he had been three years before, as directionless and unfocused, as unskilled in civilian terms. And even worse, having returned home, he realized already that he missed some aspects of Army life—the machine gun, the boxing, the camaraderie. His nephew Jerry Cutter summed it up, supposedly in his uncle's words: "I had lost the life, the calling I had found. I wasn't a soldier anymore. I was lost."

16

Back home, again a civilian, John Basilone recognized swiftly, pragmatically that "there's not much use for a machine gunner in New Jersey." If he expected much out of his hometown, he was mistaken. He went to see and seek counsel from his old priest/adviser Amadeo Russo at St. Ann's. The men talked with the old familiarity, but there were no easy answers. At home Basilone self-consciously told stories of the Philippines but not about Lolita, whom he sloughed off as just another of the generic native girls he'd encountered. Asked about the Army, he didn't feel that he could explain it very well, not so they would understand—the contradictions, the pull it had on him still, and the other, less appealing aspects of garrison life—not so that anyone "got" his mixed emotions. It was frustrating.

The Depression had eased marginally, and some of Basilone's boyhood friends were settled down and doing well. Others were as adrift as he was. No high school, no marketable skills, nothing beyond being able to field-strip and rebuild a Browning water-cooled heavy machine gun. Basilone was a good boxer in amateur circles but was sufficiently savvy to know that was a long way from being a professional paid to fight like his old idol, Primo Carnera, in Madison Square Garden. There was always the caddy shack at the Raritan Valley Country Club. As an adult, he was caddying again that summer over his father's objections: "You can't be a caddy your whole life," his father said. For a time he drove a laundry delivery truck for Gaburo's Laundry (his sleeping atop the laundry bags apparently forgiven). Then he took a job in nearby Bound Brook with the Calco Chemical Division of American Cyanamid. That job lasted a year.

Basilone's sister Phyllis and her husband, Bill Cutter, were living in Reisterstown, Maryland, near Baltimore, and Bill convinced John to become an installation mechanic for his gas company employer, the Philgas Company. Basilone moved in with the Cutters. He seemed to enjoy the work and was good at it, but after about eight months the old restlessness was working at him.

In a way he missed the orderly, organized misery of an enlisted man's daily routine on a military post, no matter how distant or alien. And he was again sensing that war was coming to his country, his home, as it had to so many other nations around the world. It got him thinking about again enlisting. But this time he wouldn't go Army.

Basilone was now twenty-three years old, a veteran, a traveled man, strong and aware of his own highly specialized skills and strengths, a solid 180 pounds, a formidable amateur boxer, and considerably larger than his father. But he didn't know quite how to break the news to his parents that civilian life wasn't working out for him and that he was going back into the service. That in fact, and without telling anyone, on July 11, 1940, the day on which Marshal Pétain, now virtually a Nazi puppet, became president of Occupied France, John had gone into Baltimore and enlisted in the Marine Corps. The Marines were apparently glad to have a man with three years of Army service behind him and a veteran machine gunner at that. Phyllis was stunned, but Bill seemed to understand and be supportive, agreeing to help smooth things over with the family and especially with the patriarch, the Old Man, Salvatore the tailor.

The two men and Phyllis drove north the next day to Raritan. The situation promised to be awkward. John seemed to have grown tranquil now that he'd made a decision and taken action. He thought he now knew how to appeal to his father, through the old man's love of his adopted country, his patriotism, and though his mother might "carry on," she would eventually fall in line. The ploy worked. Over a smoke he told his father he was concerned about threats from the country's enemies. Who would dare attack us? the senior Basilone demanded. John was prepared. "The Japs, Pop." Maybe he was still thinking of that golfing foursome at the country club, those Japanese golfers taking photos.

At Sal's insistence, John agreed to remain in Raritan for a round of leave-taking with family and friends. At first he resented these duty calls. But as the visits went on, seeing pals and relations, with the well-wishing, the ritual glass of wine, the gifts, usually money, pressed into Basilone's hands, he felt better about things. And to be candid about it, he could use the dough. His appointed date with the Marines arrived, and he left Raritan for the South, reporting to boot camp at what was then the Marine Corps recruit depot at Quantico, Virginia, just thirty-five miles south of Washington, D.C.

In her serialized newspaper account of her brother's adventures, and in his voice, this is how Phyllis describes John's formal introduction to the Corps: "A hot sweltering humid day. The processing didn't help any, however. Looking back I can truthfully say the first night at Quantico was the only night I found it difficult to fall asleep. If I thought Army training was tough, it was soon put out of my mind. When they train you to become a Marine, you either fall by the wayside or you emerge as the best damn fighting man in the service. We trained and went through exercises at Quantico until we were razor sharp. Our sergeant was a holy terror and if only one-tenth of our bitching came true, he'd never have a restful night's sleep. Later on we thanked God for our training under Sarge. It certainly paid off. Maybe he knew; he always hollered, 'Come on you guys, get the lead out of your asses. What'd you think, you're in the Army? Set up these guns, on the double.' It got so we could set them up in seconds flat. Secretly, I had the feeling he was satisfied, even proud of us."

All this may have dismayed Phyllis, but to most Marines the drill sounds familiar, routine, and rather tame. If "asses" was the worst language and "hollering" the worst treatment that boot camp drill instructors passed out back in 1940, Manila John was a fortunate man. One can assume this business of "setting up guns" dealt with the Browning heavy machine guns on which Basilone had been already thoroughly checked out during his Army hitch. As for that "hot sweltering humid" Quantico weather, I can testify as a Marine who spent three summers there (1948, 1949, and 1951) that heat and humidity was commonplace. For an American with two years in the tropical Philippines, the climate of northern Virginia shouldn't have been a shock. And for an enlisted man and trained athlete with three years of Army service behind him, a Marine recruit depot would be tolerable if not posh. Yet as Phyllis sums up in John's voice his Quantico experience, "If we thought boot training was tough, we soon discovered that compared to our training and exercises at Guantanamo Bay, Cuba, it was duck soup."

According to Basilone's USMC military service record, he boarded ship, traveling "tourist class" aboard the SS *McCawley* on September 28, 1940, and was ashore at Guantanamo on October 2. Nothing much was going on there, just a handful of peacetime Marines in canvas leggings toting Springfield '03s, guardians of one of the modest and most enduring outposts of American colonialism, held ever since the Spanish-American War. Teddy Roosevelt may have landed at or embarked from here. And in Basilone's words, "There we put in seven miserable months of maneuvers. For this we earned the title of 'Raggedy-Ass Marines.'"

Some of those maneuvers weren't at Guantanamo itself but at the Puerto Rican Island of Culebra where, as early as the winter of 1923–1924, the Marine Corps had begun a concentrated and very serious program of amphibious warfare, training troops to land on hostile beaches under fire, from small boats launched beachward from transports, destroyers, or other larger craft. By

1940 and 1941, Basilone was one of many Marines readying for amphibious warfare. There were as yet no specially designed landing craft, and photos of the time show Marines jumping into shallow-water beaches from Chris-Craft speedboats, civilian-style 1920s motorboats of one sort or another, rifles at high port to keep them dry and out of the corroding saltwater.

In a still young country like ours, it's fascinating the way history can compress and fold in on itself. Here we were in the 1940s training troops on islands and beaches won by Teddy Roosevelt and his generation at the end of the last century during the Spanish-American War, incorporating new assault tactics developed in the 1920s, to be put into action against the Japanese in the mid-twentieth century in World War II.

On New Year's Day 1941 Basilone joined the outfit with which he would first see combat, D Company, 1st Battalion of the 7th Marine Regiment of the Fleet Marine Force (FMF). On March 1, 1941, he was transferred to D Company of the 1st Marines, a different regiment. There is no explanation for this transfer. Perhaps someone was short of a machine gunner, and indeed Basilone would soon land back in the 7th Regiment.

He wrote little, nothing that came down to us through family and friends or through the years. Instead, we get the spare official record of his service, the flawed memories of his folks, most of them now dead, and beyond that, a frustrating silence.

The paucity of letters from Basilone to the family, or to anyone, is frustrating. The nuns at his grammar school and Father Russo, his mentor, must share the blame for Manila John's failure to write, even to the family, or keep some sort of informal diary. He must have had some informed, interesting things to say, one young man's commentary on being in a peacetime American military while much of the cultured and civilized Old World was at war, a war that was maybe coming, and soon, to a still peaceful, complacent America. Why should we be immune? If France with its greatest army in the world could fall, London burn, and Poland, the Low Counties, Norway, and Denmark be conquered, why would we stand untouched?

Or might not machine gunner Basilone have made pungent comparisons between the Marines and his previous employer, the U.S. Army? Did he miss General Douglas MacArthur and his paternalistic cheerleading, yearn for the boxing, ache for Lolita? Was Marine chow better than the crap they fed him in Manila? Or was there anything else from his previous enlistment and two years in a foreign country from which he took lessons? From which fellow Marines might have learned something? When he read the papers, if he did, was he following with even a narrow professional interest what was happening in Europe and North Africa? When he heard of growing tensions in the Pacific, did he once more recall that foursome of Japanese golfers he once took as spies? Might Basilone not have taken scribbled notes, worried about the future, concerned himself about a possible American war, drawn and mulled obvious conclusions?

From Guantanamo Bay, sandy, hot, wind-dried, and peaceful Gitmo, the Marines moved on to more promising exercises, those landing maneuvers at Culebra. Basilone and his heavy machine gun moved on. There were other Marine Corps "stately pleasure domes" to come. On April 19, 1941, "Patriots Day" in Boston, where they were still celebrating the battles of Concord and Lexington, Basilone and Company D arrived aboard the good ship *George F. Elliott* at Parris Island, South Carolina, later to become the East Coast's recruit training depot. It was there on May 15 that Basilone was promoted, the same day the Germans were preparing to drop their paratroopers on Crete, including old heavyweight champ Max Schmeling, to take the island from the Brits, whose numbers included Royal Marine commando officer and author Evelyn Waugh and some battered Greeks.

Basilone had been rewarded with a promotion by temporary warrant to corporal, a swift promotion in those days, which must say something about his performance, professional skills, and attitude as a relatively new Marine. When you think back to those three years of consistently "excellent" fitness reports during Army service, he seems to have been a born soldier.

There was a brief stop at his old boot camp at Quantico, a base now expanding rapidly. A short furlough later that month was followed by what sounds like seagoing duty, aboard the *Harry Lee* from June 7 to July 23 and then aboard the *Fuller* from July 24 to August 13. On September 30, 1941, Basilone arrived in North Carolina and went ashore at a new and growing base called New River. Also on that day, in Russia, Kiev having been taken, Guderian's panzer army wheeled toward Moscow. It looked as if the Soviets were next to finished, the Germans closing on victory. There was no comment on this that we know of from Basilone.

Phyllis in her account has her brother touching not on the world war but about his latest duty station in the Carolinas: "If we thought Cuba and Culebra were bad, our first look at New River made them look like the Riviera."

Marine Barracks, New River, North Carolina, what is now known as Camp Lejeune (or in Marine jargon, "Swamp Lagoon"), was a new East Coast Marine base on a big river flowing into the nearby Atlantic. In 1941 the Navy Department and Marine brass, increasingly concerned about the Japanese, were considering an expansion of the Marine Corps from a mere 7,000 troops and 500 officers to something a lot bigger, a Corps that would have need of large new bases. Basilone is quoted as describing New River this way: "Picture if you can over 100,000 acres of plains, swamps, water infested with snakes, chiggers and sand flies. No mountains or hills, just flat, swampy terrain, and you get an idea of what our playground was."

With winter coming on, Basilone's outfit was still housed in tents in the cold and damp, the heating supplied by smelly stoves prone to starting fires and very good at putting out soot, with lighting mostly limited to candles. The training concentrated on amphibious warfare drill, men climbing down cargo nets into small boats, much of the time using mockups on dry land since neither large transports or landing barges were available, though cargo nets were plentiful. There were no USO shows coming to New River, the only medium was the local weekly newspaper, and perhaps out of sheer boredom,

Basilone resumed boxing, again going undefeated, though against what quality of competition isn't clear. He enjoyed a week's furlough that ended with his return to New River on November 26, two weeks before the attack on Pearl Harbor, a shattering and historic event about which, by my reckoning, Basilone has absolutely nothing to say. The Japanese had surprise-attacked us, and Corporal Basilone issues no comment, displays no reaction.

The United States had been attacked and was now at war, the entire country was up in arms, our military men and bases were on alert, Basilone was a serving Marine, yet there is nothing at all recorded of letters or calls or any exchanges whatsoever between him and his folks. Its is tempting to say that this is vexing, but perhaps in the new wartime situation Basilone may simply have been kept busy. After all, the Marines were supposed to be "first to fight."

On January 23, 1942, Basilone was promoted, again by temporary warrant, to sergeant-line, once more a rapid promotion perhaps reflecting not only on his outstanding record but the accelerating expansion of the Corps. In the Pacific the Japanese were winning almost everywhere and rolling up American and Allied forces. And on that very date of Basilone's promotion, Japanese troops landed on New Britain, New Ireland, Borneo, and in the Solomons, on the big island of Bougainville. An enemy sub had shelled the oil fields of Long Beach, just south of Los Angeles. Incendiary balloons launched in Japan floated across the ocean on prevailing winds toward the forested slopes of Oregon and Washington State, fortunately setting no fires. But the bastards did have a helluva nerve, didn't they?

In March, reacting to continued enemy pressure and new landings in the Pacific, a detachment of Marines, Basilone among them, was assigned to the defense of American Samoa, and the entire 1st Marine Division, which had been created only thirteen months earlier, got its orders for service overseas. On April 10 Basilone's bunch embarked from Norfolk for the Pacific, and after a long, leisurely voyage, "Our convoy reached Apia, Western Samoa on May 8, 1942 and set up camp." The Battle of the Coral Sea was fought that day. A few days earlier in the Philippines, where Basilone once served, the historic 4th Marines had burned their regimental colors and sent off two officers, a field music (probably a bugler), and an interpreter to ask the victorious Japanese for terms, and then surrendered, shortly to set off on the long death march to the camps.

In peaceful Samoa, Sergeant Basilone was just barely en route to the war and, eventually, a shot at the enemy. Neither he nor anyone else could have predicted that within months he would fight heroically in desperate battles on Guadalcanal, be shipped to Australia, awarded the grandest medal we have, and then confronted with a hard choice to make, to "stay with his boys" and go back into combat, or accept a free ride home to the States as an anointed hero.

PART THREE

HOME FRONT

Major General Alexander A. Vandegrift, Colonel Merritt A. Edson, Platoon Sergeant Mitchell Paige, and Sergeant John Basilone after receiving their Congressional Medals of Honor at Camp Balcombe, in Australia, May 21, 1943, for their heroism at Guadalcanal.

17

The Marine Corps finally, in midsummer of 1943, after much backing and filling, made up its mind. John Basilone was being sent back to the States.

"The day officer came in one day and handed me orders, [to] separate from my unit. I was shipping out, going home. I was to report to Marine headquarters in New York City. There were no further instructions. Talking about coming from left field, I had to read the damn thing three times. I was going home. It didn't make any sense. My guys are gearing up for operations and I'm shipping out? [Bob] Powell looked at me as if I was Jesus H. Christ himself. He gave me his folks' address in New Haven and for a minute I thought he was going to cry. Nobody even thought seriously about home and not even in a dream. But here it was in front of me and I was going. . . . The orders said now, so I packed my sea bag." Basilone's mood had changed, his earlier elation over the medal's being a sure "ticket home" had evaporated. He would be going home, but now reluctantly.

It's exasperating that nowhere do we have a date for the man's departure. It probably was July. Basilone's service record book shows that he was promoted to temporary platoon sergeant on June 1, 1943, and the entry on the next line, partly illegible, indicates he sailed on the twenty-seventh (it had to be July) via the ship *Rochambeau*. In the next service record book entry, Basilone reports into Marine barracks at the Washington, D.C., Navy Yard on August 31, 1943. Furloughs might logically fill in the gaps covering most of August. The medal ceremony had been on May 21, 1943. Yet there was no official news about it until June 23 when it was released to the national press. The *New York Times* ran its front-page story on June 24, under a headline that read, "Slew 38 Japanese in one battle; Jersey Marine gets honor medal." The lead read, "The son of an Italian-born tailor in New Jersey took his place tonight among the great American war heroes, when a Marine Corps platoon sergeant, John Basilone of Raritan, 26, one of a family of ten children, was cited for the Congressional Medal of Honor, the highest tribute the nation can bestow on its fighting sons." John's letter to the family telling about the medal was dated June 12, and they received it June 21, did not understand its significance, and therefore didn't really react until the news broke in newspapers on the twenty-third or (as in the *Times*) the twenty-fourth of June.

Bruce Doorly in his monograph notes, "In July of 1943, John was notified that he was being sent home, but there was a catch to it. John would have to go on a 'bond drive' and on a 'speaking tour,' to war plants.

"This wouldn't be the first of these bond-selling caravansaries of Hollywood stars and actual decorated heroes to tour the country. In 1942 the luminous Carole Lombard, a glamorous figure and gifted film comedienne, the wife of Clark Gable (himself now an Air Corps officer), was killed in a plane crash during just such a trip. As John loaded up to go home he told his buddies he would be back, but they did not believe him. . . . John arrived back in the U.S., landing in California in August of 1943."

Jerry Cutter, Basilone's nephew, attempts to nail down his uncle's return to the continental United States, starting with this account, in John's voice, of the press reception at Roosevelt Base, a wartime operation on Terminal Island off Long Beach, California, possibly where the *Rochambeau* docked following its long crossing from Melbourne: "They swarmed over us, snapping pictures and yelling questions, everybody calling to me, 'Manila John, how d'ya feel when ya got the medal?' 'Hey, Johnny, were ya scared?' 'Have ya called home yet?' 'How'd ya feel when you killed all those Japs?' Talk about being in the spotlight, it was like the whole country turned its headlights on me and wanted me to tell them every last thing down to what I had for breakfast."

Sounds like the celebrity press of today, the paparazzi, the shouted questions about whether he liked being called "Manila John, the Jap Killer"? Would he be going back into the ring?

This was a guy who hated to be "gawked at" in his own barracks by Marines he knew, let alone total strangers doing a job. But here's how Phyllis Cutter reconstructed the time following the May 21 award presentation at Melbourne, in Basilone's voice, including a brief reference on a fairly important official matter. During his California sojourn in August 1943, she quotes him, fed up by all the press, as saying, "Turning down a commission, I asked to be sent back into action with my buddies and was promptly refused."

This is new, the mention of a possible commission, the Corps finally offering him an opportunity to become an officer, just as they had earlier with Platoon Sergeant Mitchell Paige. There would later be similar offers in Washington, but this reference is the earliest such bid of commissioned rank that I can find. In Phyllis's article, Basilone goes on: "I think it was during the latter part of July 1943 [while still with his unit in Australia] I was being briefed on my return to the States. Yes, I was being given leave. However, there was a hitch to it. I was given a faint idea of what was expected of me and told I would be filled in at HQ in New York City."

Phyllis describes Basilone's departure from Melbourne with one Marine, on seeing John crying, sneering to another, "I thought you said he was a tough guy." There is no account of his voyage home aboard, the records say, the *Rochambeau*, or his brief August stay in California with its welcoming if rowdy press events. There was a quick authorized visit to Camp Pendleton at Oceanside, California, to see his brother George, who was now a young Marine there in training. "A big fuss" was made, and George was given time off (he was later sent home on leave to be with his brother).

While Basilone was still in California the Marine Corps was already briefing him on an upcoming tour with movie people to sell war bonds around the country. "We kept hearing that this bond tour was going to get going but one thing or another held up the show. First it was some movie star couldn't get away, and then it was a scheduled event that was delayed and would throw the whole schedule off. So we ended up sitting in our barracks with absolutely nothing to do except waiting to be called for interviews with newspaper or radio people. They all asked pretty much the same questions. So I started telling them they could read the other newspaper and get all the answers they wanted."

So Basilone was starting to mouth off, wise-guy style. "My shadow [his guide and monitor on the tour] lit into me after that. These were all important people from important places. If I didn't toe the line he'd see about getting me shipped back to that jungle. That was definitely the wrong thing to say. He said it like being in the jungle fighting was a place where you went if you couldn't get a soft desk job like him, and his important people."

You wonder why Manila John didn't just deck the creep. Apparently the significant next step in his journey was the order to report to the senior Marine at 90 Church Street in Manhattan. Maybe they were finally getting started on the war bond tour.

Phyllis picks up Basilone's story in New York, at the Marine Corps office there, where the returning warrior would again be trotted out for the press, his first organized Manhattan press conference. A comic book called *War Heroes* had been released, his story as a superhero garishly reported in detail. There is no suggestion anyone in the Corps or in publishing even bothered to ask Basilone's clearance on the comic. He was a serving Marine and, medal or no medal, he was expected to do what he was told.

Wrote Phyllis in her brother's voice: "It was mid-morning on September 4, and sitting in the Corps office nervous, with the perspiration rolling down my brow, I remarked, 'Geez, this is something.' Well, anyway, I told the reporters who had jammed the press room my story exactly as it happened. As I once again related my experiences, I seemed to have drifted back to the 'Canal, bringing home the realization that as long as I had to repeat the experience time and time again, it would take a long time to erase its memory from my mind. Maybe that's the price a hero pays. I didn't know." You sense the confusion in the young man's mind, the understandable stage fright, almost a longing for military routine, for the structure of the unit, the outfit, his pals, the Marine Corps itself. Yet this was in a Marine office in Manhattan and the Marine Corps was more or less running the show, and the sergeant was going along with it as best he could. Things lightened up that September afternoon.

"At noon I was taken over to City Hall to meet 'The Little Flower,' Mayor LaGuardia. He turned out to be an all-right Joe. Of course the reporters and photographers tagged along, jotting down our every word to the steady pop of the flash-bulbs all over the place." LaGuardia made a little talk about the significance of Basilone's medal and the requisite pitch for Americans to buy war bonds during the bond drive coming up, and then he turned back to Basilone with a question. "Sergeant, where did your old man come from?"

Basilone gave the proudly parochial Italian American mayor chapter and verse about Italy, Naples, the name of the ship on which his father sailed to the States, and his work as a tailor, and the Little Flower beamed. There were other press conferences, with family members participating in some of them, and Marine brother George marveling to John at one point, "The whole country is crazy about you." Then it was off to D.C. and another round of press conferences, including one at USMC headquarters, on or about September 9, a session that would be pleasantly pivotal. Amid the usual shouted questions and flashbulbs going off in his face, Basilone later admitted, "I was sweating, nervous, and turning to an officer, I said, 'This is worse than fighting the Japs.' He patted me on the shoulder and told me to tell the reporters what happened on October 24–25 in my own words."

Apparently a hush then came over the big room, and for the first time the thing was no longer a circus or an adversarial process, a scrimmage between aggressive reporters and photographers and an overwhelmed Marine still unused to any of this. With Marine public affairs officers and noncoms in charge on their own turf, even the cocky press boys calmed down, stopped shouting, settled in to take notes and let the man speak. Basilone, at last and perhaps for the first time, would be able to tell his story quietly and in a measured and orderly fashion, without interruption, as he best remembered it.

"I started to talk and as the words poured out, I became oblivious to the reporters and all the confusion going on about me. I told them how there had been a heavy tropical rain all day long." Then he told them about the fight, starting with that field phone's ringing at about ten that night, warning that a Japanese attack was about to hit their ridgelines, and went on from there, taking a live audience with him through the nightmare hours of darkness and into the welcoming gray half-light of another dawn, trying to explain how an exhausted, stressed man in mortal combat felt about having lived to see yet another day.

Except for an unlikely Manila John word like "oblivious," it almost seems that this would be the press conference where Basilone made some sort of a breakthrough, realizing that if he just told the story in his own way and his own words, he might be able to handle the challenge of speaking in public. And when the machine gunner had wrapped up his story and a colonel called a halt to the proceedings, each of the newspaper reporters, not shouting now but rather subdued, walked up and asked to shake his hand.

"With that they filed out of the press room. I was a little shaken, retelling those terrible hours all over again." Shaken, sure, but he had coped, had talked at some length, and if not articulately then clearly, to hard-bitten professional journalists. He had not only responded to their questions but, it was quite apparent, moved some of those hard-shelled pros. Peter Vitelli, one of my sources in Raritan, supplied me the CD of a Basilone sound bite, so I've actually heard his voice talking to an admiring crowd. He could be an effective speaker.

Now, as Basilone's tour of the United States was about to start, Phyllis's account becomes quite detailed and precise, with dates, places, events, names, and ranks, everything but serial numbers. Her son Jerry's later but parallel version differs somewhat in the racier details of the journey.

According to Phyllis, the same public relations colonel who'd calmed and encouraged Basilone earlier now took him aside in D.C. and briefed him on the coming agenda. The tour would kick off shortly, the month of September 1943, roughly a year after Basilone and the rest of the 7th Marines went ashore on the 'Canal. "The colonel came over to me and told me to sit down and take it easy. He then outlined the coming bond tour. I was assigned to Flight number 5 of the War Veterans Airmadas [you begin to suspect a Madison Avenue ad agency copywriter at work here in the jargon, with that coined word "Airmadas"]. My companions were to be Sergeant Schiller Cohen, Bosun's Mate 2nd Class Ward L. Gemmer, Machinist Mate 1st Class Robert J. Creak, and film stars Virginia Grey, Martha Scott, Eddie Bracken, John Garfield, and Gene Lockhart [Keenan Wynn would be added]." Not precisely the A-list of Hollywood legends, but not bad. The destinations were largely and conveniently in the Northeast to start. "We were to cover the following cities, Newark, Jersey City, New Haven, Conn., Providence, R.I., Pawtucket, R.I., Worcester, Mass., Albany, Utica, and Rochester N.Y., and Allentown, Pa." And though Basilone was only one of four servicemen on the tour it was obvious he was the big catch, with the first stops in his home state. But he had questions and might as well ask them now.

"I said to the colonel, 'Sir, you mean to tell me I have to speak at all of these rallies? What in the world will I talk about?' 'Sergeant, don't worry about it, you will be introduced and asked to say a few words. Just remember, this tour is important to the war effort, in addition to raising money, you will be speaking at war plants and you of all people should know how desperately we need supplies, guns, and ammunition at the front lines. You may not think so now, but you will be serving your country as much as if you were back in the jungle killing the enemy.'"

How much of this Basilone actually bought into is impossible at this remove to say, but as a schoolboy at the time, five years before my own Marine Corps enlistment, I remember how seriously civilians took such patriotic exhortations in wartime. We had rationing and blackouts and casualty lists, so the war was hardly a far-off story. We at home were in ways also living with it. In the daily papers and in the magazines that came to our house, and on the radio and in the movie newsreels, to a boy like me seeing footage of heroic figures like Manila John Basilone mouthing the same or similar words, they meant something. We weren't yet jaded.

18

In Newark, New Jersey, the bond tour's first stop, and only a forty-minute train ride on the Raritan Valley line from his hometown, John Basilone recalled, "There were a lot of speeches by top officials. I remember Mayor Murphy saying how proud he was of what Newark had contributed to the war effort, and how he urged all citizens to buy bonds until it hurt—and then buy one extra. After a wonderful dinner and more speeches we were taken to Proctors Theatre for a showing of 'Mr. Lucky' [with Cary Grant and Leo Durocher's wife, Laraine Day]. Following the showing, the Hollywood stars in the Airmada introduced us service men. We all gave a short talk and urged the audience to 'Back the Attack.' Judging the reception we were given in Newark [where there were surely Basilones and a pride of neighbors and friends in attendance], we knew we were in for a hectic tour. There would be little rest, except for short naps, between our jumps from city to city. We were formally greeted at [Jersey City's] City Hall by the commissioners before proceeding to the Hotel Plaza, where we were the guests of about 300 leading citizens for luncheon. Commissioner Potterton was the toastmaster and thanks to him, the speeches were held down to three minutes each." Whether this was because the commissioner took up all the time with his own verbosity is not explained.

It was also in Jersey City that, according to Jerry Cutter, things started to warm up between the returning hero and one of the Hollywood stars, Virginia Grey. "Mayor Murphy made a good speech. We all got our turn at the microphone. Bracken and Garfield were completely relaxed as they told people how important it was that they support the boys overseas.

"Virginia introduced me and turned to me with a look that was a little different than the look she gave to the other guys. We did another event in Jersey City that afternoon and then a few hours off. Virginia and I managed to separate us from the others and slipped away to a hotel for a few drinks in a dark, back booth. She was from a show business family and grew up in Hollywood. I never met anyone even a little bit like her before. She was just about the funniest lady I'd ever run across, and beautiful, with real movie star looks—honey-colored hair and eyes that were deep blue, cornflower blue. She was thin, must have weighed just over a hundred pounds, and had so much energy I thought she was going to get up and tap dance on the table. We laughed our heads off. She didn't take Hollywood glamour seriously at all because to her, it was just the family business. And could she tell dirty stories on all the big stars going back all the way to the silent movie days when her dad was a big shot.

"She was too good to be true. I couldn't stop looking at her. What really got me was that she was the real McCoy—inside. The tour was more important to her than her Hollywood movies. It wasn't some put-up job just to get her face in the papers, she really put her heart into everything she said out there in front of the people. When I heard that from her and knew she was telling the truth, I was like the dog with a bone. It seemed like green lights all the way for Virginia and me. Being on the road like we were, meant that we were together every day." Clearly, Manila John was a fast worker.

Since Jersey City was only the second stop on the newly launched tour and their drinks and conversation in the back booth of the hotel bar their first hours alone, one marvels at how quickly Basilone "fell for a dame." There was another dinner at a different "fancy hotel," lots of speeches, plenty of big shots, and much pulling out of wallets and checkbooks for war bonds. There then followed at the big Jersey City theater another showing of Cary Grant's *Mr. Lucky*. Virginia had an informed take on that, you can be sure. "We laughed all the way through, even the sappy love story was okay," said Basilone. "Virginia kept whispering funny comments . . . about Cary not knowing what a woman might want."

Less laughingly, and apparently meaning it, Basilone went on: "Virginia and me were falling hard and fast even though we'd just met. It was easy to be around her when we were alone. She never put on airs. And I didn't treat her like some of the girls who just wanted to have a good time with soldier boys for an evening. She was a real first class lady. She made her own money, a hell of a lot more than I did, and didn't need anybody. She was altogether a new deal. Everything was still brand new between us and we were surrounded day and night by wild guys like Eddie Bracken who was just about the funniest guy I'd ever met. He was like me, couldn't sit still. That took the pressure off us when we were out in public because Eddie was always there making jokes and playing tricks on everybody. It was the perfect set-up. Nobody made a big deal about us. It must have seemed like the natural thing.

"We eventually got around to the talk about what I was planning for the future. I hadn't been with one woman for years, and wasn't sure if I was one-woman material any more. It was always love 'em and leave 'em, have a few laughs and then have to ship out or make it back to base. Now I was in a whole new ballgame with Virginia but I couldn't tell her. It would only have made us both feel bad. After the movie the movie stars walked out on the stage in front of the screen and introduced us vets to the other servicemen and people in the audience. The slogan was 'Back the Attack,' and we pumped a few more bond sales out of them.

Virginia was a tiger and would have taken their gold teeth if she could.

"We left the theatre, off for the evening. Orders were to report to the hotel lobby tomorrow morning. Virginia and I walked through the quiet streets for a while and didn't say too much. We got back to our hotel late and went up to our rooms. It was one of the only nights I didn't wake up around midnight and grab for a weapon. Just having her in the same building was enough for me. I slept."

There are two surprises here. This is the first time since Australia that Basilone mentions nightmares of battle, sudden awakenings and a grab for weapons. And there is an admirable discipline on the part of both Grey and himself, that business of going to their separate rooms. Well, the tour was still young. And so were they. Phyllis Cutter picks up the thread: "In Plainfield [another New Jersey town] we went through much of the same. The people listened intently when Max R. Roener, the master of ceremonies, introduced us, we got a wonderful reception and were deeply impressed when the people stood in silent tribute as seaman 1st class Elmer Cornwell, U.S. Navy told how he lost 50 pounds while adrift in a lifeboat for 36 days with rations for only 15 days. It's amazing [Basilone concluded silently, perhaps recalling his own ordeals] how much the human body can take, although I feel there must be a guardian angel that watches over us at times of great stress. How else can you account for any of us being on this platform, instead of in a lonely grave thousands of miles from home and our loved ones?"

From Newark airport, Navy bombers flew the tour group to New Haven, Connecticut for a parade. There were five thousand marchers, plus jeeps, tanks, and scout cars, two bands—one from the Army Air Corps and the other from the Coast Artillery—and the State Guard. Then came time for a freshening-up at a hotel and a big rally that evening at the Arena, a fanfare of trumpets, a parade of flags of the Allied nations, Governor Baldwin, yet another mayor Murphy, the "Hollywood singing star" Miss Edith Fellows handling the national anthem, more speeches, and an honor guard of air cadets training at Yale University. This may well have been Manila

John's first brush against the Ivy League. "Later we were introduced by the Hollywood stars in our group and each of us had a little piece to say, after which we were given a standing ovation." This
was Basilone's first such speaking date outside of his own state, and
apparently it went very well since he mentions "being sorry to leave
this pleasant city."

The PR people were apparently doing their work. At one stop
they arranged to have a general release carrier pigeons in a park. In
Rochester in upstate New York, a stop Basilone had his own personal reasons to anticipate, there was a rally at Red Wings Stadium,
after which he managed to slip away to visit with the family of his
machine-gun buddy on the 'Canal, Bob Powell, meeting his mom
at 98 Garfield Street: "Bob's sister Peggy answered the door and in
seconds I was meeting Bob's mother and sister Vicky. Vicky was 22
and a looker, in fact she was beautiful. Bob had certainly held out
on me [where was Miss Grey?]. Peggy, just eight, was cute and a
little darling. I had quite a talk with Mrs. Powell, telling her all I
could about Bob. She hung on every word. I know she was proud
and thrilled when I told her if it weren't for guys like Bob covering
up for me on the right and left flanks, I'd never have lived to get
my medal. I told her how Bob and I had become close personal
friends, training together at Parris Island, New River, and Cuba."

In Albany John looked up the mother of Jackie Schoenecker,
another Guadalcanal Marine, assuring her Jackie wasn't holding
back when he told her he hadn't been wounded but was simply
suffering from malaria. "I explained that it was a common ailment
in the tropics and as a matter of fact, I was walking around with it.
I know I eased her fears."

The tour was well organized, Basilone noting that the "publicity and fanfare" whipped up before every stop ensured a big
crowd and local enthusiasm before the traveling road show of
heroes and Hollywood stars even came to town. Some of it was
fun, some moving and emotional, some quite frankly a pain in
the ass. As Basilone put it, "No matter where I went, there was
always some guy who would ask a million questions about the
Japs and outside of the job I was now assigned to. I didn't feel like

talking about them. Too many of my buddies were still dying in the stinking jungles, which when I looked around, seemed around a million miles away. Still, they were there, fighting, praying, and dying." He asked himself, "How much longer could I continue feeling like I did?" and got no answers.

Finally, this leg of the bond tour (there were others to come), the Northeast swing, was over, and it was time to go home to Raritan, the little town where Basilone grew up. "I looked forward to spending a few days with my family." But there was still "Basilone Day" to get through.

His hometown's celebrations began the morning of September 19, 1943, at Somerset Street and Route 31, "welcomed by the honorary chairman and mayor Peter Mencaroni, together with chairman William Slattery of the Township Committee. At the welcoming ceremonies I should have expected what was to come. There had already gathered so early in the morning a large crowd, affectionate, wonderful folks all calling my name and crushing in on our car. As I waved back, I spotted some old friends. With my family and buddy, Private 1st Class Steve Helstowski by my side, we entered St. Ann's Church for a high mass, which I had asked to be said for all my buddies still fighting in the South Pacific. All during mass I prayed for my buddies and for God to give me the strength and wisdom to uphold the high honors that were bestowed on me.

"A long time ago, it seemed ages, I had knelt in this very church and prayed the good Lord to help and guide me. Now, I was back again, feeling very small and humble as I realized that God in His wondrous ways had heard my prayers. Not only did I fulfill my promise to Pop to keep his name high, but that God had seen fit to touch me with His magic, lifting me up for the whole world to see."

This was a Basilone we had not seen before, spiritual, meditative, even pious. How much of this was genuine, how much simply a reaction to all of the adulation and love on every hand, the solemnity of mass at St. Ann's, his recalling the Marines still out there in the Pacific, is impossible to say. Phyllis records what are supposed to be her brother's thoughts on his return home after the cauldron of Guadalcanal and the celebrity of the unexpected medal. "I had become a national hero, kids worshipped me, my buddies would give up their lives for me and actually did. I was featured in magazines and comic books. Newspapers had endless articles about my exploits, and the bright light of publicity shone on me day and night. To cap the whole incredible drama, the President of these great United States of America had seen fit to bestow on me the greatest honor this country could give." Does this really sound like Manila John? To me it smacks of press agentry, prepared sound bites provided the young hero by his handlers and dutifully recorded later by Phyllis Basilone Cutter in her newspaper series about her brother John.

Bruce Doorly has his turn at summarizing the war bond tour to date, echoing much of what Phyllis had written, before getting to his own detailed account of the return to Raritan, and including a fascinating insight not previously recorded: even during that first leg of the speaking tour, Basilone was drinking heavily. "The publicity and fanfare did not let up at any of the bond rallies. While Basilone himself said, 'The constant fuss is starting to get on my nerves.' He was not cut out to be a public speaker. He was a soldier, and was starting to wish that he was back in action. On the tour there were constant questions about the battle with the Japanese, which he answered over and over. The pressure of the attention got so bad that John had started drinking. One veteran [presumably another serviceman on the bond tour] said, 'He knocked off a fifth the way you knock off a beer. Whisky, gin, it made no difference.'"

Basilone's last surviving sibling, Donald, who lives in Florida, told me that when he and John shared a bedroom during his brief Raritan respite from the war bond tour, and later when he was on leave, his brother didn't tell him much. But he remembered one thing clearly: "He always had a bottle of liquor on the dresser." Donald was impressed by that.

Manila John had long enjoyed a drink. Was he simply getting back into a normal peacetime routine of social drinking? Or did he now "need" a drink? Were his tour handlers supplying the stuff to keep him relaxed, keep him performing?

Phyllis says a priest named Graham said the mass at St. Ann's; Doorly says it was Basilone's old pastor and guidance counselor, Father Amadeo Russo, which sounds more likely unless somehow a very young Reverend Dr. Billy Graham had shoehorned himself into the moment. Father Russo, in his sermon, said, "God had spared [John] for some important work," a remark that inspired Basilone later to write his sister, "The importance of bringing me back finally sank in; and I resigned myself to the role that had suddenly been thrust on me."

Here is Doorly on that September 19 in Raritan from local accounts by people like Peter Vitelli (also one of my sources), who was then a six-year-old schoolboy: "At 11:30 there was a lunch in Basilone's honor headed by the reception committee at The Raritan Valley Farms Inn, a popular restaurant . . . on the Somerville Circle where the Super 8 Motel is today. Then, at 1 p.m. the parade started. Total attendance was estimated at 30,000 . . . the groups marching included The American Legion, VFW, state and local police, service men on leave, French Navy Soldiers [their Marines, it can be assumed], Coast Guard, drum & bugle corps, Boy Scouts, Girl Scouts, Red Cross units, Air Raid Wardens, The Italian American Society, Raritan First Aid Squad, soldiers from Camp Kilmer, and various marching bands."

The whole catalog shouts quintessential Americana on parade, the local hero, whether Medal of Honor winner or captain of the high school's winning football eleven, passing the home folks in review. In a nice nostalgic touch, one marcher was John Reilly, who had four decades earlier been awarded the Medal of Honor during the Spanish-American War. "John Basilone rode in an open car with his parents Sal and Dora, who beamed with pride throughout the parade," Doorly reported. "Also in his car was Private Stephen Helstowski of Pittsfield, Mass. [who had] fought with John on Guadalcanal and had been injured in the battle."

There's a photo from that parade showing Basilone sitting happily, high atop the backseat of the convertible behind his parents, with Helstowski in the front passenger seat alongside a capped and uniformed chauffeur, Basilone waving at the crowd

and the sun-drenched crowd gawking and some waving back, little kids and a few uniformed servicemen and women visible, several people walking behind or beside the slowly moving auto, so
slowly that Basilone was able to shake hands with pedestrians
even as the open car rolled along without having to stop, some of
the handshakers aging vets from World War I.

Flags flew, the weather was perfect, and little Peter Vitelli
remembered how orderly the big crowd was as he sat on the curb
in front of St. Ann's Church watching the parade pass by and
eventually halt and morph into a "rally." At some point, the lovely
actress Louise Allbritton was kissing Basilone. There is no mention
of Virginia Grey. The disgraced though still popular former New
York City mayor James J. "Jimmy" Walker somehow showed up,
ubiquitous, beaming and shaking hands, "working the room," so to
speak. This had become commonplace, people wanting to be seen
with the hero, wanting to be associated with him. To a fallen idol
like Walker, this was the sort of event he needed and could use.
The crowd, as anticipated, was so great that "local rich girl made
good" Doris Duke Cromwell had generously invited the committee to move everyone onto her vast estate, where they'd erected a
grandstand, and to continue the festivities, holding the culminating
rally right there, which is just what they did. Father Russo gave an
invocation. A local girl, Catherine Mastice, who would later sing in
the 1949 Radio City Music Hall Christmas show, sang "The Star-
Spangled Banner." Anthony Hudek, then wide-eyed and thirteen
years old, recalls, "It was as if the world came to Raritan."

A five-thousand-dollar war bond was presented to Basilone,
and he responded gracefully, accepting it "for all my buddies
overseas on the front lines—they really appreciate everything
you wonderful people are doing by 'backing the attack' [he had
the advertising agency selling line down pat by now] and buying
these war bonds. Today is like a dream to me. Thank you all
from the bottom of my heart." Former state senator Joseph
Frelinghuysen (from a local family of considerable wealth and
distinction and himself a very appealing figure whose own son was
a POW in enemy hands) spoke, and Basilone responded again,

noting that his medal belonged in part to many others, "the boys who fought by my side."

During the Frelinghuysen remarks, Basilone's small niece, five-year-old Janice, sneaked up onstage to sit with him, drawing a roar in response, and remaining with her heroic uncle throughout. That was the press photo everyone ran the next day, the war hero and the little girl in her party dress on his lap. Fox Movietone News got it all, and the newsreel ran coast to coast the following week, including a recording of Basilone delivering a short speech about the country and its good people and promoting the sale of war bonds. His delivery is a bit stilted, but his voice is deep, almost rich. Catherine Mastice returned to sing a new song entitled "Manila John," composed by the organist of St. Ann's, Joseph Memoli with words by W. A. Jack.

Basilone at times seemed overwhelmed by what organizers called "the biggest day in the history of Raritan." But for some stupid reason, pure military bureaucracy at work, I suppose, Basilone wasn't to be permitted to enjoy the night at home. On orders, and pointlessly, he was hustled back to New York and a Manhattan hotel for the night. Maybe they feared that this close to home and family, he might go AWOL and they'd have difficulty getting their boy back to the tour. By Monday the call of the war plants was heard, and Basilone was back in New Jersey at the Johns Manville factory in Manville, just north of Raritan, meeting war production workers, shaking hands, and talking up war bonds.

The next day Basilone was at Calco Chemical, where he'd worked as a laborer. The Somerset County Bar Association beckoned that same day. One can only imagine what Basilone managed to say to the Bar Association: citing torts and precedents? Then it was off to Pittsburgh for a bond rally at a big steel plant. Within hours he was back in New Jersey, speaking to the Rotary Club at Somerville. It is not clear any of this coming and going so close to Raritan included a trip home to his mother and father's house for a meal or a night with the family. Or what Gene

Lockhart and Eddie Bracken and the actresses thought of small-town and industrial New Jersey as they were trotted around.

Doorly reports that someone, somewhere, finally decided to give the poor guy a break. A thirty-day leave came down from the top. Thirty days of no speeches, no war plants, no bond rallies. And by now Basilone badly needed a rest. He spent the time at home in Raritan, where he played with the local kids and slept late, bunking in with little brother Don, nights where he and his Raritan pals all did a little drinking and admired the local girls. But there was a letdown, a long-delayed reaction. Doorly details it. He quotes Basilone as telling friends in Raritan that as much as he appreciated the admiration and attention, he was a soldier and wanted to get back to the war. This is the first mention of Basilone's yearning for the Pacific.

19

There are men who quite literally love war, the rattle of automatic fire, the crack of a single rifle shot, the song of the bullet's ricochet, the sweet reek of gunsmoke hanging blue in the air, the heightened tension, the living (and too often dying) on the edge, the adrenaline rush, the yelling and shouting, the sound and the fury. Many of such men are Marines, veterans of different wars in different climes and down through the ages. I have myself after a firefight heard Marines coming out of the fight and back inside the wire coarsely enthusing, "Lieutenant, I love this shit." In a book I wrote about motivation, about what draws Marines to the guns rather than, more rationally, away from them, a few Marine critics carped that of all the various reasons Marines fight, I had scanted the sheer love of a fight, the appeal of battle, the call to the guns, the passion warriors bring to battle. Manila John Basilone seems to have been one of those men, one of the war lovers.

By the late summer and early autumn of 1943, Basilone had been for some months distanced from combat, death, and the war, had been home long enough seeing family and old friends, appearing before cheering audiences, consorting with Hollywood movie stars, to understand that the medal had given him some leverage, and that perhaps the time was nearing when he might start using it. He had never been much of a politician, but this could soon be the moment. Perhaps the bond tour had lost its charms, had become boring, the parroted, scripted phrases grown glib, so easily tumbling from the lips. Maybe Virginia Grey's ardor had cooled. The shrewder of the brass may have begun to sense that their pet machine gunner was no longer as docile and instantly obedient, no longer entirely on board. He'd gotten over his stage fright, his anxiety at being the center of attention, the bashful unease of being "gawked at." He'd picked up the sales jargon for the war bond drive—"Back the Attack," that sort of thing—and preached it on demand. Or was that cynical even to suggest?

For the first time, and quite specifically, Basilone bridled at being "Manila John." After all, Manila was no longer the town he once knew, where he found and loved Lolita, where he'd first tasted a small fame as he boxed undefeated, was backed in wagers and cheered on by his fellows, and where General Douglas "Himself" MacArthur, who lorded it over the poor Filipinos, vice regal in style and manner, had still found time to come back to the dressing room to shake his hand after a winning bout over a tough sailor. That Manila no longer existed, wasn't Manila any-more; it had been a "Jap" city for more than eighteen months, "Yokohama South." If there was in Basilone no longer any affinity for the place, why should people still be yammering questions at him as Manila John? Or worse, "Manila John the Jap killer"?

Basilone by now might well have been asking himself, what did civilians, even those who loved or just plain admired him, the home folks, the kids, the reporters, the girls, the fans, with their glib queries about "killing Japs," really know about war, combat, and death? So, to mollify a performer apparently growing antsy and querulous, the brass again offered Basilone a commission as a second lieutenant in the U.S. Marine Corps, the same rank that Mitch Paige, while they were both Down Under, had quickly accepted. And now six months later, the sergeant in Basilone would again turn it down. He was an enlisted man, a noncommissioned officer, and happy to be so. None of this "officer and a gentleman" snobbery for him. The brass then tried another incentive. Would Basilone like to go to Camp Pendleton at the pleasant seaside town of Oceanside in Southern California as a gunnery instructor and run machine-gun training there? He loved machine guns, knew the weapon intimately, was a proven teacher of the weapon's construction, operation, usage, its deadly effect. In a way, this would be a perfect fit, a dream assignment. Thanks, sir, but no thanks.

Then just what did John Basilone want? What would it take to keep him out there visiting war plants, selling bonds, doing interviews, boosting home-front morale? To Basilone, if to few others, the answer was simple: he wanted to return to the Pacific, to go back to the old outfit, to "his boys," to combat and the war. He was starting to mouth off about missing the Pacific, missing being a Marine and being tired of his role as a performing seal.

Every Marine senior NCO or officer who ever served knew guys like Basilone. They could be great Marines, the very men you wanted in the next hole to you in combat, but when it came to the chain of command, the regulations, to getting along, "brown-nosing" a little if he had to, the man could be a pain in the ass. There was the usual old commissioned snobbery at work still in the Corps, the occasional officer's snarl about "shifty-eyed enlisted men" or about "a guy who every morning you ought to punch right in the face because you know damned well before the day is over, that bastard is going to fuck up one way or another." Basilone was hardly that, not a troublemaker or a malingerer, not after three years in the Army with consistently excellent fitness reports, or in combat as a Marine. He was by late 1943 a thorough professional. But he was also a Marine who wanted his way and kept after you until he got it.

Basilone sent in an official request through channels to rejoin the Fleet Marine Force Pacific, the famed FMF PAC for which he had fought as a member of the 7th Marines, 1st Marine Division.

It was just as officially turned down. The Marine Corps didn't see any profit in returning a Medal of Honor man to combat and suffering the angst and second-guessing inevitable in getting a hero killed off.

And, the brass told itself, let's face it, this guy was good at selling war bonds. In a traveling troupe of heroic servicemen and Hollywood stars, Basilone was a movie star himself. The dark good looks, the hint of danger, of a coiled tension, a recklessness that appealed to women sexually and to men who wished they had something of that same aura, these were the qualities that made Basilone so good at what he did on the war bond promotional tour. The best thing about it was that he was a "movie star" who in real life had been as heroic as any Hollywood idol on a make-believe screen.

Basilone was the goods and people got it. They recognized him for the real thing, and when he spoke and cracked that lopsided Italian smile, the crowd understood this wasn't just a practiced performer. This was a genuine American legend come to town or to the gates of the big war plant just outside, to say hello, to shake your hand, to congratulate the shift worker who'd exceeded his or her production goals that month, to the factory manager whose assembly line had earned an "E for Excellence" banner from the War Production Agency, to visit the local grammar school, to kiss the baby and muss the hair of the local kid, and to do it all with an easy grin, a half-bashful hello, a dashing young man in an honorable uniform, and, above all, that pale blue ribbon on his chest or the medal itself suspended from his neck by another matching pale blue ribbon. No wonder the girls and the women loved him, the men admired him, the kids shouted and ran after him. Louis B. Mayer of MGM, President Franklin Roosevelt's close friend and financial backer, couldn't have invented him, no Oscar-winning screenwriter could have written him, the marquee part of Manila John Basilone, a hero of the Pacific. As Basilone's brother George had remarked, "Everybody loves you, John."

Basilone raised money, boosted morale, sold bonds, reaped publicity, did the damned job, a job he was continually told was every bit as vital to the nation's war effort as had been his ferocity in a fight, his mastery of the lethal Browning heavy machine gun, the man's sheer animal endurance, the physical courage, the killer instinct.

Basilone, not educated, naive but hardly stupid, must have been aware this was simply pious, full-blown press pageantry. Peddling war bonds door-to-door was important, of course, the war had to be paid for, but there were plenty of good salesmen in America selling everything else, from Fords to encyclopedias and patent medicines. There were only a relatively few men capable, strong enough, and sufficiently courageous to go into the jungle barefoot and armed in a tropical rainstorm at night and fight hand-to-hand against the flower of Japanese imperial infantry, out to kill you and your buddies, and fully capable, as they'd already shown on island after island, of doing so.

Bruce Doorly gives us this evocative and in ways shrewdly illuminating vignette of the restless hero paradoxically at rest, during that monthlong military furlough back home in Raritan as 1943 neared its end: "After bond tours and visits to war industries, John was granted a thirty-day leave which he was able to spend at home. While most of the attention bothered John, when the attention came from kids, he loved it. John's brother Carlo remembers that kids would gather outside the house at 113 First Avenue, yelling until John came out to talk to them. The kids would swarm over John, which he greatly enjoyed. His old boss from Gaburo's Laundry, Alfred Gaburo, remarked, 'his greatest pride was the kids in the neighborhood. The kids idolized him and he idolized the kids.'"

"During the time that John was home after the big celebration [of September 19] he made special visits that those present will always remember. In between public appearances, John got some relaxation, visiting neighbors, feeling somewhat like a regular guy again.

"One weekday, John took time to pay a special visit to his niece Janice's school. . . . Janice was the niece who climbed on his lap at the rally on Basilone Day and had her picture on the front page of the newspaper. Janice, now 65, when interviewed for this [Doorly's] book, lit up and described how special that day was when her Uncle John, everyone's hero, came to visit 'her' kindergarten class. He talked with kids and shook hands with many teachers. The whole school was excited and she was a very proud five year old. While Janice says she has only vague memories of the parade and rally on Basilone Day, and no specific memories of sitting on John's lap at the rally, she remembers vividly his visit to her school.

"One night on leave, John stopped by the local tavern, Orlando's. The owner, Tony Orlando, was very dedicated to the local servicemen. He posted their pictures on the wall, wrote them letters, sent them packages. To have John Basilone, Raritan's hero, stop in to socialize, was an honor for the Orlando Tavern. All eyes and attention that night were on John. His drinks were, of course, 'on the house.'"

Another favorite local hangout, for Pop Basilone's generation more than the son's, was the Star of Italy Mutual Aid Society building on Anderson Street. This was an outfit that helped recently arrived immigrant Italians to get started in America. Since Basilone was officially still "under orders," even on leave, he was pressed into service, speaking to an audience of a hundred about the appeal, patriotic as well as financial, of war bonds. The club's president, Charles Franchino, recalled young Basilone as "likable, regular" and, according to Doorly, Franchino was surprised to hear Manila John talking during his leave about wanting to get "back into action," and asked why. Basilone, possibly having fun and kidding an older civilian, said, because he liked the feel of firing a machine gun.

It wasn't all small-town, back-home camaraderie, laughter, dinner dates, and drinks on the house. Basilone was no longer on the war bond tour hustling sales, but the publicity mill, like the war itself, ground on.

"Basilone was featured on the radio a few times toward the end of 1943," Doorly recalls. "The NBC show entitled 'Marine Story' had John talk about his experience at Guadalcanal. Legendary Ed Sullivan, who had a variety show on radio, similar to his later

TV show, had John Basilone on the air. Ed and John would come
to know each other as 'friends.' They met at a bond rally at the
Capital Theatre in New York where Sullivan was the master of ceremonies. At this rally, John spoke to the crowd about his Division's
action on Guadalcanal. When he finished he received a standing
ovation that lasted several minutes. Ed Sullivan wrote a few times
about John in his newspaper column for the New York Daily News
[then the biggest circulation newspaper in the country selling
three million copies per day], John wrote that 'Ed went out of the
way to do things for me and he took pleasure in whatever he did. I
shall never forget him and his sincere friendship.' Even years after
John's death, Ed Sullivan continued sending John's family free
tickets to his newly launched and successful TV show. John's sister
Dolores recalled Ed to be very personable and caring."

Phyllis Basilone Cutter recalled her brother's new love affair
with New York, the big city just across the Hudson a few miles (and
a world) east of little hometown Raritan. "New York, supposedly
the city without feeling, took me into her heart. Every door was
open to me. Ed Sullivan of the New York Daily News and Toots
Shor took me in tow. They went out of their way to do things for
me and what I liked about them both was that they took real pleasure in whatever they did. Both are grand fellows and I shall never
forget them and their sincere friendship. It was a privilege and an
honor to know them."

To those who knew Sullivan, then or later, he was a self-
important and rather cynical man mostly involved not with others
but with himself. Basilone's and his family's impressions of Sullivan's
goodness of heart may say more about Basilone and his folks, their
own decency and their essential niceness and authenticity, than
about the worldly Sullivan. Regarding Toots Shor, a large, vulgar man
who ran a "great joint" (his own description), a Marine enlisted
man of Basilone's age and appearance, without the Medal of Honor,
might not have been entirely welcomed by Toots or his doorkeepers.
If you were famous, even marginally, it was, "Come right in, pally.
The drinks are on us." Otherwise it might be, "Beat it, Marine. Try
the joints under the El on Third Avenue."

There is a wonderful small and telling scene in Sydney Pollack's *The Way We Were* burlesquing popular nightspots such as Shor's, the Stork Club, and El Morocco during wartime, where the headwaiter at the velvet rope smilingly welcomes the colonels and the ranking naval officers and then curtly dismisses a GI and his girl, enraging Barbra Streisand's feisty character, the "pinko" scold, who promptly ushers the young couple swiftly past the rope and chews out the flunky, dressing him down as "You fascist rope holder!" That's how it was at Shor's joint back then and would have been for Basilone, had he been just a sergeant on his own, without a medal or an escort of military PR flacks.

By this time, Manila John was a star. With Sullivan and Shor, that was the difference. Basilone's youthful, innocent naiveté was never more evident than in his assessment of these two front-runners, his appreciation of the newspaper columnist and the saloonkeeper, his gratitude and their "sincerity," for the things they did for him. He didn't yet realize, and perhaps never fully would, what *his* heroism and consequent fame did for the sycophantic users around him, the leechlike pilotfish attached to the deadly prowling shark.

As Doorly puts it, "Basilone's life was no longer private. An article appeared in the Sunday Daily News [whose circulation rose to four million on Sundays] including many things about John's life, including that John had a girlfriend. The girl was Helen Helstowski of Pittsfield, Massachusetts . . . sister of John's military buddy Stephen Helstowski." The surprise here is there was no mention anywhere at this time of Hollywood glamour girl and fellow war bond trouper and reputed love Virginia Grey, the well-known if not precisely famous film actress. Where were gossip columnists Hedda Hopper and Louella Parsons at moments like this? Yet here was this publicity about an anonymous Pittsfield girl with a difficult name. John and Helen, with her brother the intermediary, had corresponded, he'd visited her while touring at Albany, not far from Pittsfield, and the two certainly became friends and saw each other several other times. There is no indication it went much beyond that. "While no one said the romance was a wild, passionate affair, John was a celebrity, and the newspapers were going to report and sensationalize the story, writing that, 'He fell in love.'" Maybe the media haven't really changed all that much.

Meanwhile, at the little house in Raritan, fan mail arrived in volume. It was mostly from young women. Some included photos. Some were outright proposals of marriage. According to Doorly, one hopeful girl said, "I think you are wonderful. I always wanted to marry a hero." A writer named James Golden had been trying for some days to get to Basilone and do an interview, to get the hero to talk about himself. When the pestering continued, an irritated Basilone had had enough. "Look, Golden, forget my part. There was not a man on the 'Canal that night who doesn't own a piece of that medal awarded to me."

Basilone had proved himself a natural at war. It was coping with civilians during a peaceful interlude at home that was giving him difficulty.

20

A gala dinner at the Waldorf and there he was on Park Avenue, up on the dais, young, handsome, bemedaled, and dashing, a man's man, somehow larger than life. But some still thought of John Basilone as the aimless, perhaps even shiftless, half-educated, hard-drinking young Italian Catholic Jersey kid with nine siblings but no "family" to speak of. A gambler and a brawler, a misfit who didn't get out of grammar school until he was fifteen, who never attended for a single day the local high school, who caddied for a living at the country club, cadging tips from the rich guys, beating the other caddies at cutthroat poker for their tips, and who was fired from one of the few jobs he ever had, working on a laundry truck. And now here he was, Basilone of the U.S. Marine Corps, sitting up there on the dais in uniform and wearing the famous medal, at the Grand Ballroom of the Waldorf, alongside such industrial giants as Alfred P. Sloan Jr. and others out of the pages of *Forbes* and *Fortune* magazines, a scheduled dinner speaker and an honored guest of the National Association of Manufacturers (NAM).

Those seating arrangements are one of the many paradoxes of this narrative, and was there ever such an absurd dichotomy?

Manila John and the big shots. Seated nearby, the closest thing Basilone ever had to a role model or an icon, a Marine lieutenant general named Alexander A. Vandegrift, honored by President Franklin Roosevelt with the same pale blue ribbon that Basilone wore, a couple of very brave men of disparate backgrounds, the commanding general of the 1st Marine Division (and eventually commandant of the Corps) and the lowly machine-gun sergeant of the same division, but both of them Marines, both of them now, and maybe forever, legends of the Corps. If only Basilone's battalion commander, Chesty Puller, were here, John could brace Chesty with his plaints. Well, then, with no Chesty on board, the "Old Man," Vandegrift, would have to do.

With the timing and instinct that in the Philippines had earned Basilone the reputation and the undefeated record of a feared prizefighter, one who recognized and would exploit an opening when he saw one, and could sense weakness in an opponent, Basilone took immediate advantage of the place and the moment. During a (men's room?) break in the proceedings he pounced on General Vandegrift, who had commanded him on the 'Canal and had that day in Australia pinned the medal on him. Vandegrift wore the same medal and additionally had a flag officer's clout, but on this night Basilone had his ear, and he didn't hesitate. The war in the Pacific raged, Basilone was a Marine who'd been there at the start, and now he wanted in at the finish. How could he get back into the fight when the big shots insisted on parading him around the country like a show pony, a traveling salesman working conventions and formal affairs like this one, when all he really wanted to do was to rejoin the war, again lead troops in the field? Could Vandegrift help? The general promised to look into it.

Maybe he did, but all John subsequently learned was that instead of being sent to join one of the Marine divisions now fighting the Japanese in the Pacific (there would eventually be six before the war ended), he found himself shunted off into the ultimate rear echelons of rear echelons, in a Navy yard a hundred miles from the nearest sea.

On August 31, 1943, while the American carriers *Essex*, *Yorktown*, and *Independence* attacked Marcus Island in the central Pacific, and in Europe the Russians advanced on Smolensk, John Basilone was reporting at and would be pulling guard duty in the Guard Company, Marine Barracks, Washington Navy Yard, with frequent timeouts to address a group or hawk another war bond.

Was this bureaucratic coincidence or was the Corps punishing the audacious SOB for having gone outside the chain of command to pester Vandegrift at the Waldorf? Whatever the situation, Basilone was increasingly pissed off.

"I felt I was still on display," he complained to his family. At another time he compared himself to "a museum piece." By now, the movie stars, including the Virginia Grey he had "fallen for," had all gone back to Hollywood. They had been freed to return to their real jobs as movie heroes, while the one actual hero among them was prohibited from getting back to *his* profession, that of killing Japanese infantry. Surely Basilone grasped the irony.

Try to analyze Basilone's state of mind as he followed in the newspapers what was happening in the Pacific while he manned a duty desk in Washington. The Marines were fighting on Bougainville in the Solomons, his old Aussie "mates" were slogging ahead in New Guinea, on Christmas Eve American naval forces attacked Buin and Buka islands to draw attention from an imminent landing by other Marines on New Britain, and on December 26 those landings took place, as General Rupertus's 1st Marine Division, Basilone's old outfit from the 'Canal, splashed ashore and headed inland as 1943 ended, to capture the Japanese airfield at Cape Gloucester. Basilone, instead of being there, was reading about the Pacific in the *Washington Post* and the *Washington Times-Herald*.

It wasn't as if Basilone had some schoolboy's romantic idea of what combat was all about. He was a realist and had known war. Maybe he felt he was letting his fellow Marines down.

Or maybe it was the country itself and its people who were driving him back to the war—his handlers, the shadows, the PR people and the ad men, the military brass, the war bond lobby, the crowds cheering him, the kids shouting his name, the newspaper reporters and radio broadcasters dogging his steps, the celebrity hunters like Ed Sullivan and Toots Shor, the legendary journalists like Lowell Thomas, the big businessmen of the NAM, like Sloan of GM who put him to use, the clergymen who preached his virtues, the heiress Doris Duke who turned over her acres to a grandstand where he would be saluted, the lovesick but ignorant girls proposing marriage, the authors who wanted to do books about him.

Then in December with the holidays coming, an impatient Platoon Sergeant John Basilone did what Marines in trouble are trained to do. He went to "the man." His commanding officer, knowing Basilone to be something of a ballbreaker, but one with an impeccable combat record and the famous pale blue ribbon, asked irritably what it was this time, what was it the sergeant wanted?

Basilone answered in five words: "Sir, I want the fleet."

Do not be confused by the phrase. Basilone wasn't asking for a shipboard assignment but a transfer to the Fleet Marine Force, to one of the Marine divisions now fighting the Japanese somewhere out there in the vast Pacific theater. And within days (it was just before Christmas), and possibly and belatedly due to General Vandegrift's intervention, Basilone at last got his wish.

Orders were cut dated December 29, sending him off to Camp Pendleton, California, to join the then newly forming 5th Marine Division, to report on January 17, 1944, to the Headquarters and Service Company of the 27th Marines, an infantry regiment. Nine days later, on January 26, he was sent up to HQ Company of the 1st Battalion of the 27th Regiment, one of the three rifle battalions that made up the fighting heart of a Marine regiment, just what he wanted and had been asking for. In November 1942, following his epic fight on the 'Canal, Basilone had been promoted to platoon sergeant, line, and now on March 8, 1944, he would be given his final promotion in the Marine Corps, to (temporary) gunnery sergeant, one of the most highly respected and important ranks a noncommissioned officer could be given, a rating that carried with it the informal and yet revered abbreviated title of "gunny." So that, as a Marine, "Gunny" John Basilone would some ten months later make a final landing on a hostile beach.

21

The Marines gave John Basilone a few days' leave over the holidays to tidy up his affairs at home, see the family, jaw with Pop and his siblings, reassure his mom, have a glass at Orlando's Tavern, say so long to his pals, attend mass in Father Russo's old church, and sing "Auld Lang Syne" on New Year's Eve. Then it was off to the West Coast and a line outfit at Camp Pendleton, a man back where he belonged and very much at ease with the place, the people, the job, and himself, once again a real Marine.

Camp Pendleton, where I've served (most Marines have), is a big, stark, parched, and rather primitive ranchlike spread of hilly brown terrain given to brush fires in the Santa Ana wind season and floods in the rainy time, covered with wartime acres of dun tentage and flat fields dotted with metal Quonset huts and the newer large, spare two-story wood-framed barracks and similar-looking mess halls and outbuildings, some of them still smelling of newly sawn wood. The landscape was populated, except for the Marines, largely by rattlesnakes, coyotes, jackrabbits, and plenty of tarantulas, the husky, hairy spiders mainly visible by night when the headlights of speeding autos or military vehicles

pick them up, slow-moving and shimmering, on the brownish hill-
sides. Pendleton is situated on the Pacific coast a half hour north
of San Diego, an hour south of Laguna Beach and its beachfront
hotels and bars, surfers and pretty California girls, and maybe
another hour south of LA and Hollywood.

I suppose there is some way to calculate how many Marines
have passed through the main gate of Camp Pendleton, California,
since John Basilone arrived there in January 1944, men either
reporting in for training or prior to shipping out later for the Asian
or the Middle Eastern wars. Named for famed Marine general
"Uncle Joe" Pendleton, it is a huge base fronting on its west side
the Pacific coastline and the garrison town of Oceanside, whose
main drags are a kaleidoscope of bars and small restaurants, uniform tailoring and pressing shops, a couple of small churches, filling stations, pawn shops, fast-food joints, barbershops and beauty
salons, and tattoo parlors, with plenty of cute young California
blondes and the off-duty, on-the-prowl Marines who hunt them.

This chunk of Southern California is an arid stretch of hills,
cut by arroyos that flood swiftly after sudden downpours, the terrain reaching mile after rolling mile to the east where further
miles away you can see the Southern California coastal range,
mountains that for half the year are topped by snow. Marines
began going to war from Pendleton in the 1940s when the
enemy was the Japanese five thousand miles away, on all those
lethal islands. In the summer of 1950 Pendleton started sending
another generation of Marines seven thousand miles to Korea, to
the Pusan Perimeter, the landing at Inchon, the desperate fight
at the Chosin Reservoir in North Korea, and to the bloody
Outpost War in which my class of young Marines fought until the
truce of 1953. Then came Vietnam and the awful decade in which
58,000 American soldiers and Marines died, most if not all of the
Marines direct from Camp Pendleton. In more recent years,
the maws of Iraq I, Afghanistan, and Iraq II, were once again
being fed through the main gate at Camp Joseph H. Pendleton.

Sensibly, they gave Basilone a platoon sergeant's job with
a machine gun platoon. The men of the platoon, most of them

young, including a kid named Charles W. "Chuck" Tatum, who would write a good book about that time at Pendleton and the battle for Iwo Jima, all recognized who Basilone was. You could hardly have been a Marine in 1943 or 1944 and not known of Manila John. The legend was now a member of the new 5th Marine Division, but his brother George was also on the base, training with the slightly older 4th Division, which would be heading out to the Pacific and the war before the 5th Division got itself organized. At the moment the 5th was nothing more than a skeleton formation peopled by newly graduated Marine boots and a cadre of seasoned noncoms and a few young officers. Basilone was by far the most famous 5th Division Marine already here.

In the months he'd been away the war itself and even the helmets and the weapons had changed. The new Garand M1 semiautomatic rifles were slowly replacing the old bolt-action Springfields that went into service in 1903, and, more to the point with a machine gunner, there was the relatively new air-cooled version of the .30-caliber Browning machine gun, much lighter. No more pissing into the water jacket with these babies.

But as an Old Breed Marine, an old-fashioned sort of fellow, Platoon Sergeant Basilone took a traditional tack in breaking in the raw Marines of this brand-new platoon in a brand-new division. He requisitioned cleaning gear, buckets, swabs, and pine oil floor cleaner and put his handful of boots to work sweeping and swabbing the wood-frame barracks. It took two days to get the place up to the sergeant's gleaming, polished standards, but that's what boots were for, menial duties, physical labor, snappily delivered orders to keep them busy and out of trouble. And now the new men began to trickle in to fill out the new division's ranks, some of them from a recently disbanded Marine parachute outfit, paramarines, a cocky bunch who thought of themselves as the "elite." Manila John wasn't impressed by what he thought of as "candy-assed" parachute training and wasn't buying much of that crap—including their penchant for tucking their trousers into their boots instead of wearing them loose outside as proper Marines did. Even the paratroopers knew about Basilone, and that in itself defused potential problems. As did the arrival of a couple of salty noncoms Basilone had known before, men who knew their stuff and didn't take any shit either from boots or from boot-wearing paramarines. We are forever being told that "sergeants run the Marine Corps," and as a brand-new and still amorphous division like the 5th was forming up and starting to organize itself, the adage was never more valid.

Basilone and his NCOs soon had his platoon out on the ground working with the two machine guns. Nobody knew the heavy better than Sergeant Basilone, but he was no slouch on the LMG (light machine gun) either. He worked them hard, snapping in (drills without live ammo), prepping them for the real thing on the firing range. Jerry Cutter and Jim Proser, in their book, possibly assisted by brother George Basilone, flesh out the Pendleton episode before, in John's voice, he sailed again for "the fleet": "A young sergeant, Biz Bisonette, checked in at the same time as the paratroopers and assisted with training of the company. [This is a mistake—Basilone had a platoon, not a company.] He was a tough cookie and an expert in hand-to-hand combat. When it came to jungle fighting we learned our lessons on the 'Canal. Any front-line fighter would need hand-to-hand skills as much as any weapon in the arsenal. The first order of business was getting the boys on the firing range with the .30-caliber machine guns, the old water-cooled Brownies and the lighter, air-cooled version. I drilled the boys on the mechanics and took them through the book, my book, on machine gunning . . . the care and maintenance, and of course, blindfold set-up, repair and tear-down, were all chapters in my book that my new boys would learn better than anything they ever studied in their lives. These new boots would also know how to operate all the weapons on the battlefield, ours and the enemy's, in case they had to use them.

"We practiced setting up various pieces of equipment until everyone could recognize any piece of a weapon by its feel and set it up in the dark. A vet sergeant named Ray Windle came on board in the next week or so. He'd seen plenty of action and knew the score on a jungle battlefield. He was a tough talker like Chesty, and a hot head, so I knew he'd be an easy mark in a card game and this gave me hope for off-duty entertainment. I couldn't fraternize with the boys to the point of gambling with them, so I was left with the non-coms. This cut my chances for extra income in half. But I was glad to have Windle with us. He was the kind of battle commander we needed around these boys. They looked so damn young, some of them. They looked like the sons or the kid brothers of the boys in the 1/7 [John's Guadalcanal battalion]. Malaria and combat hadn't touched these boys yet. Entire battalions started arriving. Many were boys who had trained to be paratroopers, like the earlier group. Once Topside caught on that you can't parachute into a jungle, where most of our work was going to be, it became our job to retrain them in amphibious assault tactics and jungle warfare. Basilone was back in business.

The only drawback, according to Cutter and Proser, was "dames." As Basilone said so himself, "Even on base I couldn't get away from the women and the truth was, I didn't want to." There were plenty of Camp Pendleton women, healthy, fit young female Marines working the mess halls, and Basilone had begun looking them over. Despite their shapeless fatigues you couldn't miss the curves.

You have to wonder why, only a two-hour drive from Los Angeles, it hadn't even occurred to Basilone to call Virginia Grey, hop a Greyhound bus north to drop by her place, send her a postcard to say hi. After all, on the bond tour, all those overnight hotel stops and their having fallen for each other, it would have been the natural thing to do. Recall Basilone's determination that there would be no more "love 'em and leave 'em" for Manila John. Not the way he felt about his movie star, Virginia, the lovely, classy, coolly irreverent actress who liked to knock back a drink with him and who made him laugh, the young woman who had nothing of Raritan about her, still less of prewar Manila.

But on her side, Miss Grey must have heard through Hollywood's gossipy bush telegraph that her good friend John Basilone had been transferred to the West Coast a few hours away. Yet she made no move that we know of, even though it would have been the simplest thing to have the studio set up a PR mission to Camp Pendleton starring Miss Grey with a couple of other pretty

actresses along for cover, a singer, and a comedian or two, to enter-
tain the troops. The studios loved to do that stuff. It was good PR,
good community relations, it was free publicity for the next movie
release, the politicians liked it; in the White House Louis Mayer's
friend FDR would show his gratitude to the industry. But Virginia
never came to Pendleton. Basilone never called her. Maybe, on
both sides, their storied love affair had been nothing more than a
flirt, or at a more basic level, a one-night stand.

Or Virginia Grey may have been off on location, making a
movie somewhere, fantasy material; the reality was these mess
hall girls on the same base. And Basilone was feeling horny and
checking out the women Marines, still in that chauvinist time vul-
garly referred to as BAMs, "broad-assed Marines," though not
usually in their earshot. Think of it, all those healthy young men
and strapping, fit young women in their late teens or early twenties, eyeing each other, young hormones raging, while wartime
husbands and wives, fiancées and girlfriends were far away. All
this against the coiled tension of a nation at war and with new battles waiting. Manila John unblushingly admits to his own sexual
frame of mind in early 1944, describing his preoccupation at the
time as that of "a pig in a pastry shop when it came to females."
However many of the mess hall girls he went through—none of
them immune to the fact he was not only handsome and a platoon (soon to be gunnery) sergeant but perhaps the most famous
and openly admired noncom on the sprawling base—there must
have been a few. "There was plenty of whispering about me being
a war hero," he admitted.

Then, and we can be sure about this, along came a BAM who
was different, who cast a spell, who wasn't just another attractive
pastry in the shop. She was sergeant Lena Riggi, a reservist with
one less stripe than John, but with other attributes. And Basilone
was hooked. Here is his account of the meeting: "I saw her as I
came down the serving line. She was dark—Italian or Spanish
kind of dark. Black hair, dark eyes, and she walked around like
she owned the place. Damn, I had to get to know that one. At
first it was just a look between us. There was nothing on it. No

wink or smile like we knew something special between us. It was just her looking at me from a distance taking stock of me and me looking back at her. I nodded and she might have nodded, or not, but she wasn't falling all over herself, to get to know me. I liked this girl. She was tough. And she was a sergeant, the rules against fraternizing [with enlisted female personnel] didn't apply."

Maybe this was the girl he'd been waiting for since Manila and his cockeyed plans to take the bar girl Lolita home to mom, or, alternatively, to stay there in the Philippines with Lolita to start up a good bar or another bicycle shop (and, as things would have turned out, to end up in a Japanese POW camp).

Lena Riggi was a beauty, dark-haired, dark-eyed, like the girls and young women he most admired growing up in New Jersey. She was Italian, probably Catholic (yes, it happened that she was), the daughter of working people like his own, in her case onion farmers back in Oregon. That little nod and look John mentioned was sufficient to get the Pendleton mess hall rumor mill working. "Sergeant Lena Riggi 'heard all from her lady friends about me. They went on and on about what a hero I was, how brave I was and that I knew all the movie stars.' Sgt. Riggi waited for the gossips to tire themselves out, looked at them and said, 'So what?' She was the girl for me. When she saw me again she pretended like no one told her a thing about me and that was just the way I liked it."

Given the exigencies of war and the accelerated training schedule of a brand-new division being formed, the romance wasn't going to be easy. The young lovers had conflicting schedules, there was little privacy, their barracks were several miles apart with very little available transport within the base to shuttle them back and forth. By day he was with his machine gunners, drilling them on both guns, the heavy Brownie of his heart and the more mobile air-cooled light. The pace picked up, the days of battle were coming, and they piled it on the new men and on the 5th Division generally: gunnery, night problems, obstacle courses, leaps into pools to simulate abandon-ship drill. They did underwater rescue and open-ocean distance swims.

Basilone, of course, concentrated on the guns, but as a veteran noncommissioned officer who had plenty of combat time and knew that more was coming, he kept up on the other skills, the intensified training the division was working on. "It was clear to everybody that because of the build-up, that we were headed toward a hell of a fight somewhere. We practiced beach landings and assaulted fortified positions. My machine gunners needed steady hands and cool heads for the work we had assigned to us. Our most important assault exercise was providing covering fire for a demolition man in an attack on a fortified position. We drilled by laying a line of covering fire about a foot over a man's shoulder as he ran toward an objective. One slip or a half second of distraction meant we would shoot our own man. Under bombardment on a beach it would be ten times worse and fatal for both the gunners or the demo man if it failed." On Iwo Jima, these drills would pay off for Basilone's gunners.

Every Marine infantryman understands, and certainly a hardened close-range combat veteran like Basilone knew, the very risky aspect of covering fire, especially overhead fire, where short rounds meant you were hitting your own men in the back. At the same time, Marines assaulting a dug-in enemy loved accurate overhead fire that would kill or distract the men bringing entrenched fire to bear on them, the vulnerable assaulting infantry. The assaulting Marines were willing to take the risk to reap the potential reward of keeping the other guy's head down. These were among the fundamental truths by which the infantry lives—or dies.

Off duty, the next time John and Lena met, he asked for her phone number and got it. They had a movie date. This was hardly the only event on the Pendleton social calendar. The 5th Division would now formally be recognized as an entity, be awarded its regimental colors: the band would play, the generals gather, the regiments march. A few Hollywood people came down—Edmond O'Brien and Ann Blyth among them, but no Virginia Grey. Basilone feared for a time he might be asked to speak, but the idea of an audience of 25,000 Marines chilled him, and he was relieved the issue did not come up. After the festivities, a remainder of the day's liberty would be authorized. Finally, an afternoon free for Sergeants Riggi and Basilone. And it was obvious John's mind was on the young woman and not on the parade, the visiting Hollywood firemen, the brass, the regimental colors, or his newly minted division, but on Lena and the way her body moved. "She walked easy, like a girl walks when she's on her way somewhere important. She didn't have the kind of sway girls can turn on when they want to impress a guy. She walked right up and stood square on her feet with a beautiful big smile. Damn, she had a big beautiful smile with a mouthful of teeth you could see from a mile away."

Evidently, John had seen plenty of women walking before, either with a sway or with a squared decisiveness as they approached him. And he knew the difference. Now, on this sunny liberty afternoon following the ritual formalities of the 5th Division's official entry into the Corps, all over the huge base, wherever there was an empty flat space, ballgames broke out, basketball but mostly baseball with one outfit pitted against another, intramural affairs, but well backed by cash-money wagering, the kind of thing on which Basilone had long thrived, betting on himself mostly. But on this particular Southern California afternoon Manila John had another sort of sporting life in mind.

Here is how in his words this rather sweet and very simple homespun mating dance began between a Marine and his girl, between a hero of the Pacific and the young woman who would become his wife. And just how, supposedly in his own words, it came down over the years through family to his nephew Jerry: "We probably walked several miles going from one ballgame to the next, talking all the way. She came from a big Italian family, onion farmers up near Portland, Oregon. That accounted for the stance she had that I recognized right away. She grew up working hard like the farm kids I grew up with. It generally made for a strong back and square shoulders, even on women. She didn't ask me a thing about the Medal. She didn't even seem much interested in war stories. That was good because I wasn't the guy to tell any. We just walked and talked like any other two people getting to know each other. Both being Italian and Catholic, there was a lot we already knew and didn't have to say. Mostly we talked about our families. She didn't mind walking which was always a good sign because I always had to walk to think clearly."

Basilone and Virginia Grey had also walked for hours the night they met, first for drinks and then back to the hotel. Walking with a girl apparently brought out the talk in the usually reticent Basilone, though this particular stroll on a military base doesn't sound like much of a romantic lovers' lane. "We walked past rows of tanks, trucks, and all types of artillery. She joined the Corps because she wanted to be with the top outfit in the war effort." It may be difficult to accept in a more skeptical age, but during World War II people in the United States actually did talk in patriotic phrases like that. Basilone continues, "It wasn't hard to figure out that with all this hardware around us, and only a few hours left of liberty, that we didn't have all the time in the world to get to know each other. The talk always circled back to family and how much we missed them."

That was February 1944. Basilone was twenty-seven years old and had a year to live.

22

For several months the young lovers saw each other once or twice a week, despite the distance between their barracks. The typical date was a movie on base and a couple of sodas at the PX since John, as he put it, had "stopped boozing," except on a few occasions when he went out with the boys to the Oceanside bars where they drank 3.2 beer, "getting dizzier" and spending more time "pissing" the weak brew than drinking it.

On March 1, 1944, Basilone had earned that other stripe, being promoted (on a temporary basis, which was the norm at the time) to gunnery sergeant. A few more bucks every payday, increased respect, additional responsibility. The promotion surely was welcomed and enthusiastically accepted, unlike those second lieutenant's commissions he'd flatly turned down.

Out in the Pacific as March became spring, fighting came to a bloody end on Bougainville, where 8,000 Japanese died or were wounded in the last-ditch fighting at a cost of only 300 American casualties, and an air and naval war raged in the Carolines with U.S. forces having the upper hand, while the Australians pushed ahead on New Guinea. Everywhere we seemed to be winning and the once "invincible" Japanese enemy losing. The great Japanese base of Truk was hammered. In a single naval and air attack the ever larger and more powerful American Navy could now typically deploy a dozen carriers. Basilone and his pals could recall bitterly when the United States was so short of operational carriers that Admiral Jack Fletcher asked permission to pull back from the Solomons entirely while we still had one or two carriers left, and in so doing left the fighting Marines ashore bereft of air support except for the handful of shore-based "Cactus Air Force" planes at small, battered Henderson Field. To a veteran of those bleak and bloody months on Guadalcanal, Marines, sailors, and GIs, it seemed another war entirely.

Then at Pendleton word went out. Another of the two big new Marine divisions, the 4th, George Basilone's division, was getting its orders and would be headed west to the fleet, to the war, to the Japanese-held islands. And in early June on the other side of the world, a huge amphibious force of Americans, Brits, Canadians, and French landed on the beaches of Normandy. It was D-Day; Europe had been invaded, Hitler would be dead within eleven months, and Germany would surrender soon after. But here in the Pacific, the Japanese would still be fighting, and few of them ever surrendered.

Once the 4th Division had shipped out for the Pacific, Basilone and his mates in the 5th knew their turn was coming. The tempo and difficulty of the training became more intense; the field exercises stepped up even further. And this just as the poor guy had fallen in love and for the first time in his often chaotic life was seriously thinking about marriage and wondering just what it took to have a lifelong and loving relationship like the one he knew at close range between his own mother and father. Was such an enviable life partnership possible for Manila John and his new love, Lena Riggi?

There were no uncertainties about the growing intensity of his daily military training grind, the pounding the Marine infantry was taking in the hardening process. No one knew precisely when or on which new hostile island it might be, but the 5th Division

Marines sensed another landing was coming, and their officers wanted them ready. The Marines themselves wanted to be ready. Basilone summed it up for his machine gunners, who on average had to carry considerably more weight than a mere rifleman, not only the heavier weight of the guns but the ammo boxes, the tripods, the aiming devices, all hard steel, as the men themselves were now hardening into. "We worked a lot on physical training, getting our lungs and legs to the point where we could hump steel and supplies uphill or through deep sand all day." It sounds reminiscent of Basilone's own training runs off Manila Bay in preparation for prizefights against the likes of Sailor Burt.

Basilone drove his men as he had driven himself, knowing how even more demanding combat could be. None of this facilitated a love affair with the girl he wanted to marry. "It was hard to have energy left over to see Lena even though I was thinking of her all the time now. She was thinking of me too and wasn't at all shy about telling me how she felt." By the start of May, John knew that his time with Lena, their time together here at Pendleton, was running out. He was trying for once to think ahead. There was much to talk about, to do, if only there wasn't the pressure of time, the need to rush. "I wanted to know how it was to love somebody the way Pop loved Mama. At least I wanted a few days, or weeks if I could get it, to know what it was like to be married. I wanted to be able to say 'I love you' a few times and mean it. Maybe it was something we wouldn't have done if we weren't in a rush, but Lena agreed to marry me. We set the date for July 10th, 1944."

There were three problems: the Marine Corps, money, and the Catholic Church. There was also John's brother George, now in harm's way. On June 15, the 2nd and 4th Marine divisions had landed on the big enemy-held island of Saipan, and hard fighting raged with heavy casualties on each side. Was George okay? No one could yet say.

Closer to home, Lena was working out things to be done, and laying plans for something she'd always hoped for: a big, white wedding. The duty chaplain, the Catholic padre of course, declared in ex cathedra tones that he needed two weeks of instruction for the bride. As a Catholic myself, I'm not sure why the priest didn't also need two weeks with John. When Lena explained to the chaplain (all Marine chaplains are naval officers, not Marines) that as a serving sergeant in time of war, she couldn't just take off for two weeks to go to wedding school, the good father was tolerant but firm. She would just have to find the time. Rules were rules, and as not only her priest but as her superior officer, he intended to follow them, and she had better as well. Fed up already, an irritated Lena Riggi demanded of the stuffy priest, "What are you going to tell me? You've never been married." And that was that.

John liked this girl better all the time. Like him, she was a bit of the maverick. Together, they went to St. Mary's Church in downtown Oceanside and found themselves a more pragmatic Catholic father, Reverend Paul Bradley, to whom they explained their dilemma, and in the end he agreed to marry the young couple with or without the fortnight's instruction, thereby rendering unto Caesar (the Marine Corps and its chaplains) the things that were Caesar's but rendering to God the things that were God's, a couple of Catholic kids in love and about to be separated by the damned war.

The ceremony was set for three p.m. on July 10 at St. Mary's. Lena was a half hour late, the single-vehicle Oceanside taxicab company having forgotten her reservation. Attending, and patiently awaiting the bride, were John's commanding officer Colonel Justin Duryea, the executive officer, Lena's sergeant, and the women in her outfit. Some local people dropped by to wish the couple well, and a few reporters from Los Angeles showed up. Standing in for her dad, Sergeant Frank Budemy walked Lena down the aisle and gave the bride away.

Father Bradley recited the vows, the couple looked into each other's eyes, John kissed the bride, and yet another wartime marriage had been solemnized in a small-town church just outside the main gate of a military post somewhere in America.

The only difference was that here were two Marine sergeants being wed and one of them was one of the more recognizable people in the country. The small reception was held down the street at the Carlsbad Hotel, a convenient and useful favorite of Hollywood studios making war movies and calling on the Marine Corps for cooperation and the use of facilities and open spaces on the nearby base's tens of thousands of acres. The studios and the Washington big shots knew the value of such films to morale and the war effort, and unless a breach of security were involved, the Marine Corps and the other branches tried to be cooperative, even to the extent of having troops appear as extras. Jerry Cutter and Jim Proser describe in Basilone's voice the place and the moment: "The reception wasn't fancy, with meat and everything else being rationed, but even so we managed to have a pretty decent dinner with some of the people from our units. Most of them didn't stay, making up excuses about a night maneuver or something they had to get back to in camp. None of us had much money. Everybody knew I was pretty well tapped after paying for the ceremony and I'd have to pay for them if they stayed to eat. A few of Lena's girlfriends stayed and a few fellas from my unit got a drink at the bar and sat with us, saying they weren't hungry." Soldiers that age are always hungry, and it's obvious that such men, who liked John and empathized with his financial straits, were giving the groom a gracious out.

"After dinner," Basilone went on, "we spent our honeymoon night in a room upstairs. We were happy together. Even though it was a rush, I know I did the right thing. I think she felt that way, too.

"We were on the train early next day to see Lena's people in Portland. The train was hot, crowded and dirty. We managed to get a seat while most of the Marines and sailors on board had to stand. We traveled until late the following morning, over 24 hours, with no place to sleep except our seats. I thought a lot about the fancy private cars and having our own plane on the bond tour. I wished I could give Lena some of that kind of treatment. She wanted the fancy stuff that women want for their weddings and it was a shame she didn't get most of it. But she didn't complain, I had to give her that. She didn't make a peep and I started to feel lucky I married her. That was our honeymoon, a stopover in Los Angeles on the way and a few days in her parents' home in Portland."

Back in Oceanside, there were no apartments they could afford, their joint income at that time being about seventy bucks a month. "Lena got pissed off after a few days and wanted to use my name and status to pry open a place to live. I was having none of that. I wasn't going to trade on the Medal for anything. It wasn't completely mine anyway. Nine boys also owned it with me. I thought this might be a hard idea for her to understand and I expected we would have our first big fight, but she surprised me again. I said what I had to say about it and we never talked about it again. She was a Marine and she understood what I was saying. It was then that I knew I had married the right one for me. We continued to live in camp in our separate barracks." So much for romance in the middle of World War II.

When the two wangled a seventy-two-hour pass they took a train north to L.A. with less than a hundred dollars between them, zeroing in on Beverly Hills and places that let servicepeople in without a cover charge. When they fell in line outside a joint owned (or fronted) by a former boxer, a very good light heavy-weight turned movie comic named "Slapsie Maxie" Rosenbloom, word quickly got out that the young Marine waiting to get into the place was John Basilone, and a flunky murmuring the words "Medal of Honor" began hustling Lena and John toward the head of the line. But John "wasn't having any of that," and he and his bride abandoned the idea of an evening at Slapsie's and went down the street to a different boîte, named for another come-dian, Joe E. Lewis, considered more of a "class place," where for some reason the young couple was welcomed without incident. Once inside, however, the two Marines found themselves expe-riencing the same sort of fuss. Basilone sets the scene: "Joe E. Lewis . . . was there. His routine was all about boozing and losing money on the horses. He had almost everybody in the place almost dying with laughter. A few people who said they were somebody in the movies came over to our table and said hello. They left business cards and told me to give them a call. They wanted to introduce me around town to movie people. Joe introduced me from the stage and I had to stand up and take a bow while everybody clapped. Joe was a real patriot. He was close to fifty [to a Marine in his twenties, apparently quite an antique] but he did shows for a lot of the fighting boys who were stranded on islands out on the Pacific."

It's possible that John might have been thinking of himself on Samoa and the 'Canal or of his brother George that day on Saipan. Or of his own new 5th Division, which would soon be headed west to the islands of the Pacific. Of Lewis, he said, "The brass didn't want him to go [to the war zone] but he needled them until he got himself flown out on a cargo transport. All he brought along, a change of clothes and a few cases of good Scotch. He made a lot of friends and brought a little bit of home out to us. He was a real good guy so I stood up for Joe and fried under the spotlight for awhile. He was a good comic for Marines since his two favorite subjects—drinking and gambling—were pretty much what we liked to do too. Lena didn't mind all the attention, it was all new to her, so I stood up there and let her enjoy it. It was our best night together. We ended up walking back to our hotel as the sky turned from black to deep blue and the stars faded out. We were getting used to each other. That 72 hours was our best time together. Our last day was just rest. We didn't get out of bed until dinnertime."

Two weeks after this Los Angeles idyll, Basilone's new 5th Division was told it would be shipping out, destination unknown. These were, of course, the days of patriotic, war-winning slogans: "A slip of the lip can sink a ship." So people, including the troops, were supposed to keep their mouths shut about troop deployments and weren't told much in the first place. One of Lena's pals, her maid of honor, in fact, a Marine named Ruby Matalon, gave the couple her Oceanside apartment for their last California night together. But it wasn't to be, not with the schedule the Marines were on. Basilone's unit was to leave its area on the base at four a.m., and there was no transport that could get John back there by then from Oceanside. So the couple couldn't spend their last night in a pleasant if borrowed apartment, and had to say their goodbyes in the place where they had first locked eyes and met, a Camp Pendleton mess hall. "We talked of our life after the war—what we would name the first boy and the first girl," Basilone said. "She held up pretty well while we talked. She didn't cry, and pretended she was okay, but she was no poker player. But I was. I told her, 'I'm coming back,' and she believed me."

At dawn the 5th Marine Division was on the move, shipping out and "in the field," as the orders read, on August 12, 1944, Basilone aboard a tub called the USS *Baxter*, hot, filthy, and crowded, with many of the new men who'd never been at sea before puking, and the chow some of the worst swill Basilone had yet experienced in the Corps. On the day the *Baxter* sailed, in France the U.S. Army crossed the Loire, and on the Eastern Front Soviet troops broke the German lines and advanced fifteen miles in a day. It was becoming clear who was winning the war.

The 5th Division Marines still didn't know where they were ultimately headed, where they would next fight, but it was surely going to be the Pacific, and the islands. The first stop would be decidedly not a hostile beach, but the romantic, lovely Hawaiian Islands, where they would arrive at Hilo harbor on August 18. Neither the voyage from San Diego nor the new base, Camp Tarawa, were the stuff of honeymoons, especially one being taken by the groom without a bride. John still had no word of brother George on Saipan.

Camp Tarawa, named for a bloody and thoroughly screwed-up epic Marine assault that nearly ruined the 2nd Marine Division, had been pitched in the midst of what they called the Great Hawaiian Desert, a tent city in a dusty bowl over which loomed the twin volcanoes of Mauna Loa and Mauna Lea. The nearest swimming beach was a day's hike distant and the division wasn't giving many days off. The intensified training schedule stimulated competition between individual Marines and units, and to boost morale and nurture unit identity, Basilone and his machine gunners shaved their heads.

And then almost miraculously out of the vast Pacific, brother George appeared, unhurt and on the neighboring island of Maui.

John wangled a pass and the brothers reunited. George had for some minor infraction been in the brig on bread and water but bragged that the Corps lost money on the deal, because he ate so many loaves of bread. Word came from Peleliu that Chesty Puller's battalion had taken a terrible beating with very high casualties. For the time being, it was finished as an effective Marine fighting force. The Japanese might be losing the war but they weren't throwing the game. At Camp Tarawa men were being trained to handle the improved and terrifying flamethrower, now an integrated infantry weapon in assaulting fortified positions.

The gunners, riflemen, demolition men, and now the new flamethrowers drilled together as a lethal team with a specific set of new tactics for assaulting blockhouses and other fortified positions. The flaming napalm would do horrific things to human flesh. As the wisecrack went, "an ugly war just got uglier."

But many Marines, including the pragmatic Basilone, welcomed anything to the arsenal that could give the machine gunners an edge, kill the Japanese, and save his men. He drilled the gunners in flamethrower tactics hour after hour, teamwork that would pay off later in the fighting.

John and George got lucky with the coincidental appearance of a Dr. John Fox, who ran the local school district nearest Camp Tarawa and got word to John that he was also from Raritan, New Jersey, and why didn't John come by for an occasional home-cooked meal, and if they could spring George, he was invited as well. To men living on field rations, you didn't turn down an offer like that. The Basilone boys and the good doctor enjoyed a jolly Raritan reunion.

In October the first Americans landed in the Philippines, and on October 20 MacArthur splashed ashore in a carefully staged landing for the newsreel cameras following the assault troops by several hours and getting the general's khakis wet. On that same day he broadcast to the Filipino people that, indeed, "I have returned." There is no record of Basilone's response, but considering his prewar years in Manila serving under MacArthur, it is difficult to believe he didn't have some variety of emotional reaction.

All through November fighting continued on various Philippine islands and in the surrounding sea, with Senator John McCain's admiral grandfather one of the key players. The Allies were fighting in and around Sumatra and other of the Dutch East Indies, and in Burma the Brits had seized the initiative from the enemy and were on the offensive. Clearly, the Japanese were being pushed back everywhere.

In December, at Camp Tarawa, the rumor mill was chattering. The 5th Division would soon be on the move. Another island would be taken, perhaps one in the chain of islands that led to Japan itself. No place names were mentioned, even in scuttlebutt form, just that it might be an island with an airfield. On December 27, 1944, two days after Christmas, the division began loading its vehicles and heavier gear and tons of supplies. In mid-January 1945, as the United States entered another new wartime year, American carriers were attacking Formosa, Nationalist Chinese were pushing the Japanese out of Burma, there was heavy fighting on Luzon in the Philippines between invading GIs and Japanese defenders, and in Europe Warsaw fell to the Russians and a Polish unit.

At Camp Tarawa, embarkation orders were cut. The 5th Marine Division, Basilone and company, would be sailing, destination still unknown, on January 17, 1945. Manila John was once again going to the wars.

PART FOUR

IWO JIMA

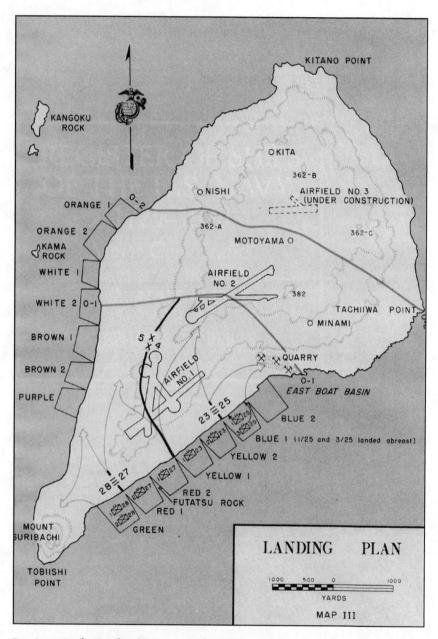

KITANO POINT

KANGOKU
ROCK

OKITA

362-B

ONISHI   AIRFIELD NO. 3
              (UNDER CONSTRUCTION)

ORANGE I   O-2

ORANGE 2   362-A   362-C
KAMA   MOTOYAMA O
ROCK

WHITE I
                    AIRFIELD
                    NO. 2
WHITE 2 O-1   382

                                          TACHIIWA POINT
BROWN I   O MINAMI

                    5 X
                    X 4
BROWN 2
                AIRFIELD   X QUARRY
                NO. I   X X
PURPLE   O-1
                                   EAST BOAT BASIN

                            23 ≡ 25
                                    X 25
                                  3/25
                                            BLUE 2
                            X 23
                         X 23   BLUE I (1/25 and 3/25 landed abreast)
                      X 23
                                       YELLOW 2
           28 ≡ 27   X 27
                    X 27   YELLOW I

                 X 28   RED 2
                 X 28   FUTATSU ROCK
MOUNT   RED I
SURIBACHI   GREEN

                                       ┌─────────────────────────────┐
TOBIISHI   │ LANDING   PLAN   │
POINT   │   │
                                       │ 1000   500   0   1000 │
                                       │ ▭▬▭▬▭▬▭▭▭▬▭▬▭▬   │
                                       │   YARDS   │
                                       │   MAP III   │
                                       └─────────────────────────────┘

Iwo Jima. In the Battle of Iwo Jima, John Basilone, now a gunnery sergeant, charged across Red Beach 2 with the 1st Battalion, 27th Marines on D-day, February, 19, 1945. He would die there on that first day of the assault, falling just short of one of his unit's primary objectives, Motoyama Airfield # 1.

23

wo Jima, Japanese for "Sulfur Island," is a volcanic flyspeck in
the Central Pacific situated roughly six hundred miles north-
northwest of Saipan and Tinian in the Carolines and another six
hundred or so miles from Tokyo, the capital and largest city of
Japan. It was this equidistant geographical position that gave Iwo
any importance whatsoever in the Pacific war. Japanese engineers
had built three airstrips on the small island (only ten square miles
of sand and rock) from where their Zeroes and other intercep-
tors could attack United States B-29 Superfortresses based in the
Carolines en route to Tokyo and other mainland Japanese targets. The same Japanese fighters taking off from Iwo could also
ambush and shoot down B-29s on their return flights to Tinian
and Saipan, especially Superforts damaged by Japanese antiair-
craft fire or shot up by Zeroes over the mainland, now limping
home, wounded, slowed, and vulnerable, the planes and their ten-
man crews. If American forces could take Iwo, the lives of hundreds, perhaps thousands of U.S. flyers would be saved and our
bombardment of the home islands stepped up in frequency and
in bomb tonnage. It would also permit American fighter escorts,

with their relatively short range, to accompany the B-29s to Tokyo and back, improving their effectiveness.

Invading and taking the rugged little island from its powerful garrison of good Japanese troops and dangerous aircraft would not be done on the cheap. Major General Harry Schmidt's V Amphibious Corps would be ticketed for the task: three Marine divisions, the 3rd, the 4th (with George Basilone and commanded by Major General Clifton B. Cates), and the brand-new and untested as a unit 5th Marine Division, a blend of raw-to-combat young Marines freshly over from the States and salty and blooded veterans like gunnery sergeant John Basilone, a total of roughly 60,000 men, about half of them having already faced and fought the enemy. There would be casualties, and some senior Marine officers expected them to be heavy.

I have been to the island once, in November 1951, almost seven years after the battle, as a replacement platoon leader being flown out to the 1st Marine Division in North Korea. Our Navy transport plane landed at Iwo to refuel, and we forty or so young officers and senior NCOs had a few hours to stretch cramped legs and wander about and gawk, very much like tourists anywhere—except that, for Marines of any generation, Iwo Jima wasn't a tourist attraction but a sacred shrine. My memory of the place is simple. Mount Suribachi was stark, bare, smaller than I anticipated; the air reeked of sulfur, the sand was black, and the wind moaned. Beyond that, nothing. Only the imagined echoes of muted battle long ago and the sense of other presences, the ghosts of the men of both sides who fought and died here. Those sensations I took with me, along with a sense of awe, long after the stench of sulfur faded. A Japanese source once described Iwo in these words: "no water, no sparrow, no swallow." More prosaically, an American source described it as being shaped like "a porkchop."

Everyone I've asked about the epic battle, from Associated Press photographer Joe Rosenthal, who took the iconic photo of the flag-raising on Mount Suribachi, to combat Marines and one Navy nurse who were there under fire in the famous fight, remembers the shifting sands, difficult if not impossible to dig foxholes in. That sand, the smell, and the wind.

As a twenty-three-year-old lieutenant in 1951, I was hardly an expert on Iwo, but I probably knew more about the island than did Gunnery Sergeant John Basilone as he sailed from Hawaii in late January 1945, one small element of a convoy of 500 ships and perhaps 100,000 men, sailors and Marines both. As he and his machine gunners departed Pearl Harbor on January 26 aboard the USS *Hansford*, it is probable that none of them, Basilone included, had ever even heard the name of their targeted destination and had not yet been told about Iwo. The Marines still took security seriously, and it was standard operating procedure in amphibious warfare not to tell the men where they were headed until they were at sea, unable to blab. Now, on the second day the *Hansford* was out of port, Lieutenant Colonel John Butler got on the horn over the ship's PA system. You know, the old "Now hear this, now hear this" announcement. Said the colonel, "Our destination is Iwo Jima, an objective closer to the Empire of Japan than any other to date." I suspect the saltier of the Marines on board took this as a good news/bad news item of information. Good in that it took us a step closer to winning the Pacific war; bad in that the closer Americans got to the Japanese mainland, the harder and more desperately the enemy would fight and the more Marines would die.

Maybe the best place to start telling about Iwo is with Marine historian Joe Alexander. In his monograph *Closing In: Marines in the Seizure of Iwo Jima*, Alexander begins with a dramatic little vignette, not at the start of the fight but two weeks into the battle, on Sunday March 4.

There was a hot war going on and gunfire everywhere, when a desperately wounded B-29 bomber called *Dinah Might*, crippled during a bombing raid on Tokyo, piloted by Lieutenant Fred Malo and carrying a ten-man crew, came in on an emergency landing. It was crash-land at sea or risk this heavily shot-over landing strip, and Malo piloted her in safe if not precisely secure, everyone glad to be alive but anxious to be swiftly away. The Air Corps was

paying its boys to fly, not to get shot at on the ground like ordinary
infantry grunts. *Dinah Might* underwent half an hour of very hurried makeshift repairs, took off safely again (every Japanese gunner
within range firing at the damned thing), and got back to its base
without further distraction. It would be only the first of hundreds
of such B-29 emergency landings on Iwo and the first ten of what
would be thousands of air crewmen saved, and it proved to at least
some of the Marines then fighting there that the place might turn
out to have been worth taking.

Colonel Alexander sets the scene, writing that by this date,
"The assault elements of the 3rd, 4th and 5th Marine Divisions
were exhausted, their combat efficiency reduced to dangerously low
levels, the thrilling sight of [the] American flag raised by the 28th
Marines on Mount Suribachi had occurred ten days earlier, a lifetime on Sulphur Island. The landing forces of the V Amphibious
Corps (VAC) had already sustained 13,000 casualties, including
three thousand dead. The 'front lines' were a jagged serration across
Iwo's fat northern half, still in the middle of the main Japanese
defenses. Ahead, the going seemed all uphill against a well-disci-
plined, rarely visible enemy."

But to the machine gunners at sea in January aboard the USS
Hansford, all this was well into the future. And, as Alexander
remarked, ten days could be a lifetime on Iwo. Bruce Doorly's
monograph about Basilone takes us on board with Manila John
and his gunners: "The convoy of U.S. ships was still three weeks
and 5,000 miles from arriving at Iwo Jima. They took time to
prepare. The men kept in shape by doing exercises. Due to the
limited room on the ship each group would have to wait for
the limited open space used for calisthenics. John worked his
men hard to ensure that they would be ready. By this time their
hair started to grow in again [remember those shaved heads that
relieved the boredom at Camp Tarawa?]. To keep themselves
busy, the 'soldiers' [Doorly uses the word interchangeably with
'Marines'] played cards and read. Books were passed around
and traded. A small pocket copy of The New Testament became
popular as they neared Iwo Jima. Letters home were written."

Knowing Basilone's tastes, you suspect he played more cards, read fewer Bible passages, and wrote fewer letters than most.

Now that the men were safely unable to pass on the information about their location (there was no way letters could be mailed until after the invasion), officers provided them with more detailed dope about the operation. The fight was expected by some on the staff to last only a few days since the island had already been bombed for two months, and the manpower advantage would be something like four to one. When informed of this optimistic projection, Basilone is quoted as remarking, "Bullshit," out of hearing by officers but loud enough for his men. Having fought the Japanese before, old salt Manila John knew that any fight against more than 22,000 Japanese soldiers prepared to die for emperor and country would be hard and drawn out, anything but a three-day affair.

On February 12, Lincoln's Birthday, and with only another six or seven hundred miles to go, the convoy paused at Saipan, where John's outfit was transferred to another ship, an LST (Landing Ship Tank) carrying a flotilla of smaller landing craft in which the Marines would hit the Iwo beach. On February 16 the LST departed Saipan on the last leg of its long voyage. Men were quieter now. Religious services were well attended.

Medics on some of the smaller ships reported an outbreak of diarrhea. Doorly suggests that some of the "new" men were getting nervy. Had Doorly never heard the popular and often uttered combat phrase "scared shitless," conveying an entirely different situation? And as for only the newer Marines being affected, seasoned Marines with a few firefights under their belts will tell you that the worst time of all is before battle, the anticipation of action, and that once the firing starts, the adrenaline flows and a man's focus becomes more acute and shifts to killing the enemy instead of worrying about oneself. But all of this is small-unit stuff, and those the humble infantrymen, not the planners or decision-makers, but only the traditional raw meat at the end of the stick that prods the enemy.

Alexander provides the bigger picture. General Schmidt, who was expecting a ten-day fight, issued operation plan 5-44 on

December 23. Despite its pre-Christmas timing, says Alexander, there was little gift-wrapping: "The plan offered nothing fancy." Another, slightly junior Marine general, Holland M. Smith ("Howlin' Mad" Smith to his Marines) said of the invasion, "It's a tough proposition," and gloomily predicted "severe casualties unless greater and more effective preliminary naval bombardment was provided." There were two potential landing beaches, both dominated by the 550-foot-high Mount Suribachi. The three thousand yards of black sand beach to the southeast appeared more sheltered and was favored by Schmidt. On D-Day the 4th Division (George Basilone) would land on the right of that black sand beach, the 5th Division (John Basilone) on the left with the 3rd Division held in reserve and to be sent in later. It was the classic triangular USMC setup, two up and one back. Alexander lists the initial objectives: one airfield, the lower one of the three, the western shore, and the hill, Suribachi. A first-night, and probably major, enemy counterattack was expected, and welcomed, cheerfully this time, by Smith. "That's generally when we break their backs," he said pleasantly of the anticipated enemy strike; he was a man who enjoys a good battle.

As Basilone's LST and scores of other ships, large and small, steamed toward Iwo, toward the waiting enemy and the battle to come, it may be that some of the more contemplative Marines reflected on the company of men with whom they sailed and would fight, their Corps, and how during only a few years it had grown. When Basilone and others, including 4th Marine Division C.O. Major General Clifton B. Cates, fought on the 'Canal in 1942, there existed in the entire Corps only the 1st Marine Division in the Pacific, with a 2nd Marine Division still forming up at Camp Lejeune. Now the Marine Corps comprised five divisions with a sixth on the way. There loomed yet another overall goal for the Corps, once Iwo and later Okinawa were digested, when the United States would be invading Japan's mainland, its home islands, probably starting with Honshu, with a huge American Army—an army that was to be spearheaded by six Marine divisions landing abreast, 120,000 men assaulting a hostile beach under fire in one of the greatest battles ever joined. Not that even in a six-division Corps would the intimacy of the Marine Corps ever totally vanish, that comforting sense that even if you personally didn't know another Marine, you knew a guy who did, and that sooner or later you would serve together—at Quantico, Parris Island, "Dago" (San Diego), Pendleton, "Swamp Lagoon" (Camp Lejeune), Twentynine Palms, or on those waiting hostile beaches of the Pacific.

There was still that fellowship, the brotherhood, no matter the overlapping of its generations, the timelessness of its traditions and lore, "the love of one drunken Marine for another." It surely must have seemed that way to General Cates, now sailing in convoy with John Basilone and his machine gunners.

One of the fighting, nonstaff generals commanding the invasion troops, Cates, who had been around for a long time, was a slim, dapper gent who smoked his cigarettes through an elegant holder, and would eventually become commandant of the Marine Corps. As a second lieutenant in World War I on June 6, 1918, he went over the top with his platoon at a place called Belleau Wood where the 5th and 6th Marine regiments would in desperate combat blunt the final thrust by General Ludendorff to take Paris and end the war. Early in the firefight, hit in the helmet by a German machine-gun bullet, Cates was knocked out, only to be revived by one of his men pouring a bottle of red wine over his face and head. "Goddamn it, Tom!" protested Lieutenant Cates. "Don't put that wine over my head, give me a drink of it." Thus revived, Cates pulled himself together, resumed the fight, and led his men into the key French village of Bouresches that was their objective, chased out the Boches, and hung on with only twenty-one men against German counterattacks until relieved. Cliff Cates was nominated for a Medal of Honor and eventually awarded a lesser decoration and fought out the rest of World War I a decorated hero.

On Guadalcanal, as a colonel, Cates commanded troops fighting to hold Henderson Field, and it may have been that Basilone then met, saw, or served under him there in 1942. Six years later, when I reported in to Quantico, Virginia, the Marine Corps Schools, as a college sophomore in the platoon leaders class, Cates was the base's commanding officer before whom all of us passed in review. I still recall seeing him strolling about with that cigarette holder. Now here he was closing in on Iwo with Manila John et al. That's what I mean about the relatively few degrees of separation between Marines of one war or another, one outfit, whatever the decade.

But in February 1945 the two men, one as a two-star general, the other a gunny, Cates and Basilone, would again be in the same fight, the general as one of the senior officers agonizing about how to get their artillery regiments ashore before dark of that first day to help handle those anticipated counterattacks against the first waves of assaulting Marines, of whom Basilone would be one. The aerial and naval bombardment of Iwo Jima was in one sense encouraging to the assault troops of the three attacking divisions. It should soften up the Japanese defenders, cave in and crush their pillboxes and blockhouses, put at least some of their artillery out of action, maybe cut some communications wire, perhaps damage, destroy, or ground some of their planes, hole their runways and break up the tarmac. All this would be good. But what of the famous element of surprise? There could be no great surprise to men being bombed and shelled for weeks. They knew the Marines were coming. And they would even know when, since the bombardment would have to lift before the first waves of Marines hit the beach.

Basilone tried to explain these things to his platoon. The men, even the boots among them, realized he knew this stuff, had fought, and brilliantly so, on an earlier island, and that if any NCO could help them get through the coming fight alive, it would be an old salt like Manila John. Even the nickname, with its suggestion of previous Asian service, of the "Old Breed" and the comforting knowledge that gunny Basilone had been there and come back alive, must have cheered his men, given them a little confidence. So what if Basilone had his doubts about the effectiveness of naval bombardment and what bombs could do or fail to do to an entrenched enemy? As for his "boys," most of them were convinced the gunny would get them through the battle to come, if anyone could.

D-Day would be February 19. Pretty soon now they would be sufficiently close to hear the sixteen-inch guns of the battleships, the heavy bunker-busting bombs of the big planes. The convoy plowed on through chill rain squalls and even sleet. This wasn't the hot and steaming tropical South Pacific Basilone knew so well. Colonel Alexander continues to narrate the story of the Iwo Jima invasion from the point of view not of the infantry and the enlisted men, who would do the fighting, but of the staff and the flag officers, the Marine generals and Navy admirals who had worked up the plan and would now issue the commands.

Like all really good Marine officers, Joe Alexander was not only a student of tactics and the capacity of his own forces, the necessity for speed, but he also believed in "knowing your enemy." He studied the most important subject, the opposing commander. He got to know and understand, and never to underestimate, the foe—in this case, Lieutenant General Tadamichi Kuribayashi, a fifty-three-year-old very senior and high-ranking officer who had once actually lived in the United States, where he was assigned to the Japanese embassy in Washington. This was quite a highly ranked officer for a command so limited and a relatively small force of only 22,000 men. But General Kuribayashi had been handpicked for this job by the very highest authorities because he was a brilliant staff officer destined for great things, as well as a fifth-generation samurai, which in imperial Japan was sort of like being an original DAR, a Son or Daughter of the American Revolution. And this being Japan with its own very particular code of military honor, rather than fail at his mission a samurai was expected to be ready to kill himself by disemboweling in the ritual manner. The Japanese were indeed sui generis.

Kuribayashi was no mindless automaton, however, but a modern and intelligent man, also very much a realist who wrote to his wife six months before the battle, "The Americans surely will invade this Iwo Jima . . . do not look for my return." Think about being a loving wife back home and receiving a cheering little missive like that! Later, during the battle, he would candidly inform his superiors in Tokyo without dramatics and flatly that he could hold the island *only* if they sent him naval and air reinforcement. Otherwise he could not, though he assured the brass he would die there. He had already demanded and received "the finest mining engineers and fortifications specialists in the Empire."

Colonel Alexander details how these experts were used. "When American heavy bombers from the Seventh Air Force commenced a daily pounding of the island in early December of 1944, Kuribayashi simply moved everything—weapons, command posts, barracks, aid stations—underground. These engineering achievements were remarkable. Masked gun positions provided interlocking fields of fire, miles of tunnels linked key defensive positions, every cave featured ventilation tubes and multiple outlets. As an American joker following the battle remarked, 'everything was buried but the airstrips.' One installation inside Mount Suribachi ran seven stories deep. The Americans would rarely see a live Japanese on Iwo Jima until the bitter end." Maybe it was just as well, in the spirit of positive thinking, that the first assault waves to hit the beach weren't too assiduously briefed on the sophistication of the enemy defense system.

Alexander also assesses the strengths and weaknesses of the three assaulting Marine divisions. Of Basilone's 5th, the newest of all, here is Colonel Alexander's reading, including a personal note about Manila John: "The unit's newness would prove misleading. Well above half of the officers and men were veterans, including a number of former Marine parachutists and a few Raiders who had first fought in the Solomons." Agreed a recently arrived battalion commander after observing a live-fire exercise back in Hawaii, "These were professionals." Alexander noted that "among the veterans preparing for Iwo Jima were two Medal of Honor recipients from the Guadalcanal campaign. Gunnery sergeant John 'Manila John' Basilone and Lieutenant Colonel Robert E. Galer. Headquarters Marine Corps preferred to keep such distinguished veterans in the States for morale purposes, but both men wangled their way back overseas—Basilone leading a machine gun platoon, Galer delivering a new radar unit for employment with the Landing Force Air Support Control Unit. The Guadalcanal veterans could only shake their heads at the abundance of amphibious shipping available. . . . Admiral Turner would command 495 ships of which 140 were amphibiously configured, the whole array ten times the size of Guadalcanal's task force." Before it was over, they would need the lot.

24

Before the Navy and the Marine Corps even reached Iwo, they were already feuding, the dispute ignited by an Army Air Corps–Navy rivalry. With a bloody fight like Iwo coming up, you marvel that senior professional officers, the best products of West Point and Annapolis, would permit themselves the luxury of jealous, pride-driven college-boy spats. But they did.

The Air Corps Superfortresses had recently flown a big mission over Japan that failed to destroy the targeted aircraft factories, and Naval Air was out to prove it could do the job. Task Force 58, assigned to batter the island of Iwo Jima with big guns and fleet aviation just prior to the Marine landings, sort of a knockout blow, was instead being lured by a new target of opportunity, within easy reach on Honshu, those Japanese factories the B-29s missed. Ambitious naval leadership allowed itself to be distracted and sent the huge task force steaming away from Iwo toward the Japanese mainland, creating for the Marines two problems. This sudden, last-minute change of plans meant that the Navy was taking away not only its big new battleships and their sixteen-inch guns so effective in shore bombardment, but also the fleet's eight Marine squadrons of specially trained, close air support fighter-bombers, experienced in working with ground air control officers to fly shotgun for the infantrymen hitting the beaches and then heading inland against formidable enemy defenses. In the end, Task Force 58 did its thing on Honshu and then belatedly returned to Iwo in time, if only briefly, to support the landings. It then hurried somewhere else again on yet another mission, not to return to Sulfur Island.

As D-Day (February 19) came closer, the commanders of both sides met with their staffs. Tadamichi Kuribayashi declared that despite all of the bombing and shelling, the bulk of his defenses were intact and functioning, and kept his message to the staff simple: "I pray for an heroic fight."

On board Admiral Richmond Kelly "Terrible" Turner's flagship, Joe Alexander reports, "The press briefing held the night before D-Day was uncommonly somber. General Holland Smith predicted heavy casualties, possibly as many as 15,000, which shocked all hands. A man clad in khakis without rank insignia then stood up to address the room. It was James V. Forrestal, Secretary of the Navy. 'Iwo Jima, like Tarawa, leaves very little choice,' he said quietly. 'Except to take it by force of arms, by character and courage.'" That reference to Tarawa was sufficient to shake any Marine in the room, since it was well-known that Tarawa was a bloody foul-up and losses there, for a three-day fight on such a small island, had been ghastly. Colonel Alexander now takes us to D-Day itself, the nineteenth (as for the brilliant Forrestal, he so exhausted and drained himself, so suffered over the casualty rolls on Iwo and elsewhere in the Pacific as secretary of the Navy, that he would eventually commit suicide). "Weather conditions around Iwo Jima on D-Day morning were almost ideal. At 0645 Admiral Turner signaled, 'Land the landing force.'"

Pulitzer Prize–winning novelist John P. Marquand, the author of best-selling New England tales of manners, covering the invasion as a war correspondent, wrote these first impressions of Iwo: "Its silhouette was like a sea monster, with the little dead volcano for the head, and the beach area for the neck, and all the rest of it, with its scrubby brown cliffs for the body."

And off they went, the 4th and 5th divisions abreast, while the 3rd Division hung back in reserve, a decision later to become controversial. Why hadn't all three powerful divisions hit the enemy simultaneously?

John Basilone and his platoon would hit the beach in the fourth wave about nine-thirty a.m. He would be under fire for the first time in more than two years, since the 'Canal in late 1942.

In Hawaii, John's brother George had questioned him closely about motivation. "You had it made. You could have called your shots. A commission or a soft berth at Pendleton. Why come back to this rat race? You of all people should know what our chances of getting back alive are." According to Phyllis Basilone Cutter, John answered this way: "When I left the theatre of operations on Guadalcanal [it was actually Australia] to come back stateside, I promised my buddies I would return and that promise I didn't make lightly." He didn't make it back, however, not specifically to them. With the brothers in Hawaii, George continued to argue. "You were lucky to get back alive. Why push your luck?" But John wasn't having any. "George, the Marine Corps is my whole life. Without it the rest seems empty. This thing I have to do, something keeps pushing me. I now know what I want. If I don't make it, try and explain to the folks. I know they always loved me. God knows I do them, but this is bigger than family and loved ones and I must do it." This sounds too pious and self-effacing to be convincing. Phyllis, with her brother George surely the source, must have attempted to quote John accurately. Why would she phony up her beloved brother's words on something as serious as the possibility of his own death? It's just that the words are so stilted.

Jerry Cutter and Jim Proser take a crack at describing what it must have been like in that landing craft carrying Basilone to Iwo and his destiny. But how much of this is to be believed? Recall that Cutter once told me that they "made up" some of their reporting.

According to Cutter and Proser, it was a bitter John Basilone who got into the landing craft. "We filed down the gangways into the ship's steel belly. Half of my boys loaded into amphibious tractor 3C27 with me. Amtrac 3C27 was an armor plated rectangular tub made for delivering men onto a beach. It rode low and slow in the water." As the concussions from the big naval guns roiled the ocean and created waves, and the small craft circled slowly waiting for orders, men began getting seasick, including some of the twenty-five Marines in Basilone's boat. And we have the sergeant unsure about whether he should talk straight to his men before they reached the beach. Should he assure them that the big guns and aerial bombing were paving the way to a successful assault, or tell them truly how bad it just might be? According to Cutter, Basilone was ambivalent: "It's going to be all right, boys. They're going to be as dizzy as shit-house rats after we get done pounding 'em. I lied—just as Topside lied to us, when they told us it would be over in 72 hours. All of us vets knew that 72 hours was pure bullshit and said so. It was like an involuntary reaction. The minute it dropped from the C.O.'s mouth, it sounded like a dozen men coughed at once. But it was a dozen mumbled 'bullshits' jumping right off the lips of us vets. We couldn't help it. There were 23,000 [sic] trained Japanese jun-gle fighters straight ahead who had been digging in and calibrating their guns for the last three months." Cutter's book leaves Basilone's dilemma unsolved. What did he actually tell his men? It is not clear that he said anything. And not to quibble, but there was no jungle on Iwo Jima for those "Japanese jungle fighters" to exploit.

The book goes on to describe the landing craft's ride toward the beach, the men puking, the shells passing overhead, Basilone's memories of prewar Japanese golfers at the Raritan Valley Country Club, his premonitions of a war to come. Then it reels off into what seems to be pure fiction in which Basilone, the hardened combat veteran and professional gunnery sergeant, behaves like a clown: "A few more of the boys tossed their steak and eggs as we came around. Tension had been ratcheting up as we turned around in circles at the rally point. This was it, we were going in. I got up behind the .50 caliber machine gun mounted by the driver. Orders were not to fire unless we saw enemy, but I knew we wouldn't see any. After three months of waiting for us, they were dug in too deep, and the Japs were too good at camouflage. We wouldn't see a damn thing. So I planned to shoot everything just to be sure. I chambered the .50 and squeezed off a few rounds. The driver [remember, the 'driver,' a Navy coxswain, was in command of the craft, not a Marine sergeant along as passenger] reminded me of orders not to fire unless we saw something, and I gave him my opinion. 'Fuck orders and fuck you, Mac.'"

This is just crazy. At a time when a veteran platoon leader should be calming and reassuring his seasick, scared, green troops about to hit a hostile beach under fire, and whatever Cutter and Proser's good intentions to show Basilone off at his dynamic, decisive warrior's best, the passage only brings into question his leadership skills, his emotional stability, and his savvy as a combat veteran at a critical moment. First, the small craft was pitching and tossing so wildly that men were "puking," which meant there was no stable platform on which Basilone could stand while firing. They were not in the first wave but in the fourth wave, so that other Marines, several thousand of them, were already ashore and in the sights of that .50-caliber gun he'd just commandeered and was arrogantly threatening to fire beachward, quite possibly at his fellow Marines! And here is the experienced, cool Sergeant Basilone, who should at this point be preparing his men to hit the beach, counseling the reluctant or afraid, soothing the overexcited, doing none of these things. Instead, he's jumping up, cursing out the coxswain, grabbing the .50-caliber to fire off a few random rounds, not at any target he can see but just generally in the direction of the beach where his most likely victims would be fellow Marines. This is not believable and is insulting to Manila John.

Cutter's story of Basilone's arrival on the beach at Iwo grows more bizarre. Now, as the amtrac rolls up on the sand and encounters steep terraces that slow and then halt its progress, the Marines leap out into deep, clinging black sand. As the Marines and their "Doberman war dogs" (first mention of those, by the way) try to dig in, Gunnery Sergeant Basilone issues his first order to the machine gunners, not to organize themselves, and then position, load, and sight their guns, but instead to "Fix bayonets!"

He tells the boys to pull out their scout knives, an order given usually when ammo is short or hand-to-hand combat is about to erupt? This is idiotic. If a machine-gun sergeant expects trouble, an enemy counterattack, he gets his machine guns ready to turn back the oncoming Japanese, wipe them out, and break the attack, what Basilone himself did with such lethal effectiveness on the 'Canal. Neither machine gunners nor assistant gunners even carry bayonets, though ammo carriers who are armed with carbines may do so ("which weren't worth diddily shit," my machine-gun expert Charles Curley assures me). The Japanese counterattack never came, not at the beach, where there were already four Marine waves ashore and a fifth arriving on the heels of Basilone's fourth. The problem now was for NCOs like Basilone to help get the men on the beach unscrambled and to head inland, in Manila John's case, toward an airstrip, Motoyama #1.

Basilone's later words on the beach itself, via Cutter, once we get beyond the just plain silly "Fix bayonets!" sound credible: "They tore us up while we were lying on the beach but me and Lou Plain [a colonel and the regimental executive officer] got this show on the road. We kicked their asses and dragged boys up by the scruffs of their necks. 'Get the fuck off the beach. Move out!' we yelled at them over the incoming fire. They were moving over the terraces now and were finding whatever cover they could in shell craters on the flat land. Bulldozers had punched gaps through the terraces and tanks were on their way up from the beach to support us. A few mixed squads of C and B Company boys were now at the edge of Motoyama #1 Airfield, our first objective. Once we took out the bunker that was slicing open the 4th Division with their cannon, we only had to worry about the snipers, the dug-in artillery looking down on us from Suribachi, and the constant hail storm of mortars that fell from the sky. Other than that, at least we were off the water's edge. Which had turned into a killing field."

25

I've tried to assess which of a number of versions of what happened the morning of February 19 is true. But are any of them?

John Basilone's sister Phyllis has her version. She loves her brother, but has never seen a war. Her son Jerry Cutter, also not a writer, and his cohort, Jim Proser, have their account. The Marine Corps records say one thing. *Leatherneck* magazine has stories by various adepts. Charles W. "Chuck" Tatum, one of Basilone's gunners, has written his own book, *Red Blood, Black Sand*, and the very professional Douglas "Bill" Lansford, a writer and a Marine who was there, has his recollection. Historian Joe Alexander writes at length of that morning. There've been movies with John Wayne and films directed by Clint Eastwood. Dozens of Iwo Jima books. Did Basilone die instantly from a mortar shell? From artillery fire? Did he linger for hours, speaking with a corpsman and even smoking a cigarette? Did he never regain consciousness? Gradually bleed to death of small-arms fire as the official Marine Corps casualty record of the time suggests? His Navy Cross citation says he was killed instantly by a shell. Phyllis says he lived for hours, discussed events, smoked a cigarette. Choose your version.

Maybe the Japanese have theirs. Or did they ever even know who Manila John was? Few survived to say. You have the sense their Sendai Division troops would have liked Basilone, even welcomed him into their own and very special pantheon of warriors—and then killed him before he could kill them, which he surely would have done and happily. General Tadamichi Kuribayashi might conceivably have greeted Basilone as a fellow samurai, gallant, impassioned, fierce, if a bit crude perhaps, a warrior not overly given to politesse or ritual.

I believe this was how it really was on that February morning in 1945: Basilone and other Marines headed down into the hold of the LST to board the smaller landing craft that would actually take them through the surf and up onto the black sand beach, the medium LCMs and the smaller personnel-carrying LCVPs, the tractorlike amphibians they called amtracs. Navy coxswains piloted the assault waves to the shore, backed out, returned to their mother ships, and loaded up again to return with fresh meat for Iwo, men or supplies. There was some wishful thinking in the scuttlebutt men heard that the brass figured it for a seventy-two-hour fight, over in three days, maybe five. "Bullshit," said others, including vets like Basilone. But what the hell, anything was possible.

Historian Joe Alexander sketches the scene. "The massive assault waves [two reinforced infantry regiments from each of the two attacking divisions, the 4th and the 5th] hit the beach within two minutes of H-Hour. A Japanese observer watching the drama unfold from a cave on the slopes of Suribachi reported, 'At nine o'clock in the morning several hundred landing craft with amphibious tanks in the lead rushed ashore like an enormous tidal wave.'" The executive officer of the 28th Marines recalled, "The landing was a magnificent sight to see, two divisions landing abreast; you could see the whole show from the deck of a ship." If you were closer than shipboard, it wasn't all that "magnificent." It was too close. The tracked amphibious vehicles bellied down in the soft sand, and the wheeled vehicles simply spun their wheels. Some of the smaller landing craft swung sideways in the surf, a few capsized, men had to bail out heavy-laden in deeper water, some drowned. But from the distant vantage points on the ships, everything looked great. If you have enough rank, and are far enough from the gunfire, the perspective is always terrific. I attended only one war, a small one, but I was an infantryman, a rifle platoon leader. I never enjoyed that luxury of distance. At that point, from the ships, it was still a "show"—but not for long.

On shore, the enemy patiently waited for orders. Kuribayashi had made only one small blunder so far: when the underwater demolition teams going in before the first wave had been spotted, instead of ignoring the mere handful of invaders, the general had permitted some of his artillery targeting the beach to fire at the demo teams, tipping off their hidden positions to the counterbattery crews of the bigger guns on the battleships, the eight-inch-gun heavy cruisers, Marine aviation, and the big bombers, causing the Japanese guns considerable counterbattery damage. Otherwise, the Japanese were smart. They accepted that the Marines, some of them, maybe a lot, would reach the beach alive and in condition to fight. The enemy had no illusions of stopping them all on the way in or in the surf before they landed. If there had to be Americans on the three-thousand-yard black sand beach, why not withhold fire until there were plenty of them, thousands of Marines instead of mere hundreds of potential targets? Let the first waves land and be reinforced, and then when the narrow beach was clogged with Marines and their weapons and supplies amid the usual chaos, confusion, shouting, and mixed signals, exacerbated by the nerviness of men fresh to the fight, the contradictory orders and wild firing at nothing, hit them hard. Hit them with everything. *That* would be when the Marines were most vulnerable. What a target of opportunity. What a slaughter. The disciplined Japanese held back, held back, held back.

As Kuribayashi assessed his intelligence reports from the many observers, including the handful of Zeroes overhead surveying the scene and dodging the American fighters, he at last gave the orders for his artillery to fire their beach concentrations, target areas already zeroed in on weeks or even months before, crosshatched down to the last square meter of black sand. Sand now covered with American Marines, their weapons, and their packs, their sergeants and officers trying to get the men organized into fire teams, squads, platoons, and companies and saddled up to push inland to engage the enemy. And to get the hell off the soon-to-be lethal beach. It was at that delicate stage of operations that the artillery crashed down murderously on the first four or five waves of Marine infantry, as they admitted, "bare-assed naked," because you couldn't dig foxholes in the soft, shifting and blowing black sand. Shovel with your entrenching tool, watch the sand slide back into the hole, and shovel again. Corporal Ed Hartman, a 4th Division rifleman, said, "The sand was so soft it was like trying to run in loose coffee grounds." Shoveling it was worse; you dug and dug and still didn't have a deep hole to shelter in. And by then you might be dead.

Bill Lansford, a World War II Marine and one of the legendary Carlson's Raiders, later a Hollywood screenwriter, still residing in California, gives us this account of Basilone's and his own first hours on the island. Lansford, an old pal of Basilone's who was by now in a different outfit (a job at regimental HQ) and in a later wave, wrote about it for *Leatherneck* magazine:

"On the morning of 19 February, 1945, we hit Red Beach on Iwo and started climbing its black sides under a storm of enemy mortar and artillery. Basilone had landed one wave earlier and apparently moved in. He didn't know how to stand still. 'Let's go in and set up them guns for firing,' a correspondent later quoted him. Whose guns the correspondent is talking about is hard to imagine. From the moment we landed it was total confusion: platoons and companies mixed up and in the wrong places; men and equipment sinking into the black sand while officers and NCOs drifted about, looking for their men. All that as Kuribayashi's presighted weapons tore our battalions to pieces.

"In the midst of the hellish noise and confusion," Lansford wrote, "two Marines were seen moving among the stalled troops shouting, cursing, and moving them out. One was Colonel Louis C. Plain, the regimental executive officer of the 27th Marines, who would soon be wounded and evacuated, the other was John Basilone. Having cleared a path for the troops on the beach, Basilone gathered several more Marines, set up a base of fire, and ordered them to hold while he went back for more men and weapons. On his way Basilone spotted three M-4 Sherman tanks, their water-cooled V-8s grinding like hell as they struggled up the beach under heavy fire. Knowing their value for knocking out bunkers, Basilone immediately took over."

There is usually a telephone on the exterior rear of tanks, and it may be that Basilone was using that to communicate with the crew inside and give them the benefit of his superior field of vision outside the buttoned-up vehicle.

Lansford continues: "Sergeant Adolph Brusa, a mortar squad leader, remembered he suddenly looked up and there was this lone Marine with those tanks. 'And I said to myself, that's John Basilone! What the hell is he doing standing up when everyone else is hugging the ground?' What Basilone was doing was guiding the tanks through a minefield and pointing out targets while completely exposed to the fire aimed at the Shermans."

We've got to wonder, how would a machine-gun sergeant just off the beach know where the enemy minefields were located? There is no description I can find of Basilone's going ahead of the tanks on hands and knees, probing with a bayonet for the telltale clank of metal on metal as Marines were trained to do when traversing mined areas. And defenders don't usually leave marking stakes to alert an oncoming foe. I accept the other suggestion, his pointing out targets of opportunity to the tankers. Good infantrymen do that.

"Leaving the tanks on high ground, Basilone returned to round up more troops for the assault team he had started building near the edge of Motoyama Airfield #1 (one of his unit's several first-day objectives). To do this he'd have to re-cross the steep volcanic beach where he had met the tanks and where many Marines were still pinned down by Kuribayashi's relentless shelling and well-camouflaged pillboxes." To one who's read descriptions and the citation for what Basilone did on Guadalcanal in October 1942, there is an eerie resonance, this business of going back, under heavy fire, small arms as well as shelling, and more than once, to pick up ammo or water or even a few stragglers he could use in the fight.

Lansford cites one of the officers in the battle who was an eye-witness: "Among those trying to reorganize their scattered units was Major (later Colonel) Justin G. Duryea of the 1st Battalion, 27th Marines. Duryea, who would lose an arm in an enemy mine explosion on D118, (and who) was so impressed by Basilone's heroism that he later recommended him for a second Medal of Honor." The second medal he once joked with buddies about going after?

"Basilone had landed with the fourth wave approximately at 0930. It was now almost noon and throughout the battle he had risked his life repeatedly, disregarding every danger, to restore momentum to the stalled attack. It seemed nothing could touch him [as nothing had touched him on the 'Canal two years before], and yet by ignoring fire that would eventually kill or wound thousands of men, Basilone had finally pushed his luck beyond its limits."

Before the landings George Basilone had warned his brother about pushing his luck. Now Bill Lansford picks up the theme, just before going on with his account of Manila John's death that first day on Iwo Jima. "Many men have said they saw John Basilone fall on the beach, which he did not. One said Basilone's legs were blown off by a mine. Several claim they heard Basilone's final words, and one said Basilone begged to be put out of his misery with his own pistol. Perhaps the most credible witness is Roy Elsner, the headquarters cook who had watched our machine gun drills back at Pendleton and was now on Iwo. He said that when he and some buddies were hunting for their headquarters, 'A few hundred yards from Motoyama Field #1 we heard an explosion, which caused us to look a bit to our right, toward the field. We saw Basilone and the three guys who were with him fall. We reached him almost immediately.'"

There are the other versions, not only from Marines in the Iwo fight but from members of the family, some of which I will cite. First, though, a moving note from Lansford in *Leatherneck* magazine: "Some time after noon I came across a group of blackened bodies on the edge of Motoyama Airfield #1. Company C was advancing half a mile ahead, sweeping the flat field clean, when one of the dead caught my eye. He was a thin, pallid kid. His helmet was half off, and he lay face up, arched over his combat pack. With his jacket torn back and his mouth open I vaguely recognized someone in that lean, lifeless face beneath its dusty stubble of hair. 'That's John Basilone,' said one of the men standing around. 'He just got it.'

"That's bullshit. I know Basilone. We were in the same company.' Someone else said, 'That's Basilone.' A guy I knew said, 'Yeah, he was briefing his guys when a mortar scored a direct hit. It killed them all.' I went and studied the dead man closely, but I didn't touch him. The shell had landed at his feet and sent shrapnel into his groin, neck, and left arm. He looked incredibly thin like an undernourished kid, with his hands near his stomach as though it hurt. This was the hero of Guadalcanal, the joy of a nation, the pride of the Marines, and my friend Manila John Basilone."

Reading that, I was unsure whether Lansford really accepted that the "thin" body was John's. So in June 2008 I phoned Bill again in California to ask. He said, "It was about noon of the first day and getting shelled to hell and all of us were in some state of shock. And of course it was John. I saw his pack with his name on it. And when the burial detail came up this cook was in it who knew our outfit and knew John and he made the same ID. I used to stay in touch with him [the cook Elsner] down in El Paso and then we lost contact. And I certainly knew Basilone from our time in the same machine-gun outfit. I was a section leader and he had a squad. We had gone on liberty together, gotten drunk together, and remember how we all shaved our heads that time?"

When I mentioned the several versions of Basilone's death that I'd read, Lansford reacted contemptuously. "There's a lot of scuttlebutt and bullshit out there, a lot of self-promoters. I've seen the different versions."

I then cited the official casualty report from the History Division in Quantico attributing Basilone's wounds to "GSW," gunshot wounds. Lansford wasn't buying that either. "That's absurd. I saw the body." I then mentioned the report's detailing three different hits, right groin, neck, and left arm. Lansford agreed that part sounded like what he'd seen but held to his insistence it was a single mortar shell that did it, not gunshots. We'd both seen dead bodies and knew that shellfire and small arms usually make different-looking entry wounds. He then continued with a last description of the living Basilone from memory. It's worth hearing.

"I was trying to round up all my guys at the foot of Motoyama Airfield #1 and the assault groups had gone through and there were a lot of Japanese dead lying around. It had been raining intermittently and I went over to one of the dead to go through the body for papers or maps or whatever, which we did for intelligence. He was wearing a raincoat and their [Japanese] raincoats were better than our ponchos and we would take things like that. And John Basilone came out onto the plaza near the lip of Motoyama Airfield #1 and he was calling his men together, you know with his hand circling above his head [the 'gather on me' gesture] and five or six guys came over. That was when a mortar shell came in and killed all of them, I don't know, four or five. I saw the medical report from the people who do the examination and it was one mortar shell. Just one."

I said, "One is all it takes," or something like that, and I again thanked Bill Lansford, a wonderful writer, who was writing a new book of his own and had worked on other projects with Ken Burns and Steven Spielberg.

26

There are as many descriptions of John Basilone's last firefight and where and how he died as there are Alamo legends about a wounded Jim Bowie's final fight in the old monastic cell where he lay waiting for the enemy with a knife and a gun or two. In Texas, they tell to this day of platoons of Mexicans found dead around Colonel Bowie's last bed.

I don't mean to be flip about this, but the Basilone family has been of little help in establishing the facts of just how John died and what he accomplished that terrible morning under heavy fire against the Japanese. Phyllis Basilone Cutter provides us perhaps the most colorful and probably the least credible account of her brother's heroics, in her hagiographic depiction of the fighting and of his unspoken thoughts and what he supposedly said and actually did in the battle. This is entirely understandable. Phyllis was a civilian writing about the brother she loved and lost, for a local audience, many of whom knew young John, remembered him as a boy, and revered his memory. Whether in Phyllis's family biography of the Basilones or in the fourteen installments of the same story she wrote for the Somerset County, New Jersey,

Messenger-Gazette newspaper, there is a "lives of the saints" quality to her account of his heroics, the stuff of B-movie, Republic Pictures films of the era when John and his sister were growing up and going to the local movie theater ("the Madhouse") in Raritan.

To begin, Phyllis talks throughout of Basilone's having landed with the first wave of assault troops, as if this makes him somehow braver than men who came later. In fact, Basilone was in the fourth wave, landing at about nine-thirty that morning, perhaps twenty-five or twenty-eight minutes after the first wave, a position every bit as perilous and courageous as the three waves that hit the sand earlier. Phyllis's account of Basilone's Iwo starts as he and his men board their landing craft, first circling, then taking a direct line to the hostile beach, and their landing under fire.

At this point, with battle about to be joined, a platoon to be steadied and encouraged, weapons and gear to be checked, Phyllis imagines, in Basilone's voice, that he isn't focused on Iwo and the battle coming up fast, but on December 7, three years earlier. "We thought of Pearl Harbor and had no compassion for the enemy." There may be Marine gunnies who speak or think like that as they go into combat, but I don't know any. Phyllis has her brother next describing the situation on the beach as the Marines come in for a landing: "The Japs lay stunned and helpless under the curtain of fire. Our landing was met by only weak small arms fire. The beach was coarse volcanic ash which made for a bad landing. We sank deep into the ash, slowing us down, as well as practically miring our vehicles. The boys were all together gathering their equipment so that we could work our way off the beach inland to our predetermined points, when we were suddenly peppered by machine gun fire. 'Down, fellows, hug the beach! Pull your helmets in front of your faces.'" This line is nonsense.

The ostrich buries its head in the sand; Marines in a firefight rely on their vision to target the enemy, to return fire, to figure out what's happened, to look for orders. If you cover your face with a helmet, you're blind. And this is an order given by a seasoned gunnery sergeant to his Marines? Phyllis goes on with her account, quoting Basilone: "As if struck by lightning, we hit the ground fast. Carefully tilting our helmets a bit we could see where the machine gun fire was coming from. It had to be silenced or we would be pinned down indefinitely."

Phyllis picks up Basilone's early moments on the black sand beach of Iwo with her "tale of the blockhouse," a dramatic vignette of which there are multiple versions. And she shifts from first to third person and back, in retelling what Basilone did next to silence the enemy gun. "Telling us to stay put [who is 'us,' who is narrating here?], Basilone crawled in a large semi-circle toward the blockhouse, which was spitting fire and death. He was able to crawl underneath the smoking gun ports. As he rested his back against the wall of the blockhouse, we counted with him the seconds before each machine gun burst. Waiting for the interval, he pulled the pin on his grenade, slammed it in the gun port and ran like hell down the beach. He tripped in the deep ash and as he buried himself protectively we heard the muffled roar of the exploding grenade. The blockhouse was smoking and the gun at the port had disappeared. Basilone ran back, dropping another grenade in for insurance. There were no signs of life, nothing but silence and the sickening smell of burnt flesh and scorched hair. Working his way back to us Basilone yelled, 'well, boys, there's one bunch of slantheads who won't bother anyone. They're fried.'"

Why would a machine-gun platoon sergeant be carrying hand grenades? I don't insist it never happened, but it puzzles me. Riflemen tote grenades, but machine gunners already have such heavy loads that they don't need to pile on additional gear.

Alternating between third and first person, Phyllis continues, describing the heavy enemy bombardment chewing up Marines on the beach. More disconcerting is Basilone himself explaining from the beach what the Japanese strategy is and what orders General Tadamichi Kuribayashi is sending to his various commanders. How the hell can a gunnery sergeant under fire know what's going on with general officers at the enemy headquarters as he and his men attempt to mount up and move on against hostile resistance?

When an American tank passes through Basilone's position and is hit by shells, one of its crew members scrambles out of the hatch to safety, only to be killed by Japanese small-arms fire. "Basilone was raging," Phyllis wrote, "rising to his feet as he charged over to the tank cradling his machine gun in his arms [machine gunners in the platoon usually carry the guns; the platoon sergeant doesn't]. Spotting a flash from a tree top [were there many trees on Iwo?] he stood upright and sprayed it furiously. We heard an unearthly scream as the treacherous sniper plummeted to his death. By this time there were other tanks, unaware of the heavily mined path. Basilone yelled and waved his arms, motioning them to follow him. As we watched [who is 'we?'] he led them in a wide circle into the safety of the wooded area."

So now Basilone is commanding a tank platoon, and again, how does he know where the mines are? "By now Basilone was as if possessed, ignoring the flesh ripping death all about him he rushed back to us shouting 'OK, fellows, let's get moving. We got to get these guns set up.'" Now, either they're going to set up the machine guns where they'll make a stand or they're going to move out; they can't do both. "We began to work our way off the beach. Without warning the whole beach erupted. The enemy had recovered and was fighting back."

This is terrible stuff, and it goes on like this, making little sense, such as Phyllis's statement at this point that "it was hours before another Marine landed on the beach." Other sources say the fifth wave had landed on the heels of the fourth (Basilone's), adding to the confusion. But Phyllis makes it sound as if Basilone's platoon was the famous "Lost Battalion" of World War I, abandoned and alone, out in front of the lines, facing 22,000 Japanese all by itself, when it was actually still on or trying to advance off the beach with thousands of other Marines. Basilone sends a scout named Sammy ahead to look over the way ahead and report back. "Fragments of white, steely death were whining and singing all about us. It was a miracle that up to this point, any of us had escaped injury, much less death."

The fevered prose of a bad war movie goes on. And Phyllis is not alone in this. Another Marine, Charles "Chuck" Tatum, a member of Basilone's platoon, in his book *Red Blood, Black Sand*, offers this capsule description of Manila John in a firefight, from the point of view of the assistant gunner who feeds the belted ammo into Basilone's gun. "Basilone's eyes had a fury I had never seen before. Rigid, hard clenched jaw, sweat glistening on his forehead, he was not an executioner but a soldier performing his duty."

This aside, Tatum does tend to clear up questions about Basilone and the famous blockhouse. Tatum's B Company had gotten bogged down, and as the confusion grew worse, Basilone was seen stalking up and down the beach trying, with Colonel Plain, to get his own men and the remnants of the earlier waves organized and heading inland. Tatum and the B Company machine gunners recognized Gunny Basilone and, knowing his reputation, were only too happy to fall in line when Basilone gave the "gather" signal and tried to get everyone moving forward.

Tatum writes that in the beach chaos, while trying to get men from different units organized, Basilone came across a demolitions assault team headed by Corporal Ralph Belt. It was not Basilone, but one of Belt's men, who, on Basilone's order, and given covering overhead fire by Basilone's machine gunners, rushed the looming blockhouse and tossed a heavy satchel charge of C-2 plastic explosive at its steel doors. According to Tatum, no one got up on the roof during the attack. And it was a Marine flamethrower operator, a hulking corporal named William N. Pegg, also on Basilone's orders, who finished off the blockhouse and cooked the men inside, again assisted by overhead machine-gun fire. Those Japanese able to flee, some of them actually aflame, would be shot down by Tatum, PFC Alvin C. Dunlap, PFC Steve Evanson, and Private Lawrence "Cookie Hound" Alvino.

These men and Tatum himself credit Basilone for organizing, ordering, and directing a brilliant blockhouse operation, but not for having carried out the demolition himself. It was a perfect example of carrying out a perfect plan of assault, a Marine Corps "school solution," employing flamethrower and demolitions, the sort of live-fire maneuver Basilone had drilled into his men over and over at Pendleton and later Tarawa. It was a feat of cool, superb leadership that could easily all by itself have earned Basilone a decoration.

Which is why it's exasperating that the Navy Cross citation needlessly includes an imaginary single-handed Basilone appearance on the blockhouse roof. Tatum's book adds clarification on that point, saying that *after* the position had been destroyed, Basilone grabbed Tatum and his machine gun and they took to the roof of the wrecked fortification for a better vantage point from which to pick off fleeing Japanese.

Phyllis now resumes her own version of Basilone's final orders and actions. As Sammy the scout gives the all-clear, the unit prepares to move inland: "Turning to the rest of the boys, Sergeant Basilone snapped, 'Okay, boys, stick close and follow me. Remember, if anyone gets it, the rest keep going. That's an order. We've got to get those guns set up. Let's go.' Single file we followed him. He never once looked back. He knew we were right behind him. Progress was slow. We had to detour and work our way around our knocked-out, still blazing vehicles. Dead Marines in our path received silent salute as we passed them. Every one of them had fallen face toward the enemy, rifles still in their hands." This is an unlikely picture to anyone who has ever walked over a heavily shelled, chaotic field of battle and seen the contorted limbs of the dead.

"The ground was rising and slowly settling back under the thunderous impact of heavy mortars and artillery shells. Slowly, it seemed hours, we crawled for the comparative safety of the first rise of ground. The figure of Sammy loomed larger and larger through the haze as we approached the end of the beach area. A second later, just when we thought we'd make it, suddenly there was a horrible screeching, whining sound picking up in intensity until we thought our eardrums would burst.

"Sergeant Basilone yelled, 'Hit the dirt, boys!'

"As if in rehearsal, we all hit the ash. Just at that moment, there was a terrifying roar, indescribably loud and angry. As we were slammed into the ground, we saw Sergeant Basilone hurled bodily into the air. It was as if a huge hand had reached down, smashed him deep into the volcanic ash. As we picked ourselves up, dazed, groggy and numb from the concussion we saw Sergeant Basilone lying half-buried in the swirling volcanic ash. He was unconscious and from the peculiar position he was in, appeared to have been hit bad. Sammy, who until this moment was too shocked to move, recklessly ran over to Basilone and was trying to rouse him."

There are additional contradictions here. Other accounts have Basilone killed with three other men in a group as they advance on Motoyama Airfield #1, not on the beach. Here he seems to have been the only one in the unit to have been hit. Though later Phyllis has the scout Sammy telling the wounded Basilone, "Sarge, it's horrible. Most of the group got it," the official Marine Corps casualty record blames small-arms fire, not a big shell. In Phyllis's version Basilone is still alive but unconscious. Several of her sentences later, he is awake and trying to shove his intestines back inside his body, and he is speaking. Others say he died instantly. Some say he lived half an hour. Phyllis has him living for hours and his men calling for help: "Medic, medic!" In the Marine Corps the call is always for "Corpsman, corpsman!" our term for a medic.

But these are details, and perhaps I'm nitpicking. Phyllis's account of her own brother's death deserves a hearing. Without my injecting further critical commentary, this is how she narrates the story in the *Somerset Messenger-Gazette* on Valentine's Day 1963, eighteen years after his death, of Manila John's last hours:

"You could see Sergeant Basilone fighting his way back to consciousness. In deep shock and tottering on the brink of complete unconsciousness, the sergeant was fighting back. His face, twisted and contorted with pain, was set in grim determination. By now Sammy was crying as he cradled Basilone protectively in his arms. Basilone slowly and with great effort, opened his pain-wracked eyes and said, 'Sammy, what happened?' Sammy, convulsed with grief, could only mutter, 'Sarge, it's horrible. Most of the group got it.' We watched silently, knowing the rest of us should move on, yet not wanting to leave the two of them alone on this God-forsaken beach. As we leaned over, Sammy was removing Sarge's hands which were clasped tightly over his stomach. The sight before our eyes was horrifying. Basilone's hands were drenched with deep scarlet blood, which trickled back to his wrists when Sammy elevated Sarge's hands over his head. The hot nauseating smell of blood and torn guts swirled slowly under our nostrils. We gulped back hard, but Sammy couldn't take it. He started to heave, horrible, retching, vomiting. It was then Sergeant Basilone displayed the intestinal fortitude he was so noted for. Ever so slowly and with a deftness surprising in such a muscular man, Basilone reached down into the sickening bloody mess that were his intestines, and placed them back into his torn and gashed open stomach. The effort must have been exhausting, as he lay back breathing heavily, biting huge gulps of the dust-laden air. Sammy had reached the dry retching stage. Suddenly, as if propelled from a catapult, he dashed madly down the beach, shouting, 'medic, medic!'

"Don't ever discount the courage and bravery of our medics. This lad was typical. There he was, oblivious to the hell and destruction being showered upon him as he tenderly ministered to the wounded. We watched as Sammy talked to him and gestured in our direction. No doubt Sammy told him the wounded Marine was Sergeant Basilone. It made no difference to the medic. A Marine was a Marine, Medal of Honor or not. To his credit, and keeping in the spirit of the Corps, he calmly finished bandaging his patient. Then, and only after making the wounded youngster as comfortable as possible, did he accompany Sammy back to us and Sergeant Basilone. We watched hopefully as the medic silently, and with tender hands, examined Basilone's wounds. Reaching for his kit, he fished out a hypo and bending loosely to Basilone's ear, he said softly, 'It's OK, Sarge. I'm going to give you a shot of morphine. That'll ease your pain until we can get you to a doctor.' The enemy by this time had succeeded in stopping any more landings.

"Basilone's only chance to live was to be taken back in one of the empty assault boats as it returned for another load. Seeing Basilone tug at the medic's sleeve, we edged closer to hear his words. 'Level with me, Doc. Am I going to make it?' Hanging on for doc's reply we heard him tell Basilone, 'Sarge, I'll give it to you straight. If I can get you back to the hospital ship in a couple of hours, you have a chance. Right now we're pinned to this god-damned beach. Your guess right now is as good as mine. I'm going to stay with you and the first boat that hits the shore will have you and I as passengers on the way back. Meanwhile, when the pain gets unbearable, yell out. I'll give you another shot. That's the best I can do for you now.' Basilone nodded he understood.

"We watched fascinated as his life blood slowly and relent-lessly kept oozing out, trailing brilliant crimson streamers down his side, turning the black volcanic ash into a dark purple spot which spread out ever so slowly. He was bleeding to death before our eyes and we were powerless to stop the flow."

In the Taebaek Mountains of North Korea in January 1952 I watched a Marine bleed to death coming back from a combat patrol. We had him on a stretcher, and it took the wounded man maybe seven hours to die. Toward the end he thought he was Jesus. Loss of blood eventually kills you; along the way it weakens not only the body but the intelligence, the judgment, the brain. Lose enough blood and you don't make much sense anymore. In Phyllis's story, Basilone was not only physically tough, he was still remarkably cogent.

In her account, as hour after hour passes, Sammy and Basilone have a discussion of what Basilone wants the young Marine to tell his brother George when and if George hits the beach. Basilone says he's had it, that he knows there's no chance. Sammy argues with him. Then Sammy pulls out a pencil and takes down Basilone's instructions about his brother. Basilone asks the corpsman, "Doc," for a cigarette. Doc then lights a cigarette for Basilone and places it between his lips. But the wounded ser-geant coughs and the butt comes away soaked with blood. Then Sammy reaches inside the pocket of Basilone's "tunic" and pulls out the miniature Bible many combat soldiers were given and carried during World War II, worn as protection in a pocket over the heart. Sammy begins to read the Lord's Prayer. As he finishes, Basilone's face, "now in peaceful repose, turns toward us." The Marines drop to their knees in prayer, as John Basilone "slipped away." Sammy, unbelieving, tries to rouse him, but the corpsman tells him, "Kid, it's no use. He's gone."

Here is Colonel Joe Alexander's briefer account: "On the left center of the action, leading his machine gun platoon, in the 1st Battalion 27th Marines' attack against the southern portion of the airfield, the legendary 'Manila John' Basilone fell mortally wounded by a mortar shell, a loss keenly felt by all Marines on the island."

Did he die on the beach, on the approaches to the airfield, from a mortar round or gunfire? On this last question, the official USMC casualty report backs up neither the family biographies nor Colonel Alexander. No mortar explosion is cited. Basilone's death in this report, drawn up on March 7, 1945, two weeks after he died, reads like this: "Nature of wound, GSW [gunshot wound], right groin, neck, and left arm." Robert Aquilina of the Corps' History Division reference branch in Quantico concludes that Manila John probably bled to death from these gunshots.

Marine casualties that first day ashore amounted to some 2,400 wounded and 501 killed, and Alexander reports in a small but very human sidebar that survivors of that deadly February 19 still remember how cold it was the first night after the landing, so unlike the tropical Pacific many of them knew from earlier fights.

Jerry Cutter, Basilone's nephew, has his version of his uncle's death, conflicting dramatically with his mother's more detailed version. Here, probably no truer but less flowery and imaginary, is what Cutter and writer Jim Proser wrote: "Sergeant John Basilone was killed by an enemy mortar shell at approximately 10:45 a.m. February 19, 1945. He suffered massive abdominal wounds but lingered for approximately twenty minutes before succumbing from shock and loss of blood. Four Marines died from the same explosion. His last words were spoken to a Navy corpsman who attended to him following the explosion. That corpsman has vowed never to reveal those final words."

So the two Cutters, mother and son, differ. In Jerry's story, no final message to George, no last cigarette, no Lord's Prayer, only twenty minutes of life, no three or more talkative hours, no peaceful look on his face. As to death by mortar shell or small-arms fire, Joe Alexander and the official casualty report are also at odds on that one specific item. There are other versions of his death as well. But it is the family versions that appear to stray furthest from the facts.

Clearly, they love the man, but trying to make a great warrior even better—a superman, an icon, conjuring up dialogue never spoken, prayers never prayed, inventing scenes that never happened, laying it on thick about feats of arms surely within Basilone's competence, but which never happened—is no service to a great man.

The service record book on Gunnery Sergeant John Basilone, his dates of enlistment, promotions, duty stations, transfers, and the like, filed at Marine Corps Schools, Quantico, Virginia, ends with this simple entry on his death: "Killed in action, February 19, 1945, Buried in grave 41, row 3, plot 1, 5th Mar Div cemetery, Iwo Jima, Volcano Islands." That's all there is, no poetry, no flourishes, no heroics.

PART FIVE

COMING HOME

Gunnery Sergeant John Basilone, originally buried on Iwo Jima, was re-buried in 1948 at Arlington National Cemetery with full military honors. Marine comrades are seen holding the American flag during services as members of the family look on. (Seated left to right) Basilone sister Phyllis (in light jacket); his mother, Dora; and his father, Salvatore.

27

In the traditional Marine Corps protocol of death, the family must be officially notified before any media are contacted. Inadvertently, though quite properly, it was a Basilone clan member who first learned of John's death on Iwo long before anyone at home got the news. George, John's brother, whose Marine unit went ashore several days after the first waves, was approached by a sergeant assigned to seek him out with the bad tidings. The sergeant saw the name Basilone stenciled on a backpack, and according to Bruce Doorly's account, called out, "George, I need to talk to you." Alarms went off, since George had never seen this sergeant before. "How come you know my first name?" A subsequent and famous photo shows George kneeling, a thoughtful, wry half-smile on his face that resembled John's so closely, at the simple white cross marking the temporary grave on Iwo. Coincidentally, another Raritan Marine named Tony Cirello would find John's pack in the sand and return it to George.

When the word finally came to Raritan on March 8, sixteen days after Manila John's death, there was some confusion. A reporter that morning phoned brother Angelo Basilone's house on Second Avenue. His wife answered, then went directly to the parents' home on First Avenue to ask the matriarch of the family, Dora Basilone, if she knew anything. Dora didn't, and for a time the two women took comfort in the possibility that this was all a mistake and the reporter had gotten it wrong. Ten minutes later via Western Union a War Department notification (I suspect it was actually a Navy Department wire, which would be standard operating procedure for a Marine death) arrived, not at the Basilone family's front door, but at Pop Basilone's new place of work at Holcombe & Holcombe (he had sold his own shop). It went to Sal Basilone because he was officially listed as next of kin in John's service record book. This is how the telegram read: "Deeply regret to inform you that your son, Gunnery Sergeant John Basilone, USMC, was killed in action February 19, 1945 at Iwo Jima, Volcano Islands, in the performance of his duty and service to his country. When information is received regarding burial, you will be notified. Please accept my heartfelt sympathy."

It was signed, "General Alexander Vandegrift," who had been John's commanding officer on Guadalcanal and later presented him with his medal. The circle was closed.

In Camp Pendleton, Sergeant Lena Riggi Basilone, John's wife, got a similar wire.

Salvatore immediately phoned home and broke the news. It was official now, official and confirmed—no more comforting doubt, no hope there'd been a mistake. Bruce Doorly writes in his book, "Dora was in a state of shock and described as being on the verge of collapse. Salvatore quickly came home and soon word of John's death sped throughout the town. When a local Raritan boy died in the war, the word always spread quickly. Police Chief Lorenzo Rossi went around town informing people of John's death. The station master at the Raritan Train Station told commuters as they walked to the train. The church bells at St. Ann's were rung. Father Amadeo Russo [the youthful John's mentor] soon arrived at the house to comfort the family. The Basilone house was quickly flooded with visitors offering their sympathy. John's sister Dolores described for Doorly's monograph how she was notified. She was in class at Somerville High School when the principal of the school came in and said her dad had called. She and her younger brother Donald had to go home. No other information was given them but when the principal himself drove them both home, they started to realize that something major had happened. They were informed of John's death when they arrived home."

Both local newspapers, the *Somerset Messenger-Gazette* and the *Plainfield Courier News*, were afternoon papers, and on that same day, March 8, Basilone would be their front-page lead story. On a larger scale, the *New York Times* commented editorially, "Being a Marine fighting man, and therefore a realist, Sergeant Basilone must have known in his heart that his luck could not last forever. Yet he chose to return to battle." Also that day, March 8, Marines were still fighting on Iwo, pushing forward against fierce opposition. In Germany U.S. infantry and armor crowded onto the congested Remagen Bridge across the Rhine while desperate Nazi counterattacks continued. In Burma, British and Indian divisions broke out of their bridgeheads across the Irrawaddy, west of and "on the road to" Mandalay, where in Rudyard Kipling's poem "The Road to Mandalay" "the old flotilla lay."

Back home in Raritan, while everyone mourned John Basilone, the family thought about and prayed for another son, George, still believed to be on Iwo. How dreadful it would be to lose another boy on the same lousy little island. On Saturday the tenth there was a requiem mass at St. Ann's. Town flags flew at half-staff, and the American Legion post changed its name to "Sgt. John Basilone Post 280." Word arrived that Basilone had posthumously been awarded the Navy Cross. One of his officers on Iwo, Justin Gates Duryea, had submitted Basilone's name for a second Medal of Honor, only to be informed by higher echelons that all the Congressional Medals they could give were already gone. Heroism was one thing, bureaucracy remained very much another.

At St. Ann's they held a memorial mass later on Sunday, April 29, 1945, with Father Russo saying the high mass and the chaplain of nearby Camp Kilmer (named for the New Jersey poet killed in World War I), Reverend Raymond Kilmera, there to concelebrate. The Marine Corps dispatched a Marine color guard and a colonel, Harold Parsons. Governor Walter Edge sent the state adjutant general, and other local officials attended, as did people from the VFW and American Legion and the Army and Navy Union. Two Boy Scout troops were on hand, a band from Camp Kilmer, a detachment of troops and WACs from Fort Dix, and civilians from other New Jersey towns—Camden, Perth Amboy, South Orange, Trenton, and Newark.

A month earlier, on March 26, after thirty-six days of battle (remember that optimistic estimate that this might be a seventy-two-hour fight?), combat on Iwo ended with a final suicide attack by 500 Japanese troops against Basilone's 5th Marine Division. By the time the guns fell mute, 25,000 Americans were casualties, 7,000 of them dead. On that day on the Western Front the American 7th Division began to cross the Rhine. In the Philippines 14,000 American soldiers landed against hostile opposition near Cebu City.

When I first went down to Basilone's hometown that January morning all those years later on the early train out of Newark, and those three old boys from the Basilone Parade Committee met me at the depot in the red truck, they told me that when news of Basilone's death came, it was like the world ended in Raritan, just came to an end, not as literally but just as certainly as it had out in the Pacific for Manila John.

But worlds don't come to ends. Amid the grief, life goes on. And the war itself went on, until it eventually ended, too late for Sergeant Basilone and for so many more. Among them were small-town boys from burgs like Raritan where local people put up markers and ever after recalled.

Germany surrendered in May, Japan on August 15, 1945. On that mid-August day an impromptu parade of thanksgiving made its straggling way along Somerset Street in Raritan, and when the VJ Day march ended, the celebrations continued at local places like Orlando's Tavern, where John Basilone used to drink, and where Tony Orlando hosted a victory party. Surely toasts were drunk to Manila John's memory. He would have liked that. One unnamed local serviceman was quoted as saying on that last day of the war, "I keep thinking of my buddies who won't come back." But many of the dead *would* be coming back.

During World War II, we often buried the bodies of our men where they died—Italy or Normandy or the Pacific islands—with the tacit understanding that our people would eventually be brought home and planted here where they grew up and where they belonged. In 1948, three years after he died on Iwo, John Basilone came home from Iwo Jima.

And so it happened that in April of that year Raritan would have yet another opportunity to mourn and celebrate their local hero. The government had begun moving bodies back from Iwo's ad hoc cemeteries, giving families the option of choosing a burial near home or a plot at Arlington. Dora initially preferred to have John buried at Raritan, where the family lived and where he grew up. But local funeral director Anthony Bongiovi, nearly one hundred years old when I interviewed him, told me there was indecision at first. He admitted he didn't want to be in the middle of it, didn't welcome having to handle the job with its possible complications.

Well, after my talk with undertaker Bongiovi I was still getting differing versions of whether the body had passed through Raritan, where a mass was said at St. Ann's Church, several sources insisting they had seen the casket. So I asked Deacon John Pacifico of the church to clear up the mystery. On September 2, 2008, he wrote back: "Dear Jim, Both Anna Marie Bongiovi and Steve Del Rocco have confirmed that the body of John Basilone never came to Raritan. The body was at Arlington."

So at some point the decision had been made to bury their son at Arlington, instead of in New Jersey. Some sources say Bongiovi recommended Arlington. He didn't say that to me but continued telling me what then happened.

According to Doorly it was the undertaker who convinced Dora being buried at Arlington was a big deal, would do honor to her boy, and that Arlington was where Basilone belonged. I don't believe that any of them, including the undertaker Bongiovi, suspected what was coming. They all expected an intimate little funeral, a prayer from Father Russo, some friends, the family, a rite appropriate to a small Jersey town and a blue-collar family and their boy who never made money or much of a splash when he lived there, who joined the Marines, and then died in the war.

The burial was on April 20, 1948, but the Basilone funeral was going to be relentlessly small-town. Police chief Rossi volunteered to drive the limo, Bongiovi volunteered the undertaking services, Father Russo drove up front with the chief, with Dora and Sal, the parents, in back. A couple of other cars made up the cortege, carrying Basilone brothers and sisters and some neighbors. Al Gaburo the laundryman came, the man who once fired Johnny for goofing off and sleeping on the laundry bags; the mayor Rocco Miele; a future mayor, Steve Del Rocco. It was about two hundred miles, but the traffic was lighter then and they made it in under four hours.

Bongiovi told me they expected a simple affair, a couple of guys with rifles, maybe a bugler to play Taps, that was about it. Doorly gives this account from the family and Raritan vantage point: "When they arrived, they were amazed. First, they were picked up from their vehicles and driven in jeeps to the grave site. There they saw dozens of military dignitaries, a Marine band, and uniformed soldiers [Marines, surely] who would fire a gun salute. It was a most impressive, inspiring service, a true tribute to an unselfish hero. Father Russo blessed the casket. An American flag had first covered the coffin, and then as is customary, it was later taken off, folded in the ritual manner, and given to the Basilone family. Anthony Bongiovi, when he spoke with Doorly, said the funeral was simply unbelievable. He recalls that it was during the playing of Taps that everyone became emotional. The family and friends all drove back the same day."

More than four hundred miles down and back and eight hours behind the wheel. No one thought to have reserved a couple of hotel rooms or a motel, what was then called a travel court. Maybe they didn't have the dough. But they had properly buried their Johnny. Lena Riggi Basilone, the widow, wasn't there. She had come east after the war to meet John's family, though only the once. Her niece, an actress and dancer, lives in New York, where in 2007 I interviewed her.

Doorly contacted Virginia Grey for a comment to use in his monograph, asking if she remembered Basilone. She was eighty-seven by then and still living in California, and she sent a statement: "How I do remember John. Every time I pass Basilone Drive at Camp Pendleton, it brings tears to my eyes."

Curiously, there is very little about Basilone's widow, though there is a photo from 1949 when she and the family attended in Boston the commissioning of the destroyer USS *Basilone* on July 26. Doorly writes this brief passage about her: "Lena did not meet John's parents until after his death when she came to New Jersey. A picture of them together appears in this book. She never remarried, as she was very content with her life. She told a friend 'Once you have the best you can't settle for less.' Lena was described by her friends as a great cook, who enjoyed inviting people over for special dinners. She worked at an electrical plant. Always active in military affairs, she volunteered at the Long Beach Veterans Hospital, the American Veterans Auxiliary, and the Women Marines Association. She died on June [11] of 1999 at the age of 86." Former Marine Clinton Watters, the best man at their wedding in 1944, told me in admiring tones, "When she was in her eighties, she looked fifty."

With the widow so relentlessly offstage in the various accounts of Basilone's life, I contacted her niece, Fiddle Viracola, an Emmy-winning actress, singer, and dancer who appeared on Broadway in such plays as *The Beauty Part* and *The Rose Tattoo*, and who lives in Greenwich Village. She told me she had met with a writer for a new Steven Spielberg–Tom Hanks television series about the Pacific war, and has on her own been collecting material about John and Lena for a screenplay. She's also had an exchange of letters with the Spielberg office and with the casting people, so she's anxious to see the finished project. "I'm working on the script now [her own script, not theirs] and I've got eighty-eight pages. It's a powerful love story. Lena was so strong, and they were very compatible. He was very lost, always losing jobs, and Lena gave him a center. She knew his passion to go back [to the Pacific and the war]."

According to Ms. Viracola, Lena met the Basilone family only that one time in Massachusetts and never in New Jersey (as other sources insist she did). "They met up in Boston for the commissioning of the ship. The Basilones had been horrible to her. Raritan was resentful. I gather his sister wanted to run the show, getting all the limelight and the plaudits. There were a lot of self-serving people around."

To my knowledge, the widow did not attend the 1948 reburial at Arlington. "I don't know if she was invited," Viracola said. "I hear the mother [Dora] wanted Lena to come back to Raritan and live there, but that wasn't her style. She became a master sergeant and left the Marine Corps eventually and ran a company that was in air-conditioning and things like that and was involved in many things for the vets. People were drawn to Lena."

What about that line explaining why she never remarried, "I was married to the best"? "Yes," said the niece, "that quote is true. She also said, 'Great love only happens once.'"

Had she as reported handed over her ten-thousand-dollar government check as next of kin to the Basilone family? "Yes, she gave it to them. And when Lena was asked if she wanted to be buried next to John at Arlington, she said, 'I don't want anything to do with them.'" Was "them" the government or the family? "The family. They did not treat her well. And when she died Lena was buried in California wearing his wedding ring."

28

Sixty-five years after he earned the Medal of Honor fighting on Guadalcanal, sixty-three years after his death on Iwo Jima, there remains within the Marine Corps controversy about John Basilone. Not that anyone seriously disputes his heroism or questions the Medal of Honor, but you encounter differences of opinion about him, and he has his critics.

For instance, did Chesty Puller recommend Basilone not for a Medal of Honor but for a lesser award, a Navy Cross? No, reported Bob Aquilina, of the Marine Corps History Division, who sent me Puller's formal recommendation of October 30, 1942 (just a week after the October 25 battle), for a Medal of Honor for Basilone.

Aquilina also provided more information about what exactly happened on Iwo. According to a dispatch from Marine combat correspondent Henry Giniger, shortly after the landing Basilone was "wounded fatally" when "he was about to lead his machine gun platoon forward through a heavy barrage."

More descriptive is part of a cover story in the *Marine Corps Gazette* of October 1963, which also brings into question the account in Chuck Tatum's book of the famous blockhouse attack that first day on Iwo. It quotes former Marine corporal Ralph R. Belt (also cited in a disparate version by Tatum): "Basilone and I were both in the 27th Regiment—he was with C Company, I was in B Company. We landed on Red Beach 2. Right after we'd landed, my squad ran into a Jap block-house firing canister shells at the 26th Marines, and doing a lot of damage, too. There was a Marine standing on top of this pillbox, shouting for flame throwers and demolition men, I was a demolition man, and my buddy right alongside, PFC William N. Pegg, was a flame-thrower man. Before I had time to prepare demolition, Pegg moved to one side of the pill-box and knocked it out. He got a Silver Star. The Marine standing on top of the pill-box—shouting instructions, yelling for a machine gun, shaking a Ka-Bar knife at the Japs trying to get out—was Manila John. He would turn his back on the Japs to yell at us—wave his knife and laugh, then turn around toward them again—wave his knife and laugh right in their faces. I think Manila John was a great Marine. I'm very proud to have served with him in the Marines and on Iwo Jima. With the block-house out of the way, Manila John and his platoon fought their way across those bullet-torn sand dunes toward Airfield Number 1."

Corporal Belt then also corroborates the yarn about Basilone's guiding the tanks ahead before winding up his eyewitness account. "They had reached the edge of the airfield when the end came for Manila John a bursting mortar shell got him along with four others of his platoon." Later, crossing the airfield itself, "Pegg and I ran across a kid from our company by the name of Sorenson who had a very bad shoulder wound. A few feet away a corpsman was working on another wounded Marine. It was Manila John. He'd been hit bad. It looked like a mortar shell had landed right in front of him and ripped him wide open from his chin on down. As bad off as he was, he spoke to us—and he wore that grand smile of his. I have thought about that smile many, many times since. He died soon afterwards."

In 1992 a couple of newspaper reporters named Laurence Arnold and Regina de Peri Whitmer of the *Bridgewater (NJ) Courier-News* Sunday paper, for a feature about Basilone, got hold of a letter sent by a Lieutenant Hector R. Gai Jr. to his own sister on March 7, 1945, writing this about Iwo. "When a Japanese mortar struck Basilone's position, I was with him when he died on the south edge of [the airfield] Motoyama 1. He certainly did a hell of a fine job before he got it. He was only in action about two hours and a half.... John lived about an hour and a half but was in a coma. Surgery was the only thing and, of course, at that time it was out of the question. There wasn't any."

Aquilina also highlighted a copy of Basilone's posthumous Navy Cross citation signed by Forrestal and cited earlier. In part it reads—according to Corporal Belt, inaccurately—how Manila John, on top of the blockhouse, destroyed it single-handedly with grenades and demolitions.

As *Time* magazine reported in 1945, it was a mortar shell that killed Basilone. That story was also appended by the reference branch, as were other newspaper clips from the *Journal-American* in New York, a 1943 story bylined by Burris Jenkins Jr., headlined "Fought full regiment of Japs, Now he has Congressional Medal."

Regarding Corporal Belt, how just plain wacky is it that a veteran Marine machine-gun platoon sergeant in a firefight would be on the roof of an enemy blockhouse waving a Ka-Bar hunting knife around and taunting the Japanese instead of firmly on the ground commanding his gun crews and directing their fire? Tatum's earlier version seems more credible, that Basilone ordered demolitions man Belt and flamethrower Pegg to attack the bunker while his machine guns provided overhead covering fire.

Then again, as in Tatum's memory and book, was Basilone firing off a storm of bullets at the enemy in a fury, eyes blazing, or had he never fired a round just before he was hit? You can't have it both ways. Was his final action on the beach? Clearly not. Or inland on the approach to Motoyama Airfield #1? Probably there. The contradictions escalate with each different source. I'm not quite sure just which of the competing accounts is the most reliable. Some seem more bizarre than anything else with their obvious fabrications.

As far as Basilone's performance on Iwo is concerned, we have the official citation for his Navy Cross with attachments, including the signature of the commandant of the Marine Corps, who by that time late in the war, six months after Basilone died, was General Alexander Vandegrift, his commanding officer on the 'Canal and the very officer who in Australia in May 1943 presented Basilone with his Medal of Honor.

Here is the documentation for the Navy Cross on Iwo and the citation itself, starting with the recommendation for an award: "From the commanding officer, Company C, 1st Battalion, 27th Marines, 5th Marine Division, 24 April 1945," and sent upward through the chain of command all the way to Vandegrift:

> Subject: Navy Cross, recommendation for, case of Gunnery Sergeant John (n) Basilone (287506). USMC (Deceased). (A) Simple citation. (B) Statement of Witness.
>
> It is recommended that Gunnery Sergeant John Basilone be considered for the award of the Navy Cross. On 19 February, 1945, Gunnery Sergeant Basilone was serving in combat with 1st Battalion, 27th Marines, 5th Marine Division, on Iwo Jima, Volcano Islands.
>
> On this date, Gunnery Sergeant Basilone, moving forward in the face of heavy artillery fire, worked his way to the top of an enemy blockhouse which was holding up the advance of his company. Single handed, through the use of hand grenades and demolitions, he completely destroyed the blockhouse and its occupants. Later, on the same day, Gunnery Sergeant Basilone calmly guided one of our tanks, which was trapped in an enemy minefield, to safety, through heavy mortar and artillery fire. Gunnery Sergeant Basilone's courage and initiative did much to further the advance of his company at a time vital to the success of the operation. His expert tactical knowledge and daring aggressiveness were missed when he was killed at the edge of the airstrip by a mortar blast later the same day.

This was signed by Edward Kasky.

Rereading this "simple citation," a sort of preliminary sketching out of the facts for the authorities to review before writing and approving the formal citation itself and the award, I'm struck by several problems noted earlier in other accounts. Why would a machine-gun platoon sergeant be toting hand grenades and demolitions enabling him to knock out a blockhouse? Earlier stories seemed to indicate he destroyed the blockhouse from ground level, running toward it, not on its roof. And how is it that Basilone, just arrived on the scene, is able expertly to guide a tank through enemy minefields?

Then there is the statement of a single witness, PFC George Migyanko, dated April 24, two months after John's death: "I, George Migyanko, while serving with the 1st Battalion, 27th Marines, 5th Marine Division, saw Gunnery Sergeant John Basilone (287506), USMA, single-handedly destroy an enemy blockhouse which was holding up the advance of his company. Later in the day he led one of our tanks from a trap in a mine field in the face of withering artillery and mortar fire." End of statement.

That April 24 document was approved and forwarded to the secretary of the Navy on September 13, signed by H. G. Patrick, senior member of the board looking into the matter. Attached are other endorsements from lower-ranking officers of the 27th Marines, including Gerald F. Russell on April 25, T. A. Wornham on April 27, and K. E. Rocket on May 25. On June 27, 1945, it is the commanding general himself, "Howlin' Mad" Smith, who adds a fourth endorsement and sends the whole package on to the secretary of the Navy, via the commander in chief of the Pacific Fleet (Chester Nimitz, I would suppose) and to the commandant of the Corps. Next, on August 10, the commander, Pacific Fleet, sends along his approval to the secretary, again via the commandant, this letter signed by J. A. Hoover, deputy CINCPAC and CINCPON. On August 27 Vandegrift, who was by now the commandant, sends along his okay to Forrestal, the Navy secretary, noting, "recommended that Gunnery Sergeant Basilone be awarded the Navy Cross, posthumously."

There's a little more confusing bureaucracy at work here, it seems, since James Forrestal, SEC/NAV as they say, would not date until August 12, 1946, the official award of the Navy Cross, a year after the war ended. Who can explain that one except to suggest the office rubber stamp was incorrect in dating the sheet of paper with Forrestal's signature 1946 instead of 1945 when all the other material is dated? Clearly, in wartime, paperwork in the Corps or in the Department of the Navy was often sloppy.

Here, in any event, is the final version of the citation for his Navy Cross, verbatim:

> For extraordinary heroism while serving as a Leader of a Machine Gun Section of Company C, 1st Battalion, 27th Marines, 5th Marine Division, in action against enemy Japanese forces on Iwo Jima, Volcano Islands, 19 February, 1945. Shrewdly gauging the tactical situation shortly after landing when his company's advance was held up by the concentrated fire of a heavily fortified Japanese blockhouse, Gunnery Sergeant Basilone boldly defied the smashing bombardment of heavy artillery fire to work his way around the flank and up to a position directly on top of the blockhouse and then, attacking with grenades and demolitions, single-handedly destroyed the entire hostile strongpoint and its defending garrison. Consistently daring and aggressive as he fought his way over the battle-torn beach and the sloping, gun-studded terraces toward Airfield Number One, he repeatedly exposed himself to the blasting fire of exploding shells and later in the day coolly proceeded to the aid of a friendly tank which had been trapped in an enemy mine field under intense mortar and artillery barrages, skillfully guiding the heavy vehicle over the hazardous terrain to safety, despite the overwhelming volume of hostile fire. In the forefront of the assault at all times, he pushed forward with dauntless courage and iron determination until, moving upon the edge of the airfield,

he fell, instantly killed by a bursting mortar shell. Stout-hearted and indomitable, Gunnery Sergeant Basilone, by his intrepid initiative, outstanding professional skill and valiant spirit and self-sacrifice in the face of fanatic opposition, contributed to the advance of his company during the early critical period of the assault, and his unwavering devotion to duty throughout the bitter conflict was an inspiration to his comrades, and reflects the highest credit upon Gunnery Sergeant Basilone and the United States naval Service. He gallantly gave his life in the service of his country.

Among the multiple copies one is directed to "Public Info," and with a brief notation at the bottom, "Raritan, New Jersey . . . Buffalo, New York," I assume this meant that the media in those two cities, of John's rearing and his birth, were to be notified of the honor.

It is the accuracy of details in these battle accounts of Basilone's conduct that comes under criticism. But despite all the brass in Washington signing off on his Navy Cross, there remain to me some questions. We know Basilone was brave, a great Marine, a heroic man. But where did the blockhouse-busting grenades and demolitions come from? Was he on the blockhouse roof or down below? Was he really waving a hunting knife around? How was he sufficiently familiar with alien ground to guide that tank through the mines? Was he killed instantly by that mortar? Then why all those accounts of his living for hours, speaking with the corpsman, dictating messages to be passed on to brother George, and gradually bleeding to death? And what about that sole witness, the private who signed the citation recommendation? Where were the others? Questions remain.

Epilogue

Despite what Bertolt Brecht said, I believe having national heroes is healthy, giving us people to admire, role models, perhaps helping us to *be* somehow better than we are. Maybe heroes are just plain good for us; they make us feel better about ourselves, about the country, to know that among us are men and women who under pressure behave in exemplary ways and do things most of us don't even try. And it's not only wars that make heroes; newspapers and the local television stations regularly run features about "everyday heroes," urging nominations. There was even a time when America really *needed* a hero like John Basilone.

I'm neither a scholar nor a historian, just another old newspaperman who once fought in a war, but I remain fascinated and often puzzled by John Basilone, a professional Marine machine gunner in two climactic battles, one at the very start of a Pacific war we were losing and then in a second fight near the end of a war we knew we were going to win. He was a man already dead when I was a Catholic high school boy reading about him in the *Daily News,* and most of what I later knew of Basilone came from Marines and Marine Corps lore and the memories of old men in New Jersey, what they told me, the black-and-white photos at the Raritan library, when they drove me to the big bronze statue and took me to visit the little frame boyhood home, to see his hangouts.

I mentioned earlier a resemblance to the youthful Sly Stallone. Basilone *was* Stallone's Rambo, a real-life Rambo. And despite the wars and the years that separate the generations of Marines, I feel I knew a man I never met—because every Marine knew Manila John.

Even though . . .

More than sixty years after his death at age twenty-eight on Iwo Jima, Basilone remains an enigma. There are still questions about the famous decorations for his heroic battles. Some of these are insignificant points, matters of detail, an incorrect stat here, a confusion of names there, the chaos of battle, the tendency of loved ones to boast a little. Other questions were more substantive. This was the exasperating part of Manila John's story.

It goes without saying that neither sergeant, Mitchell Paige nor Basilone, campaigned for a decoration of any sort, never mind the top medal we have. Marines don't recommend themselves for awards; their superiors write them up.

The Navy Cross awarded posthumously on Iwo Jima is a strange affair, more complicated than any doubts about Guadalcanal. And being dead, Basilone can have no responsibility for what was subsequently written, said, or sworn to. The facts seem to be that Gunny Basilone, when confronted by a Japanese blockhouse, did precisely what the moment called for. He demonstrated initiative by getting a demolition assault team to send a man forward with a heavy explosive charge and another, the giant William Pegg, with the flamethrower, while Basilone's machine gunners gave them overhead covering fire.

Sergeant Basilone did his job perfectly, and so did the demo guy and the flamethrower, as did Basilone's machine gunners. The Japanese position fell to the combined Marine operation of explosives, flame, and machine-gun fire, and the stalled Marine drive inland got going, thanks in large part to Basilone's gutsy, intelligent leadership.

If that's the story, those the precise facts—and Chuck Tatum, there as a machine gunner, writes that they were—it is both rational and believable. If "Sergeant Basilone directed this operation 'by the book,' the way we practiced it at Pendleton and Camp Tarawa," then why conjure up a fantastic story about how Basilone scaled the roof and single-handedly destroyed the position with grenades? Or spent his time waving a hunting knife around, taunting and capering?

Basilone made the thing happen. It wasn't a solo performance, but it was heroic. Two other men backed up by his machine guns carried it out.

Then reread the official Navy Cross citation. The story of the tank in the minefield. Why pad the already impressive résumé? Did the Department of the Navy have so much invested in Basilone that he couldn't just die, he had to die gloriously, capable of superhuman feats? Maybe they had to make it up to America for permitting its hero to go back one more time to the battle. How else do you justify an official citation signed off by so many while so rife with apparent exaggerations?

Maybe, as has been charged, the Basilone of the war bond tour, with his handlers and packaged speeches and appearances, was to an extent a product marketed and merchandised by imaginative young officers doing PR for the Marine Corps. They were out to sell inspiration to a country that needed heroes, and Basilone must have looked like a good bet, a superior salesman. The kid out of Raritan was everyman from everywhere, an ordinary Joe, a small-town American; the darkly handsome, undefeated boxer Manila John, a poker-playing roughneck from the caddy shack, the guy with a knockout punch—and that marketable nickname. If this is true, none of it was Basilone's idea.

Basilone has surely been ill served even by people who loved him, family and friends, and by others, publicity professionals and inventive journalists, who damaged his reputation with fanciful stories and memoirs, their cartoon-styled exaggerations of feats of arms never performed, the hero lost behind his deeds.

The Basilone statue in Raritan, New Jersey, haloed by the sun.

But this is what makes him a legend and an American icon. Maybe we should just embrace the colorful lore, memorialize John Basilone as a Marine and honor his service, take him on faith, forget the disputation and the skeptical theories, mine and others, and just love the guy, saluting him with a well-earned and final Semper Fidelis. Always faithful. Perhaps we should leave it just as simple and as wonderful as that.

Bibliography

This bibliography was compiled from the author's notes after his passing. Any omissions or inaccuracies are, therefore, those of the editor.

Alexander, Joseph H. *Closing In: Marines in the Seizure of Iwo Jima.* Washington, DC: History and Museums Division, Headquarters, U.S. Marine Corps [Supt. of Docs., U.S. GPO, distributor], 1994.

Alexander, Joseph H., with Don Horan and Norman C. Stahl. *A Fellowship of Valor: The Battle History of the U.S. Marines.* New York: HarperCollins, 1997.

Doorly, Bruce W. *Raritan's Hero: The John Basilone Story.* Privately published.

Lansford, William Douglas. "The Life and Death of 'Manila John' Basilone." *Leatherneck.* October 2002.

Leckie, Robert. *Challenge for the Pacific: The Bloody Six-Month Battle of Guadalcanal.* New York: Da Capo, 1999.

———. *Helmet for My Pillow.* New York: Bantam, 1995.

Paige, Mitchell. *A Marine Named Mitch.* Santa Fe Springs, CA: Wylde & Sons, 1975.

Proser, Jim, with Jerry Cutter. *"I'm Staying with My Boys . . .": The Heroic Life of Sgt. John Basilone, USMC.* Hilton Head, SC: Lightbearer Communications, 2004.

Santelli, James S. *A Brief History of the 7th Marines*. Washington, DC: History and Museums Division, Headquarters, U.S. Marine Corps, 1980.

Shaw, Henry I., Jr. *First Offensive: The Marine Campaign for Guadalcanal*. Washington, DC: History and Museums Division, Headquarters, U.S. Marine Corps [Supt. of Docs., U.S. GPO, distributor], 1992.

Sledge, Eugene. *With the Old Breed, at Peleliu and Okinawa*. New York: Bantam, 1982.

Tatum, Charles W. *Iwo Jima: 19, February, 1945, Red Blood, Black Sand, Pacific Apocalypse*. Stockton, CA: C.W. Tatum Pub., 1995.

Tillman, Mary, and Narda Zacchino. *Boots on the Ground by Dusk: My Tribute to Pat Tillman*. New York: Modern Times, 2008.

United States Marine Corps, Historical Division. Lieutenant Colonel Frank O. Hough, USMCR; Major Verle E. Ludwig, USMC; and Henry I. Shaw Jr. *History of U.S. Marine Corps Operations in World War II: Pearl Harbor to Guadalcanal*, vol. I. Washington: GPO, 1958.

Illustration Credits

Index

Page numbers in *italics* refer to illustrations.

Sian, Joe, 94–95
Sims, Amor LeRoy, 73
Slattery, William, 140
Sloan, Alfred P., 155
Smith, Holland M. "Howlin' Mad,"
186, 193, 231
Smits (soldier), 112
Solomon Islands, 19, 22, 169
Somerset County Bar
Association, 144
Somerset Messenger-Gazette, 6, 22,
29–32, 207, 212, 221
See also Cutter, Phyllis Basilone
Sorenson (Marine), 228
Spanish American War, 16, 107,
118, 119
Spielberg, Steven, 205, 225
Star-Ledger, 96
Star of Italy Mutual Aid
Society, 151
St. Ann's Roman Catholic Church, 10,
89–90, 115, 144, 220
Basilone Day and, 140
memorial mass for Basilone,
221–222, 223
St. Bernard's parochial school, 80
St. Mary's Church, 172
Sullivan, Ed, 5, 151–152, 153, 158
Sumiyoshi, Tadashi, 35, 41

Tatum, Charles W. "Chuck," 161, 198,
210–211, 228, 229, 237
Terminal Island, 129
3rd Marine Division, 182, 186, 194
Thomas, Lowell, 5
Thomason, Clyde, 9
Tillman, Mary, 10
Tillman, Pat, 10
Time, 229
Truk, 26, 170
Tulagi, 18, 22, 25
Turner, Richmond Kelly "Terrible,"
191, 193

U.S. Army
Army Air Corps, 89, 128, 138, 183,
192
Basilone and, 81–82, 97–100,
101–106, 107–114
Depression-era pay by, 101
at Guadalcanal, 45
U.S. Army Air Corps, 89, 128, 138,
183, 192
U.S. Marine Corps, 2, 10–11, 146
Army Air Corps-Navy rivalry and, 192
Basilone's enlistment in, 82, 116–123
casualty report on Basilone's
death, 215
as "first to fight," 122
growth of, during World War II,
186–188
Marine Corps History Division
(Quantico), 48, 53, 205, 215
Marine Corps Schools (Quantico),
187, 216
training and, 53, 117–118, 121
women in, 164
*See also individual names of battles;
individual names of enlisted
Marines; individual names of
officers*
U.S. Navy, 29–30, 45, 192. *See also*
U.S. Marine Corps
USS *Ballard,* 27
USS *Basilone,* 225
USS *Hansford,* 183
USS *Jarvis,* 26
USS *Republic,* 105, 108

Vandegrift, Alexander A., 2–3, 24–25,
27, 34, 35, 37, 73
Basilone's Australia assignment
and, 59–60, 63
Basilone's death notification signed
by, 220
Basilone's Navy Cross citation and,
230–233